D1478858

Where the Rhododendrons Bloom

A THRU-HIKING ADVENTURE ON THE APPALACHIAN TRAIL

Audrey Payne

Where the Rhododendrons Bloom. Copyright © 2024 by Audrey Payne. All rights reserved. No part of this book may be used or reproduced in any manner without written permission from the author, with the exception of brief quotations within critical articles and reviews. For information: audrey.marie.payne@gmail.com.

Cover design and map illustration by Monica "Moss" Aguilar of Chasing Trails Art (chasingtrailsart.com).

Disclaimer: The stories in this book reflect the author's recollection and views of events using memories, photos, journal entries, and blog posts which were originally published on TheTrek.co. Dialogue has been recreated from memory. Some names and identifying characteristics have been changed to protect the privacy of the people involved.

Audrey Adventures Publishing Paperback ISBN: 979-8-218-35569-2.

DEDICATION

To my ever-changing tramily, who made the trail pure magic.

And to my family, for always supporting my life choices, even when they don't understand them.

Appalachian Trail

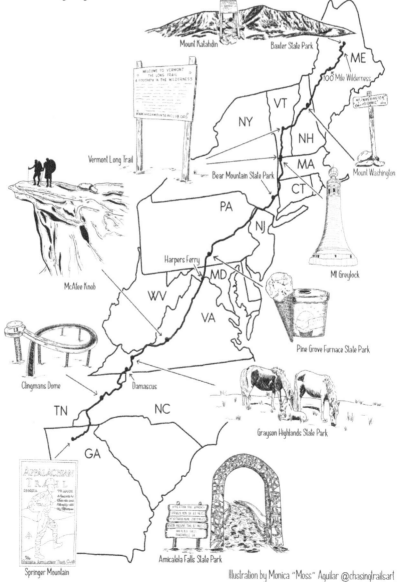

Mount Katahdin

Baxter State Park

ME

100 Mile Wilderness

WELCOME TO VERMONT
THE LONG TRAIL
A FOOTPATH IN THE WILDERNESS

WWW.GREENMOUNTAINCLUB.ORG

VT

NY

NH

MT. WASHINGTON

Vermont Long Trail

Bear Mountain State Park

MA

CT

Mount Washington

PA

NJ

Mt Greylock

Harpers Ferry

MD

McAfee Knob

WV

VA

Pine Grove Furnace State Park

Clingmans Dome

Damascus

TN

NC

Grayson Highlands State Park

GA

APPALACHIAN TRAIL

Springer Mountain

Amicalola Falls State Park

Illustration by Monica "Moss" Aguilar @chasingtrailsart

PROLOGUE

It is one in the morning, way past hiker midnight, and I am wondering how I'm going to make it through the night. I am slumped against the wall of the privy, my hands held up in prayer as I support my head. My hair is matted with sweat, and my legs are covered in sawdust and upchuck. I listen intently as fat raindrops bounce off the wooden roof of the structure, desperate to focus on anything aside from the razorblades in my stomach. It is spring in Virginia and the night air is warm and muggy, but I am shaking with sick and cold.

I wrap my arms around my stomach protectively as bile forces its way up through my esophagus. I lunge toward the makeshift toilet, heaving as the last remnants of my Kraft macaroni and cheese dinner force themselves out of my body. I try not to look down as the sleek, wet vomit splashes into the pile of waste below.

I am feeling sorry for myself. While my trail family sleeps soundly, cozy inside their tents, I am awake and alone, curled into a ball on the floor of an outhouse. I have angered the trail gods somehow, and this is their vengeance.

Of all the sleepless nights that I have experienced on the Appalachian Trail so far, this is by far the worst. Forget about the bear that plodded around camp in the night, threatening to swipe my dangling food bag and eat me alive. Forget about the wild ponies that decided the only grass worth consuming was directly under my tent. Forget about the six-degree night when the wind howled ominously through the trees and I shivered in my sleeping bag the whole night through. This is far worse, and it's not over yet.

CHAPTER 1

As I sat on the plane, about to embark on what I hoped would be the greatest adventure of my life so far, my feet would not stop tapping. Tap, tap, tap. Sitting still in my tiny seat felt like torture, and I probably drove the person sitting next to me crazy. I shifted this way and that, sighing audibly and wishing that I could pace up and down the aisle.

Anxiety had been plaguing me for weeks, and it was coming to a head. It started the day that I handed in my resignation to my boss, letting him know that I would be leaving my position to hike the 2,200-mile Appalachian Trail (AT) from Georgia to Maine. That's when the nightmares began. Each night, I would wake up with a gasp, shaking and clammy, my pajamas soaked in cold sweat. I would toss and turn in bed while the world slept, gripped with worry over my future and the decisions I was making.

I asked myself the same few questions on a loop. Was I crazy? Quite possibly. Irresponsible? Most definitely. Would I regret it? I couldn't know, but I also couldn't shake the question.

It would have been much easier, and perhaps smarter, to stay the course in Washington, D.C. For seven years, I had worked my butt off to create a life and build a career there. I had put an exorbitant amount of time and energy into my education, relationships, and especially my jobs—only to drop it all like an old hat as soon as things finally seemed to be falling into place.

But I was burned out, and I felt deep in my bones that it was time to go.

When I first arrived in the city that I would call home for the next several years, jonesing for the chance to work in environmental conservation, I didn't even own a smartphone. By the time I left for the AT, I was exhausted from constantly having to stay plugged in. Checking email and taking work calls in the evenings and on weekends were not just expected, they were required. I quickly learned that changing the world, or having a fast-paced career in a big American city rather, does not allow for great work-life balance. At least not in my experience. That did not make leaving any easier, though. To leave stability—a meaningful job, a regular paycheck, a boss I respected, friends that I loved—behind to chase a dream, one I didn't know if I was even capable of achieving, seemed bonkers, even to me. But the idea of hiking the AT had sunk its teeth into me, and despite my attempts to brush the idea aside in favor of furthering my career, it just wouldn't let go. Finally, I was giving in.

As time marched on toward my leave date, panic set in. Each night, I'd wake up shaking from another bad dream. Each day, I'd find myself scouring the blogs, social media posts, and YouTube channels of thru-hikers from years past, hoping to find evidence that all this anxiety was both normal and worth it. I ached for confirmation that I was making the right choice, that everything was going to be okay.

But life doesn't offer that sort of certainty, and no amount of reading could assuage my fears. I had to leap into the void without being able to see what lay ahead.

Thankfully though, the peace that I'd so desperately searched for in the weeks leading up to the start of the trail finally found me as I stepped through the famous arch at Amicalola Falls State Park in Dawsonville, Georgia, where the approach trail begins. Once my feet started moving, my brain could finally rest.

CHAPTER 2

Before deciding to sweep my responsible adult life to the side to hike the AT, there had been some amount of buildup. It wasn't just an idea that came to me one day and made me think "Why certainly, after years of working to get where I am, and while I have thousands of dollars of crippling student debt to my name, and while I have some pretty significant back problems that might flare up and render me useless as soon as I find myself in the backwoods of Georgia, unemployed, with a 40-pound pack on my back, I should, *by all means*, quit my job to go prance about in the woods with a bunch of (possibly dangerous) strangers and bears. Yes, that sounds reasonable."

It did not happen *quite* like that. It was more like a tiny *what if* that began to build and build as time went on. It wasn't an immediate obsession so much as a constant pulsing thought in the back of my mind that became larger and larger. *Don't forget that someday you've got to go do that thing.* My brain just wouldn't shut up about it. Eventually, I figured I was going to have to do something about it.

I've always been adventurous. I grew up on a dirt road in rural western New York, the fringes of my backyard stretching into forest. "Go play outside" was often bellowed lovingly but firmly in my house. Instead of staring at a screen for endless hours a day, I climbed trees, built forts, played hide and seek, chased fireflies, and got dirty. My family only had two TV channels, powered by an antenna on the roof, and they did not even work half the time. I went camping with my family often when I was a kid, but my relationship with backpacking did not begin until high school. When I was 16, I was granted a scholarship to spend a summer abroad. I wanted to go to France—I had fallen in love with the language and wanted to practice it. But my first-choice program was full by the time I was selected for the scholarship. Rather than chasing romance in Paris, I wound up at an outdoor pursuits center halfway around the world in New Zealand, a country I had not even heard of before. There, I took my first backpacking steps in the land of "The Lord of the Rings." I was immediately hooked. It would be almost two decades before I would set foot on the AT, but this is where I caught my first glimpse of jagged peaks and took my first steps on a trail with a heavy pack on my back.

In college, I managed to peel myself away from my robust social calendar long enough to fulfill a childhood dream to study lemurs in the rain forests of Madagascar. I spent three months sleeping in a tent in spectacular Ranomafana National Park during a study abroad program run by Stony Brook University. There, I lived a life that belonged in National Geographic Magazine for a semester. In between classes, daily life consisted of chasing lemurs through steep cloud forests, scouring tree trunks for elusive chameleons, following frog calls in search of their owners, trekking through streams and climbing up waterfalls, and getting covered in glittery golden mud and itch-inducing leeches. It was glorious. While there, I befriended Natalie, who will become important later in this story.

Post-college graduation, I wound up parked at my parents' house for a few months unexpectedly. My beloved dad was given a pretty dire diagnosis after asking my mom, who is a nurse, why his face looked so yellow. Cancer had infected his pancreas and snaked around his bile ducts, causing jaundice. As he peered into the mirror, he found Homer Simpson staring back at him.

I was sitting in the Los Angeles airport, returning from a long vacation abroad, when I found out. I had a 12-hour layover before my homebound flight to Buffalo. I called my parents to confirm that my dad would be picking me up when I landed. "Your aunts will be coming to get you instead," my mom told me. That felt off; I hadn't seen my family in several weeks, and my dad always came to fetch me after these trips. I pushed back, questioning why he wouldn't come this time. She told me that my dad might be dying and that he was scheduled for surgery in just two days. He'd be sliced open, half of his innards scooped out, the cancer cut off at the source. I wandered tearfully around the airport, baffled as to why she would admit this to me while I was stuck in the airport on the other side of the country alone and wondering how I was supposed to cope with the news.

While cancer is never a promising diagnosis, pancreatic cancer is especially ominous. The five-year survival rate is only five percent; most people are given only weeks or months to live. My dad was told that if the surgery to remove his cancer was unsuccessful, there wouldn't be much more the doctors could do for him. I was terrified. So I put off life for a bit, working part-time as a bartender at a local Italian restaurant and keeping my dear old dad company. I was convinced that if I dared to drift, he wouldn't pull through, and I couldn't bear the thought of losing him. After a few months, as he began to recover from surgery, chemotherapy, and the cancer, my mom insisted that I get on my way. "You can't sit around making sure he doesn't die," she told me. I took her words to heart and found a job out of state for the summer. Miraculously, my dad pulled through.

My aspirations that summer, then, were to get out of town, make a buck, and cut loose from the stress I had endured during the past several months. I landed a seasonal job working for an environmental education center owned by a Presbyterian church down in the mountains of Eastern Tennessee. I had been scheduled to work as a naturalist during their spring program, but my dad's illness had thrown that plan off the rails. Three days before I was supposed to be there to start training, I had to call and cancel. Generously, they allowed me to come down for their summer camp instead. I was told that although they'd be running a Christian-based summer camp, I would be working for the environmental education center, which was separate. As an agnostic, that was a relief to hear, but it wasn't quite the truth. Actually, it wasn't the truth at all. Soon after arriving at camp, I found myself singing gospel music and leading prayer circles at the demands of my boss.

I only spent about half that summer in Tennessee. My then-boyfriend and I, along with two of our friends, were fired in the middle of the night for having had the audacity to consume alcohol on our day off. There were no campers on the premises at the time, but it was a Christian camp and they had their Christian rules. I knew there would be consequences if we were caught, but the stress I had been under for the past several months had taken its toll on me and I was feeling rebellious.

We were fired at 11:00 pm, minutes after we had returned from taking the campers on a night hike. As we sat down at a table in the mess hall, our boss, Teresa, told us that we would be better off if we told the truth. Then, she took us into the kitchen one by one for questioning. We were all honest with her. We had, indeed, dared to consume the devil's drink days before.

Teresa, of course, already knew this. Someone had snitched on us and she had climbed into a dumpster that was taller than me to search for and fish out our discarded beer cans. After interrogating the four of us separately, she ordered us back into the dining hall. She slammed a small plastic bag containing the empty cans onto the round table where we were seated and ordered us off the premises by 8:00 am. I was devastated. Despite the religious aspects of the camp, I loved my job, my coworkers, and the campers. And my relationship with my boyfriend, whom I met at the camp, had only just begun to bloom. But it was what it was. And being fired, in a roundabout way, brought me ever closer to the AT.

I spent the rest of that summer road-tripping across America and falling deeply in love. As I tearfully asked my boyfriend what he would do after leaving camp, he told me that he might hitchhike to Colorado. He had a friend living there for the summer who could probably get him a job. "Do you need a ride?" I asked hopefully. I wasn't ready to head back home to New York just yet. We hurriedly packed up all of our clothes and threw them into the trunk of my car. We hightailed it out of the camp in the middle of that lovely late-June night, strategizing as we went. My boyfriend was in no hurry to get to Colorado—we could take our time.

We stopped by a gas station the next day to buy a road map of the United States, circling the areas we'd like to visit. We had next to no money, but we had a car and we had freedom. We drove north from Tennessee until we arrived at the Indiana Dunes National Park. There, we splashed in the frigid waters of Lake Michigan and cowboy camped on the beach under the stars. Next, we headed west, aiming for Montana. A farmer let us camp for free on his land en route, and a kind man handed us some cold sodas and beers as we napped in a gazebo in Wisconsin to wait out a rainstorm. "You look like you could use them," he told us.

We arrived in the Badlands of South Dakota in the middle of the night. I was awestruck when I awoke to the sun hitting the buttes and spires of the national park in the morning. I had no idea that such a place existed. We stopped at every national forest and park that we could along the way. I was discovering the incredible ecological diversity of the United States, and I couldn't get enough. I fell in love that summer with not just the guy, but with the expanse of America as well. From the Grand Tetons and Yellowstone, we headed north across the Canadian border to Calgary then Edmonton, west to Vancouver, then finally south to Washington state. I dropped the guy off in Seattle and headed home to New York. We never did make it to Colorado. My friend Colleen, who had met us out in Yellowstone, and I had a stint lined up to teach English in South Korea and we needed to go home to prepare. That summer didn't last and neither did the relationship, but I carried the experience forward with me and my interest in exploring more of the U.S. remained.

After a few years of low-paying seasonal jobs, I decided that it was time to get serious about my career and my future. I wanted to help better the world and aspired to work in communications for one of the large environmental non-profit organizations that were headquartered in Washington, D.C. So when I was accepted into a prominent public relations program at American University, that's where I headed. At first, everything was going according to plan. I earned my master's degree, interned at the Environmental Defense Fund, and landed a job at a fast-paced public relations agency where I was learning a ton, regularly dining with celebrities, and making valuable connections. But disaster struck one day as I was working out at the gym across the street from my office.

At the public relations agency, I was regularly pulling 12-plus-hour days, and sometimes 16-hour days. I was rubbing elbows with the rich and famous, yet I could barely pay my bills. Finding the time to exercise was critical to keeping my mental health in check, so I would squeeze a workout in any chance that I could. During this fateful occasion, I joined a lunchtime boot camp class with my coworker, Jenna. The instructor commanded us to jump up from a squatting position and push a heavy bar over our heads. Suddenly, something felt off in my body. I left the class early and returned to my office to pop some Advil. I was concerned, but not overly so. By nightfall, I could barely stand. Each time I moved, it felt like I was being electrocuted. The move put too much pressure on one of the discs in my lower back, which act as shock absorbers between the vertebrae in your spine. The disc cracked open, pushing a jelly-like material onto the nerves in my lower back, irritating them. For a long time, I was in so much pain that I couldn't run, travel, work out, or even sit at my desk for more than 15 minutes at a time.

I had always been physically active. I was a regular gym-goer and running was my daily meditation. But with my injury, I couldn't handle the impact; I had to quit cold turkey. Just walking down the street could send me into spasms of agony. My daily commutes via the metro were torture. Getting treatment for a herniated disc is tricky though. Some people who herniate a disc don't even feel it; they have no idea it happened. For others like me, it's debilitating. I was only 29 years old when my injury occurred, so the many doctors that I saw wanted to wait it out to see if it would heal on its own. Insurance companies don't want to pay for surgeries for people so young without exploring all other options first. I tried nerve blockers, painkillers, cortisone shots, physical therapy, a chiropractor… anything and everything that would potentially make my back feel better. But nothing helped.

I was in so much pain from even the most mundane activities that aside from work, I had no energy left to do anything else. Sitting was the absolute worst thing for me, so I couldn't even meet my friends for a quiet meal at a restaurant without falling into excruciating pain. When I was finally cleared by my health insurance company for surgery a year after the initial injury, my orthopedic surgeon told me to think about it. "I don't have to," I told him tearfully. "I can't keep living like this." If I had not been able to get the surgery, or if it had been unsuccessful, I truly do not believe that I would be here today. I would not wish that kind of pain on my worst enemy, and I don't know how long I could have continued to deal with it while holding out hope that I would make it to the other side.

During that time, I read *a lot*. It was my great escape when I had no other outlet. And one of the books that finally made its way onto my lap was Bill Bryson's "A Walk in the Woods," about his journey along the AT. That book had been trailing me for years. It was on the bookshelves of several offices that I worked in and of numerous friends, but I'd never had a desire to read it. It just didn't interest me. But finally, while I was down for the count, spending a miserable couple of years confined to the adventures of books, I picked it up. As I read through it, the idea of hiking the AT took hold. I promised myself that if I was ever healthy enough again to do so, I would thru-hike the trail. And five years later, after a spinal fusion and a long, painful recovery, I fulfilled that promise to myself. I stepped onto the Appalachian Trail, following in Bryson's footsteps.

I had peripherally kept in touch with Natalie, my aforementioned friend from my Madagascar study abroad program, in the 13 years since. I think we saw each other two or three times. We linked up once when her dad came down to D.C. to play a show with his band. And she'd write to me when she was serving in the Peace Corps in Fiji. On one particular occasion, she wrote to tell me about how she'd had to shave off her waist-length dreadlocks because her hair had become infested with lice.

Natalie and I had always gotten along, but 13 years was over a third of our lives—we barely knew each other anymore. We had become adults. She'd gone from being a young, cool, punk chick to a granola grownup with a full-time job working in a quality control lab. But she dreamed of thru-hiking the trail too. I reread "A Walk in the Woods" in 2017 and I posted about it on Instagram, describing how much I loved the book and hoped to hike the AT someday. Natalie reached out.

A few months later, in the fall of 2017, we found ourselves reconnecting for a weekend of hiking in the middle of farm country in Pennsylvania. She was living in Upstate New York, so this was about halfway between our cities of residence. We decided to give the whole backpacking thing a whirl—to test the waters and see if, just maybe, it would feel right to set off together on a journey through the wilderness. I was set on it before we even arrived. I'd been diligently saving all year and was listening to podcasts about thru-hiking every day on my commute home from work. She, on the other hand, wasn't quite sure. She told me so as I hopped into her car, hitching a ride with her to the trailhead.

We'd planned to hike in a state park that weekend but found when we arrived that overnight parking was not allowed. A quick Google search for other local options showed that the AT was only about a half hour away by car. "Well, I guess we'll really get a taste of what it's like," I said. We changed course and headed toward the AT. By the end of the weekend, Natalie's mind was made up as well. "Alright, I'm in," she said as she dropped me back off at my car. Cue the panic attacks. We were doing this.

I spent the next six months listening to podcasts about thru-hiking, reading trail journals, working two side gigs in addition to my full-time job, squirreling away money the best I could, hiking during my free time, collecting gear, and doing my best to prepare. I wasn't entirely convinced it was happening, but I believed it just enough to live with constant heartburn. Could we really leave our jobs and our lives behind? Could I throw away everything I'd worked for—just for a bit of fun? But I'd had a hard few years and the idea of spending the rest of my life wondering "what if" was too much for me. My dad's health scare made it very clear to me that our time on Earth is not guaranteed. And my back injury made me acutely aware that my physical health is not a certainty either. The trail was calling me, and I felt strongly that despite the ifs, ands, or buts, I had to go, and I had to go now. Was I afraid? Yes. I'd never been so afraid in my entire life. I constantly waffled between extreme excitement and outright panic. I was afraid of everything—of unemployment, of murderers and bears, of running out of money, of dark nights playing tricks on my overactive imagination, of adjusting to life without daily showers, of loneliness, of injury, of my body not being able to handle it, of my mind not being able to handle it, of hating the food, of endless days of rain, of missing my friends, of throwing my life off the rails. But I made a deal with myself—I'd go and fear would just have to come too. We'd have to learn how to live with each other. After all I'd been through, I decided that I couldn't allow fear to rule my life. It could occasionally make a decision, or usher me into debate, but it could not be in charge. I'd miss out on too much that way. So here we were. Me and Natalie and Fear. And we were going on an adventure.

CHAPTER 3

It felt like I didn't have a moment to breathe as I scrambled to tie up loose ends in the days and weeks before leaving Washington, D.C., for the Appalachian Trail. I opted to work for as long as possible, not knowing when I'd next have a steady income. So between my full-time job and my side gigs, donating stuff I didn't need, packing up the stuff that I wanted to keep, and saying goodbye to friends, my schedule was jam-packed until the day I left D.C. for good.

On my last morning in the city, I got my first taste of Appalachian magic. I met up with a couple of friends at my favorite local coffee shop to say goodbye before hitting the road to New York, where I would leave most of my belongings with family during my trek. From there, I would head south to Georgia to start the trail. I was chatting away anxiously about my plans and my insecurities when two older men at a table kitty-corner to us politely interjected. They explained that they had hiked the AT in the 1980s and had absolutely loved their experience. Afterward, they ended up gainfully employed in Golden, Colorado. Everything had worked out perfectly well for them and they cherished their experience. They expressed how excited they were for me.

This had to be a sign. I was planning to hike the AT and then start life anew in the mountains of Colorado. And here these guys were, a few decades ahead of me, having taken that exact path. And they both seemed so genuinely happy.

There's a saying on the trail that probably sounds a bit cultish to outsiders—"the trail provides." Thru-hikers say it constantly. It doesn't necessarily mean that the trail gives you everything that you want. The trail gods are not the sentimental type, in my experience. It means that the trail gives you what you *need* when you really need it. There are probably thousands of stories out there of hikers in desperate situations saved seemingly out of the blue or wanting something *so badly*, only to have the very thing they desire so strongly appear. It is a belief that the trail and its people will take care of you; that you are exactly where you're supposed to be when you're supposed to be there. I saw and heard enough examples, and lived through plenty myself, to know that if magic exists, it's definitely on the Appalachian Trail.

These coffee shop dudes? That was the trail providing.

I finished up breakfast, hugged my friends tight, and made the half-mile stroll back to my house. I took one last look around the room that I'd lived in for almost five years. Then, I ducked into my car and started the engine. I pulled out of the alleyway behind my garage and into the street. I pointed my car north and never looked back.

As I drove north through Maryland, I passed under a footbridge built over the highway. It was labeled "Appalachian Trail" with a big green sign. "I'm coming back for you," I said aloud, glancing up at the bridge. Minute by minute, it was all beginning to feel more real.

After a restless seven-hour drive, I pulled my car into the driveway of my parents' house in Western New York. I had approximately 36 hours to squeeze in some family time, pack and repack my backpack about 100 times, and try to convince myself that this was still a great idea.

My parents thought I was nuts. They didn't want me to give up the job that I'd worked so hard for. They had watched me struggle through long days and low pay at the public relations agency and they were thrilled when I landed my dream job on the communications team at World Wildlife Fund just two years earlier. But they supported me in their own ways regardless.

My dad, for example, drove down to D.C. before my last week of work to take most of my possessions home to New York. My cousin, Kellie, and her husband, Tim, generously allowed me to store my belongings in their basement while I was away, so my dad hauled them to their house. The day before I left for the trail, my mom spent hours in the kitchen fixing up a huge homemade spaghetti dinner complete with crispy, butter-soaked garlic bread. I needed to carbo-load, she reasoned. I agreed and wolfed down as much as my stomach would allow. It tasted like home, and I wouldn't be back for a while.

The gear and clothing that I'd accumulated for the trek did not want to fit into my 65-liter Osprey backpack, and I was starting to wonder how I was going to survive the frigid nights up in the mountains. I wished that I had the space to stuff an extra parka in there. My family laughed hysterically every time I tried to load that bursting-at-the-seams beast onto my back. My cousin, Katie, who is decidedly much stronger and more capable than I, balked as she tried it on herself and went for a quick jaunt down the hallway.

"You're going to be carrying this on your back?" she asked incredulously. "For *hours a day?*"

I nodded glumly, trying my best to put on a brave face. "It's only 35 pounds," I said, with much more conviction than I felt. "That's totally normal! I've done it before."

Sure, 10 years prior when youth was on my side and I had not yet had my fitness regimen ruined by a desk job and a back injury. I picked up the backpack with as much grace as I could muster, suppressed a groan, and walked carefully down the hallway. I felt crushed under its weight. I took out a pair of Teva sandals and an extra fleece top and set them aside, wondering woefully how many layers I *really* needed to keep warm during the upcoming blustery nights in a tent.

"I'll be fine. I'm sure I'll get used to it!" I said. I hoped I sounded surer than I felt.

The next day, as my dad drove me to the Buffalo airport, the newscaster on the local radio station talked about the opioid crisis in between musical numbers. The crisis was afflicting the people of our quiet, sleepy region, along with methamphetamine. I am from Allegany County—one of the poorest counties in New York State—and during even my short visits there as an adult I could see the presence of poverty and addiction in the faces of many of its people. Like much of Appalachia, the populations of numerous small towns in the area have been dwindling for decades due to limited economic opportunities. Factory jobs used to be a dime a dozen, and now many of the factories have shut their doors and moved on to cheaper pastures.

It was a strange topic to be pondering just as I was about to say goodbye to my dad for the next six months and embark on one of the biggest journeys of my life so far. But I'd later see the same issues afflicting many of the towns that I'd walk through on the AT.

As we pulled up to the airport, I loaded my backpack onto my back and posed for a quick photo before heading to the check-in counter. My dad walked with me to the security line, giving me a big hug.

"Be real careful and safe out there," he told me.

I would do my best.

CHAPTER 4

After disembarking the plane, I wandered through the Asheville, North Carolina, airport wondering where I was supposed to meet Natalie. I followed the shuffle of passengers down to the baggage claim and watched as my silver and purple Osprey Aura backpack tumbled into sight and circled the carousel. I grabbed the straps and swung it off the platform, lugging it to a nearby bench before lifting it laboriously onto my back. I buckled the hip belt and chest strap, then I steadied myself. As I looked up from the straps, I spotted Natalie's newly shaved head bobbing in the opposite direction. I attempted to jog toward her. However, with my backpack already weighing me down, my pace was more of a hobble. I caught her only as she stopped to use the ATM. "We're really doing it!" she exclaimed joyfully, wrapping me in a big hug.

She explained that her mom, Jolie, was waiting in the car with some leftover Indian food, which I was welcome to snack on as we drove south to Georgia. They had been visiting some old friends of Jolie's from her days as a receptionist at a recording studio at their lake house in South Carolina, so Jolie agreed to drive us to the trailhead at Amicalola after. Natalie's dad is an old British rocker who had some success in the 1970s and early 1980s, and they met while Jolie had the receptionist job.

I helped myself to some fried okra and vegetable tempura in the backseat as they chatted about their weekend of fun at the lake. As we drove through the mountains, I recognized a few trail town names on highway exit signs, like Franklin and Hiawassee, making it seem all the more real. Natalie wasn't nervous at all— just a bundle of excitable energy, which I would come to learn was her norm.

Once we arrived in Dahlonega, Georgia, we checked into our room for the night and planned our last meal. We had originally planned to start the trail on this day, March 19, but had pushed it back a day to give ourselves more time to prepare. We were glad that we did as we watched the local news from our hotel room, learning that a tornado was possible in this part of Georgia that very night. We took a moment to commiserate with the poor hikers who had already started their treks, then headed out to a lovely little Greek restaurant along the main stretch of town for our last supper. I made a point to get a green salad with my meal, thinking I would soon miss fresh produce, and happily agreed to split a bottle of red wine with Natalie and Jolie. We would probably miss that soon enough as well.

We woke up bright and early the next morning, and I took an extra hot, extra long shower, knowing this would be my last for some time. I repacked my backpack and headed over to the dining room for the hotel's complimentary continental breakfast. As I sipped my coffee, I noticed that my nerves had subsided a bit.

We had a short drive from the hotel to Amicalola Falls State Park. While the Appalachian Trail officially begins at Springer Mountain, at least for northbounders like me, the trailhead is located on a four-wheel-drive-only road and is difficult to get to. As a result, most northbounders start their journeys 8.8 miles south of Springer at Amicalola and hike an approach trail to the official start of the AT.

Roughly 80 percent of thru-hikers choose to go northbound. This is because the northbound season is longer and northbounders don't have to tackle the most difficult sections of the trail right off the bat. While hiking through the mountains of northern Georgia is certainly not easy, it doesn't come close to the tremendous difficulty of climbing through the White Mountains in New Hampshire and Southern Maine. Some people do choose to go southbound, however, starting in Maine. There is also a small subset of hikers that "flip-flop" and start somewhere in the middle. For example, a flip-flopper might begin in Virginia, hike to Maine, then flip back to Virginia and head south to Georgia from there. There are several reasons to do it in this non-traditional way—to beat the cold, to beat the heat, or to better fit one's schedule. But logistically, it's easiest to simply go northbound or southbound and hike straight through.

Typically, it takes between five and seven months to thru-hike the AT. As I began my adventure, this meant if all went well, I would spend about six months of my life immersed in the wilderness of the Appalachian Mountains, carrying everything that I needed on my back. According to the Appalachian Trail Conservancy, only 20 to 25 percent of people who set out to thru-hike the AT finish the trek successfully. Half drop out within the first 500 miles. One in four allegedly drops out by Neels Gap—the first major road crossing of the AT, only 31.1 miles into the trail. Most commonly, people quit because they get injured, run out of money, or just plain don't like the experience.

Upon entering the visitor center, we were invited to attend a talk on the 10 essentials of hiking. We sat in a small, windowless room with several other hikers. The tension in the air was palpable. These people were clearly nervous too.

The ranger in charge of the class asked everyone how many days of food we had packed. When I responded that I had six, he laughed heartily and told me I needed a "shakedown." A shakedown, I learned, is when an expert rifles around inside your pack, removing items that you do not need, to make your pack weight more bearable.

He was right. My pack, despite having weighed in at 34 pounds on my parents' scale, read 48 pounds on Amicalola's scale. A ranger by the name of Bob offered to help. By the time he took out my journal and half my food, I had shed several pounds. I was a little embarrassed. I had been backpacking a few times before and felt like I shouldn't have been such a novice, but apparently I was. But Bob didn't seem to judge. He was pleasant, paternal, and a big help. He chuckled merrily as he gave encouraging advice, explaining that I wouldn't need to make big miles at first. Stopping at Springer Mountain the first day was perfectly acceptable, he told me, and highly recommended as far as he was concerned. I was happy to oblige—the first leg of those 8.8 miles from Amicalola to Springer includes 604 stairs up the side of a waterfall.

Ranger Bob also told me and Natalie that he had been doing this a long time and could pick out the hikers who were going to make it all the way to Maine. "You two girls are going to make it, I can just tell!" he declared. I'm sure he tells that to everyone, but hearing it brought huge smiles to our faces and a renewed confidence in our abilities. If Ranger Bob said we were going to make it, then by golly we were going to make it!

We snapped a photo under the stone archway that signals the beginning of the approach trail, and after some more encouragement from the rangers, we were on our way. The first mile was gorgeous but miserable. I could feel every single pound on my back with each of those 604 stairs. As I reached the top of Amicalola Falls, I was soaked with sweat and my face was bright red. I huffed and puffed as I shoved my pack off my back and threw myself on the ground, panting. "I'm dying!" I told Natalie.

Natalie, whose pack was a good 10 pounds lighter than mine, eyed me calmly, her face dry as a bone, without a hint of perspiration. "I didn't think it was so bad!" she said cheerfully. I couldn't pretend to agree.

Luckily, the trail mellowed out quite a bit once we got past those godforsaken stairs. Natalie and I strolled on together for a bit and soon caught up to another group of hikers. Katie and Francis were an engaged couple from Austin, Texas, Akuna was a military veteran from the south who had hiked the Pacific Crest Trail (PCT) the year before, and Jamie was a ski shop manager with a nose ring from Boston, Massachusetts.

I chatted with Katie and Francis for a bit while Natalie hiked with Jamie and Akuna. I learned that Francis was mostly deaf, having had a brain tumor a few years prior. He and Katie had been friends for years before falling in love at work, and she stuck with him when crisis struck. The AT had been his dream, but she asked him to wait a year so she could join him. After they finished, they were planning to move back home to the Midwest, where they were both originally from, to get married and start a family.

I caught up with Natalie as Katie and Francis stopped for a break, and the two of us continued with her waiting for me at the top of each hill. We passed several other thru-hiker hopefuls throughout the day and made small talk with most of them, asking where they were from and what made them want to hike the trail. Two older gentlemen made big impressions on both of us: Kevin, a short, blunt but jolly man from Massachusetts, and Mickey, a stoner with wild hair who had done the trail in pieces a few times before.

We also met and conversed with another friendly guy, a 20-something named Mark from Alabama, as we collected and filtered our water. He cut a water bottle in half, keeping only the bottom portion to use as a cup to scoop water out of slow-trickling streams rather than waiting for it to sluggishly run into a water bag. I would use this trick for the rest of the AT. It not only saved a lot of time, but it also saved my fingers from freezing every time I needed to refill my bottles. Though his legs were much longer than ours and he was clearly fitter than us (well, fitter than me, at least), he hiked on with us for a good while, chatting about his life as a software developer in Alabama and what brought him to the woods.

It was a lovely day—60 degrees and sunny. I was in shorts. But that quickly changed as we reached the summit of Springer Mountain. As we officially arrived on the AT, a dark, ominous cluster of gray clouds rolled in. Rain began pelting my bare legs and the air temperature dropped by probably 20 degrees within just a few minutes. The trail gods were showing us what we were in for.

As the rain came in, we rushed ahead to the Springer Mountain Shelter and began hastily setting up our tents. We wanted to get everything ready before the weather got any worse. Once my tent was up, I crawled inside. There, I found a canary yellow glow stick. It was emitting a bright light as if it had just been cracked.

"Hey look at this!" I said to Natalie, giggling. "This must be from the last music festival that I went to!"

Natalie laughed, rolling her eyes at me as she continued making camp. As we were getting settled in, Ducky, a charming former PCT thru-hiker from Oregon whom we had met at the summit, asked if he could set up next to us. The three of us chatted merrily. Natalie and I were thrilled; we had made our first friend. He asked if we'd gotten our photo with the official Springer Mountain plaque. We hadn't, because we hadn't known it existed. We decided to make a quick run back to the summit to do so and to sign the logbook.

Since the rain seemed to get heavier as we made our way back to camp, we decided to head into the shelter, a three-sided lean-to, to cook dinner and meet some of the other folks who had started the trail that day. Everyone was friendly but seemed exhausted and cold. We met John from Norfolk, AJ from Florida, Michael from New Jersey, and Sarah from Minnesota, among others. I immediately felt drawn to Sarah. She was confident and friendly, offering me her lighter when my waterproof matches wouldn't ignite. I had a quick meal of instant mashed potatoes and would have liked to hang out longer, but I had begun to shake from the cold, so I cleaned out my pot and called it a night. It was 6:30 pm.

CHAPTER 5

I awoke my first full morning on the trail stiff and sore. A dusting of snow coated my tent. Spring had reverted to winter overnight, and I groaned as I forced myself out of my cozy sleeping bag. Ducky had disappeared around dawn; I heard rustling as he packed up his tent before first light. He'd told Natalie and I the night before that he wanted to get an early start. *He wasn't kidding about being an early bird*, I thought.

We decided to cook breakfast inside Springer Mountain Shelter, hoping it would give us some respite from the frigid wind. At the very least, we had others to commiserate with in there. We chatted with the same crew who had been there the night before. AJ, one of the younger hikers, had already decided to call it quits. He turned back for Amicalola early that morning, already on his way home. We chatted with Sarah from Minnesota a bit more and learned that she'd already ripped her cheap Frogg Toggs rain pants by trying to stretch her legs out too far. Jamie tried to name her "Crotch Toggs" but she declined the name.

Tradition mandates that hikers pick up trail names during their journeys. Some people name themselves, and some do so even before beginning the trail, but that is frowned upon. The general rule of thumb is that someone else names you once you're on trail, for some silly thing you've done, or a personality trait that sticks out, or the like. You are allowed to reject a name for any reason, though. You are the only one with the power to accept a trail name, and once you do so, you begin to introduce yourself as such. Your legal name is no longer of any consequence, and most people don't even know what it is. Your trail name is how you are known henceforth.

After a quick breakfast of oatmeal and black tea, I made my way down to the stream to gather and filter water. I had opted to buy a Sawyer Squeeze mini water filter and quickly found that it was a much slower model than the full-sized Sawyer Squeeze that Natalie had. It took me several minutes longer than her to filter my water, and in that time I was not unconvinced that my hands were going to freeze solid, also finding that my brand new filter leaked. Much to my chagrin, I finished up with both hands intact.

As I passed the shelter on my way back to my tent to pack up my gear, Sarah followed. "Would you guys mind if I hiked with you, just for today?" she asked. She explained that she was solo, and thought it would be nice to find some other women to tag along with. We happily agreed. She had made a positive impression on both of us during our meals together, and we were ecstatic to already be making a friend to hike with. Our twosome was now a threesome.

We packed up, shaking as much snow off of our tents as we could before stuffing them into our packs, and got a move on. We were anxious to get our blood pumping so we could warm up a little. Wearing 90 percent of my clothing, I was freezing but happy. I'd made it through my first night on the AT.

As we rejoined the AT, we followed the signature white blazes that are painted on tree trunks along the trail to guide hikers on their way. We stopped to admire some huge icicles that were hanging off the boulders on the side of the trail and mused at the rhododendron trees creating tunnels for us to walk through. None of us had seen rhododendrons in the wild before, and we wondered how long it would be until they bloomed. The AT is often referred to as the "green tunnel" because hikers pass through thick forests for the majority of its 2,000 miles, missing the big sweeping mountain views of the long trails of the West. These woody flowering plants are a main player in creating that effect.

We stopped for lunch at a waterfall not far off the trail, and while it was lovely to have a scenic lunch, by the time we started hiking again I was convinced I would never be warm again. As long as I kept moving, I was fine, but stopping for even a short amount of time was enough to trigger violent shivering. Our threesome hiked together as a group all day until we reached our campsite for the night at Hawk Mountain Shelter, 8.1 miles north of Springer Mountain Shelter.

The air temperature continued to drop throughout the day, and after stopping to set up camp and scooting into all my dry clothes, I was once again absolutely freezing. It was so biting cold outside that my fuel canister froze to the wooden picnic table in front of the shelter. Another hiker had to roundhouse kick it to lodge it free for me.

Luckily, some other hikers had gotten to camp earlier in the day and built a roaring fire. I bundled up next to that campfire for hours. I honestly don't know how I would have gotten through the day without it. Everyone had the same idea, so it was a social afternoon and early evening. We were entertained for hours by the tales of a former army ranger who had been through survival training in the Arctic, and I pestered him for all of his tips on how to stay warm in these frigid temperatures. He recommended that I take off my extra layers of clothing once in my sleeping bag. This way, I could put them on again in the morning before leaving my tent, which would make me feel warmer. I tried this method as I got settled into my sleeping bag, but I was so uncomfortable that after a few minutes I changed course and opted to wear every single piece of clothing that I owned instead.

Jamie was there once again, and I also met Chuckleberry Finn and Ken, a pair of best friends from Florida, and Mary and

Firebug, a sweet couple from southern Illinois and Tennessee who had met while training for their thru-hikes in the Smoky Mountains. Firebug was named for his penchant for building fires. He was the hero of the day, having built this fire, but he was not the type to go bragging about it. He was the quiet and unassuming one of the pair. Mary, on the other hand, was a talker and an entertainer. She shared story after story after story about her life.

That night was the coldest of my life. Even with my zero-degree sleeping bag, between my violent shivering and the ferocious roaring of the wind through the trees, I barely slept a wink. When I did finally doze off, I dreamed of cuddling up with a space heater. It was the one thing in all of the world I desired more than anything else. Unfortunately, I had to go without. I slept with my arms over my head for half the night, convinced that the loud cracking in the trees meant one was about to fall on my tent.

I was rewarded for surviving the night by waking up to sunshine and blue sky as far as the eye could see. It was a welcome sight after the frigidity of the past two nights and the gloom of the previous day. That morning, as I hiked down the trail behind Natalie, I began to notice hints of spring in the forest around me. Tiny purple, white, and yellow flowers dotted the path, rhododendron leaves sprouted out from their branches, dangling over the trail, and I swear I even saw the beginnings of little green strawberry plants. Things were looking up.

Sarah asked if she could join us for another day. As far as we were concerned, she could stay forever. We adored her—she was sweet, smart, and hilarious. It already felt like she belonged with us. We were meant to find her.

As I climbed down a long and winding hill, I found Mary and Firebug from the night before having a snack break on the side of the trail. I stopped for some water and chitchat, and they began to grumble about their tent. They had a Big Agnes Fly Creek 2, one of the more common lightweight tents on the trail. It was a great tent, they explained, but the thing was that most people on the trail weren't sharing that tent with another person. It was about big enough for one person and their pack, they told me. But for the two of them, it was a tight squeeze.

"It's a great tent, don't get me wrong," said Mary, in her thick southern Illinois accent. "I just think we would get along better if it was bigger."

They asked me what tent I was carrying and how I liked it. "I have the opposite problem," I explained. I loved my tent, a Kelty Salida 2 that my brother had bought for me as a birthday gift a couple of years before, but it was much too heavy. Weighing in at four pounds, it added unnecessary weight to my already oversized pack. I often felt like I was being crushed under the weight of all my gear, even after my shakedown.

"Well, uh, why don't we just trade tents then?" Mary asked eagerly. I considered the proposal for all of two seconds, nodding vehemently in agreement. We decided that we'd meet at camp that night where we would check out each other's tent. If we still thought it was a fair proposal, we'd trade in the morning. And that's what we did. The trail provides.

Sarah, Natalie, and I stuck together for most of the day and arrived at Gooch Mountain Shelter, which was built on the side of a mountain with steep rows of tents descending toward a cliff, to another fire and lots of unfamiliar faces. Some hikers were making quick time—16-mile days already. We were sticking with eight, following Ranger Bob's advice to take it easy for the first couple of weeks to avoid quick burnout and injury. Slow and steady was the name of our game. Dylan from California, who wore John Lennon Glasses and had the scrawny but strong look of a long-distance runner, had hiked 24 miles on his first day.

The first of our trio accepted her trail name on this day. Sarah was no longer Sarah; she was now Girl Scout. I came up with her new name myself because she was always prepared. If you had a headache, she had you covered. If you couldn't sleep and needed some Benadryl, she had you covered. If you tore a hole in something and needed it repaired, she had you covered. I originally tried to name her Spam because she kept going on and on about what a fantastic trail food it was—she and Spam were both from Minnesota, after all, and she loved nothing more than Minnesota—but she ultimately rejected that trail name. Girl Scout, though, stuck. From then on, no one called her Sarah on trail again.

The sun continued to shine for the remainder of the afternoon, so the torturous cold of the previous night was at least temporarily behind us, and there was a shift in the mood at camp reflecting this. Everyone seemed to be in much higher spirits than the evening before, myself included. I even led two expeditions to collect firewood. Mary and Firebug had saved me the day before with their roaring fire; I was determined to pay it forward. We chatted with a bunch of other hikers around the fire, including Katie, Francis, Jamie, and Mickey, all of whom we had met the first day on trail. Mickey invited everyone to join his "safety meeting," referring to the joint that he was passing around the campfire. I declined but chatted with him for a long while anyway.

Mickey was a real southern character. A genuinely nice, jolly man, but a little rough around the edges. He told me that he had completed the trail once before and was planning to hike as far as he could get this time around before early June when he had to be back to work at his construction job. "The trail gets into your blood," he told me. "You can't shake it once you've been here." The trail had called him back again, and it probably wouldn't be the last time. His wife understood.

I didn't yet understand what he meant, but I knew that after only three days on trail, I felt more at peace with the world and my place in it than I had in years. I had the strong sense that this was where I was supposed to be. There was already so much joy here.

CHAPTER 6

The next morning, we opted to hustle out of camp without having a sit-down breakfast. We had to reach Lance Creek campsite, which we knew had limited space, before it filled up. Otherwise, we'd have to hike five extra miles through a patch of forest closed to camping due to aggressive bear activity. And none of us wanted to hike an extra five miles.

It was a crisp but pleasant morning, and I felt like I was flying down the trail after having lost two pounds in tent weight. About a mile in, we rounded a corner to find a giant party tent set up in the grass off the side of the trail. A friendly man hollered at us to come sit down. He and his three companions had come out to the trail from Tennessee for an annual long weekend to help hikers on behalf of their church.

The AT community is robust. Even though only about 20,000 people have ever completed a thru-hike, the community stretches far and wide, and there are so many people out there not just willing, but *enthusiastic*, to help hikers on their way. This help, known as trail magic, manifests in various forms. Sometimes, it means giving hikers rides to town. Other times, it entails letting them pitch their tents in your yard and take a shower in your home. Most often though, it's in the form of food. Because there is nothing a thru-hiker values more than food.

This trail magic was of the food variety. The men sat us down in camp chairs and demanded that we put our feet up and relax. They offered us hot breakfast sandwiches, apples, coffee, and cocoa. Our first morning without a hot breakfast, and here was one for the taking on a beautiful sunny morning. The trail provides. They also weighed my pack for me and it came in at 37 pounds. 11 pounds lighter than when I'd first weighed it at Amicalola. I was thrilled!

"That's still pretty heavy," one of the men told me. But I was on cloud nine.

After having our fill and chatting with these kind souls for a while, we let some new hikers take our seats and then ambled down the trail. A few more miles in, we found ourselves being hollered at again to come on over and rest our weary bones. Trail magic number two—and on the very same day as trail magic number one! Obi-Wan, a 2015 thru-hiker, had coffee, cocoa, and bananas ready for us. He asked in return that we leave no trace and say hello to Katahdin for him when we completed our journey. We promised that we would.

From there, we entered Blood Mountain Wilderness and made our way to Lance Creek campsite. We set up our tents side by side and immediately became concerned about the quality of the water coming from the creek. White roses of used toilet paper visibly covered the hillside behind the creek, and the entire place smelled like human feces. A quick Google search told me that this very creek had been linked to a bad outbreak of norovirus the year before. We weren't taking any chances. We'd only hiked about 7.5 miles that day, and after our double trail magics, we all felt like we had some extra energy to burn. We had passed a clear mountain stream about a mile back, so opted to drop most of our gear and backtrack in search of some cleaner water. We spread the word as we passed other hikers that they may want to skip the water at Lance Creek, and many of them turned around and followed us. We ended up leading a parade of hikers back to the stream.

None of us fell ill, so we decided in retrospect that the search for clean water had been worth the extra hiking.

Since there was no shelter to use as a home base, upon returning to camp, we headed to the largest tent site around to socialize with some of the other hikers who were also staying at Lance Creek for the night. Our friends Katie and Francis were there, as well as some new faces, including Erik from Maui, who I estimated to be around my age and seemed reserved but friendly, as well as Jill and Monica, two recent college graduates from Massachusetts. These two women were already talking confidently about the quick miles that they were making, and I doubted I would see much of them from here. We chatted about Erik's favorite hiking trails in Hawaii then eventually moseyed off to hang our bear bags. This was the first site that didn't have bear boxes for us to store our food in. Girl Scout took the lead and strung our bags up on some bear cables near our site, as she would often come to do for us in the following weeks. Then, after much debate on where we could safely and privately use the restroom without stepping in toilet paper or worse, we headed to bed, exhausted and happy.

The next day was going to be a tough one. We had to go over our first big climb—Blood Mountain—and *everyone* was talking about what a beast it would be. We didn't know yet that trail talk is often exaggerated. Information spreads fast and loose, but like a game of telephone, information is not always accurate by the time it gets to you. Conquering Blood Mountain, though, daunting as it was, would come with a heavy reward for our efforts. Following the descent, we'd pass through Neels Gap, home of Mountain Crossings, an outfitter and hostel where we would resupply our depleted food stocks. Rumor had it that in addition to grocery items, they also sold hot food and had hot showers available to hikers. Five days into the trail, this was our first taste of civilization. And during each hard climb and violent fit of shivering thus far, I daydreamed about the hot, steaming, gooey pizza that I'd buy myself at Neels Gap. Needless to say, we were all a little antsy to get up and over Blood Mountain. Treats were waiting!

The night was warm and muggy and I slept well for the first time since we'd started hiking, having not been awakened by my own shivering. Natalie, on the other hand, was sleeping just fine every night. While I am a naturally cold sleeper, she is a hot sleeper. I would put on every piece of clothing that I had with me each night while she'd strip down inside her sleeping bag. I'd shiver myself to sleep while she'd wake up sweating. Each morning, she'd find water droplets clinging to her tent walls. On the bright side of being such a cold sleeper, I didn't have to worry about condensation dripping down onto my sleeping bag and dampening it like she did. I just didn't seem to naturally produce that much heat.

In the morning, we were happy to find that no bears had come along in the night to ransack our food bags. We packed up quickly as some rain clouds moved in, and immediately we began climbing. We had a pretty steady climb for most of the day, the only major descent occurring on the far side of Blood Mountain. Since we had so much uphill to conquer, we decided as a group to simultaneously pop in our headphones, rock out to our best trail playlists, and meet at the top of Blood Mountain. I was feeling strong as I climbed and ran into Kevin just as I noticed some foreboding mountains in the not-too-far distance.

"Which one do you think is Blood Mountain?" I asked, eyes screening the horizon in trepidation.

"Kid, you're *on* Blood Mountain!" he exclaimed in amusement. I was surprised; I had thought that the monster climb everyone was talking so ominously about would be tougher.

As it turned out, not only was I *on* Blood Mountain, but I was pretty darn close to the top of it. I started to see little patches of snow on the ground as I climbed higher, and before long, I stumbled upon the shelter that signifies one has conquered his majesty. I ducked inside to seek refuge from the wind, as I found once again that the temperature had dropped tremendously. I later learned that for every 1,000 feet of elevation gain, the air temperature typically drops by about three to five degrees Fahrenheit. I was soaked in sweat and definitely noticed the change. Inside, I found a gaggle of hikers, including Jamie, Chuckleberry Finn, Ken, and Jay, a big guy with a thick accent from South Carolina, huddled inside, cooking up instant mashed potatoes for lunch. As usual, Natalie had beat me up the mountain, so we munched on some snacks together as we waited for Girl Scout, who was close behind. Once she turned up, we snapped a few photos and got a move on, joined by Jamie and Nick, a weekender from a nearby college who seemed a little smitten with her. The Neels Gap pizza was calling!

The climb down Blood Mountain seemed to wind on forever. But at long last, we finally made it to the bottom of the descent, and more importantly, to Mountain Crossings. As we walked toward the entrance, we passed by the infamous hiking boot tree, where allegedly, hikers who couldn't hack it strung up their shoes and headed home. There were a healthy number of shoes on that tree.

Inside, we inquired about paying for some hot showers. However, showers were unfortunately only available to those staying at the hostel. We planned to camp up the trail, so we were out of luck. We were a little dejected; the hot water would have been a godsend. But Girl Scout, Natalie, and I ordered a whole pizza each, and the anticipation of our hot pies was enough to keep our spirits high, even if the dream of the hot shower had to wait. We chilled out in the back room of the store, charging our phones, sipping on hot coffees, and eyeing other hikers' hot meals enviously as we waited for our own. When our pizzas finally came out of the oven, you would have thought we hadn't eaten in weeks. We devoured them. It was pure ecstasy. I didn't look up from my plate until half my pie was gone. I saved the other half for breakfast the next morning. Finished with my meal, I sat directly in front of a nearby space heater in a satisfied food coma for at least an hour. If I couldn't have a shower, this was the next best thing. I also bought a silk sleeping bag liner to add additional warmth to my bag. It cost me a whopping 70 dollars, but I would have paid anything to guarantee warmer nights.

　　　While there, we met a friendly guy around our age named Chet who came in after us to wait on his pizza. He was from Bozeman, Montana, and had a mohawk. That, along with a West Coast cool guy vibe, gave him a bit of a rock star quality. He laughed easily and I was immediately drawn to him. I was hoping, like us, that he was planning to move on to the next campsite, but he had booked a room at the hostel for the night. I crossed my fingers that we would see him again.

　　　With full bellies, charged phones, and newly restocked food bags, we joined another group of hikers, including Jamie, Jay, Michael from New Jersey, and John from Virginia, whom we'd met the first night at Springer Mountain, on the mile trek up to Bull Gap campsite. We all pitched in to gather firewood, then spent the rest of the day huddled around the fire ring together. I got to know Jamie a little better and decided that we were going to be friends. We were eventually joined by another 20-something hiker that I hadn't met before named Floyd from Georgia. Standing over six feet tall with an easy demeanor, he was a gentle giant.

　　　"Hey Floyd," I called. "Isn't Georgia supposed to be warm?"

　　　"It usually is!" he responded, laughing. "I swear, it's never like this in March!"

That night, I awoke to the sounds of my first "maybe bear." I heard what I thought was a large animal plodding around camp, but when I bravely stuck my flashlight outside my tent and peered into the dark night, really only because I had to relieve myself, I didn't see a thing. *Impossible*, I thought. I just knew there was something out there, and it was colossal. Just because I couldn't see it, didn't mean I wasn't going to lay awake wondering if I was about to be its supper. The next morning, John told me that he'd heard something as well.

Luckily, I made it through the night fully intact, and as I was taking my tent down in the morning, a tall, middle-aged, high-strung man came through camp armed with a camera.

"Gather round, everyone!" he called. "Time for your interviews!" His name was Adrian, and he was a Canadian sailor. Or at least he had been until a car accident left him with a traumatic brain injury and forced him into early retirement. He now dealt with memory loss issues and was making videos on the trail for a class of fourth graders in the United Kingdom who faced similar injuries.

"I'll never remember you unless you really make an impression on me!" he told us impishly. He forced us to stand around in a semicircle as he grilled us on our favorite parts of the trail so far, camera in our faces. I wasn't sure at that moment that I liked him. He was bossy and abrasive, and he flirted with Jamie. But he demanded that we hike with him for a while that morning, leading us down the trail like the Pied Piper. I was surprised to find that the more that he chatted, in his confident, cocky way, about his life as a sailor and how he was finding the trail, the more my irritation turned to amusement. He won me over. It didn't hurt that while my energy was waning as we climbed up an especially steep hill near the end of our day, he offered us all some candy out of his hip belt pockets.

"Sugar will get you up the hills when your muscles won't!" he told us knowingly. This was a mantra that I would carry forward in perpetuity. I'm a sugar addict, and if sugar was going to help me get up the tough climbs, then I certainly was not going to fight it.

"And another thing, ladies," he said. "You're going to watch the men on the trail drop a bunch of weight their first weeks on the trail. In a month, their bodies will have completely changed, but yours will look the same. Don't fret. It's just going to take you longer. In three months, you'll be looking like supermodels!" I liked the sound of that.

After hiking for 10 miles through thick, cold fog, we arrived at Low Gap Shelter to find a city of tents. I'd estimate there were almost 100 of them, at least double what we'd seen even at Springer Mountain on our first night. We found space for our tents on the outskirts of the massive site, changed into our dry clothes, and then went in search of a bonfire, which was rumored to be down a steep incline next to the shelter.

The rumors were true, and after we found the fire, we parked ourselves there for the evening, only leaving it to gather water. There, we met On Step, a lively, open 30-something with a Southern accent. I talked with him for a long while and learned that he was a former minister who had "gotten off track" as he put it. He was recently divorced and had three small children, whom he no longer got to see regularly. His wife was already remarried, though his kids were still practically babies. He was on the trail to get his life back together. He'd made bracelets for each of his family members before he left home, meaning to inscribe them with the words "one step at a time." One step at a time he'd get to Maine. One step at a time he'd get his life together. But instead, there had been a typo. He'd accidentally gotten them printed as "on step at a time" rather than "one step at a time." And so, he was dubbed On Step.

Chet had set up his tent next to ours and appeared at the fire not too long after. He was now known as Wintergreen, named by his brother-in-law because he carried wintergreen oil with him to protect him from vicious… mice. Mice are known pests at AT campsites and shelters, sneaking into packs and chewing through gear to get to hikers' snacks. Chet learned that they are deterred by wintergreen oil so brought some along. However, despite sprinkling it generously around his tent, he'd managed to unwittingly bring one inside his tent during his very first night on the trail. He'd heard it rustling outside around his backpack, so grabbed his pack and brought it inside to safety. But the mouse was already inside his pack, which was now inside his tent. Panic ensued, likely for both Wintergreen and the mouse, and he managed to knock over the trekking pole that was holding up his tent, caving it in on himself.

As we cooked dinner around the fire, Girl Scout, Natalie, and I discussed plans for our upcoming stop in Hiawassee, Georgia, for my thirty-fourth birthday, only a couple of days away. Alarmed by the number of tents at the current site, we decided we'd better book a room in advance to be on the safe side. We invited Jamie to share a room with us and join in the birthday festivities, and soon we had wrangled a group of guys to come along with us as well, including Wintergreen, John, Erik, and Michael. The eight of us decided we'd camp at the same tent sites for the next two nights and then catch a shuttle into Hiawassee together.

And so, the original trail family, or "tramily," was born.

CHAPTER 7

As someone who grew up on the outskirts of a small town but had long ago left it behind for a big city, I was keen to experience small town America while on the trail. Especially *southern* small town America, in my mind about as charming as a place can get. So I was thrilled that I was going to spend my birthday in my very first trail town: Hiawassee, Georgia.

After a couple of long days full of tough climbs, all that was standing between me and the gigantic birthday cake that I planned to buy myself was an easy 3.6-mile hike to Dicks Creek Gap and an 11-mile shuttle into Hiawassee.

As we sat and waited for the shuttle to arrive to whisk us away to the Budget Inn, the first of many seedy motels that we'd stay in along our journey, our anticipation only grew. It was midmorning and our stomachs were grumbling audibly, but we didn't want to spoil our appetites with trail food. There were much bigger and better things awaiting us down US 76. After eight days in the woods, we were more than ready to trade in our granola bars and Pop-Tarts for a real meal. We had a hard time deciding which was more important: food or showers. The ladies chose showers; the guys chose food. Half of the men had already showered at Neels Gap, making their decision easy.

Upon arriving at the Budget Inn, we found that we had rooms directly next to each other on the back side of the building. The guys immediately dispersed, while us ladies had some valuable girl time in our motel room as we got cleaned up. Freshly showered for the first time in over a week, we put our laundry into the coin-operated washer across the quad and headed over to Barney's Tap & Grill for some comfort food and iced cold beers. While wintery shades of brown and gray dominated the mountains, here in town, flowering trees popped with color every which way you looked. The sun was shining bright and, even given the opportunity to dine inside, we chose the patio. I devoured my grilled cheese and house-cut fries, and as I was finishing up the last dregs of my draft beer, On Step showed up with a birthday India pale ale for me. I'm not normally an IPA drinker, but I was trying to say yes rather than no to things on the trail. Plus, it was a sweet gesture from a new friend.

We spent the majority of the afternoon sipping beers and conversing with whichever hikers happened to stroll or stop by. Because Hiawassee was the first major town on the AT, everyone stopped there. After just a week on trail, I felt like the mayor of the town. I recognized *everyone*. And as far as the ones I didn't know, it wasn't too difficult to pick them out as thru-hikers. Thru-hikers have *a look*. Once you see it, you can't unsee it. And you start to pick them out even beyond trail life.

Later that afternoon, we meandered about a mile down the town's main drag to the grocery store to resupply. From Hiawassee, we had about 50 miles, roughly five days, to our next town stop. We would have to make sure our rations would last us until then. We needn't worry; at that time, our eyes were still much bigger than our stomachs, and I left Ingles Market with enough treats to last me a month. This, of course, included a giant marble sheet cake that I intended to share with the entire hiking community as part of my birthday celebration. My friend Allison had sent me $20 to get myself a birthday treat, and I could think of nothing better to spend it on than this massive cake.

As I finished ringing up my groceries at the self-checkout station, an older man with a big white beard stopped me. "Are you a thru-hiker?" he asked. His name was Tom Kennedy, and he was an avid hiker and the co-founder of Hike for Mental Health, a non-profit that encourages people to hike as a way to raise money for mental health research. Tom and I made small talk for a few minutes, and his obvious love for the trail shined through his stories. He invited me to drop by his booth at Trail Days in Damascus, Virginia, to say hello, and he left me with a warning. "The Smokies will kick your ass," he said. "But they'll be worth it."

Word spread quickly that we were intending to dine on Mexican food that evening for my birthday dinner, and what had begun as a table of eight quickly became a party of more than 20. Adrian, our boisterous Canadian friend, showed up last with Thumper, his more reserved but kindly hiking partner. Adrian was now known as One Up because he was always one-upping people with his elaborate stories.

I sat next to Wintergreen and Michael, and across from Natalie, Jamie, and Girl Scout. Margaritas flowed and the chatter at the table grew louder and louder. One Up secretly ordered me a dessert of fried ice cream, and when it arrived, the staff sang obnoxiously, placing an oversized sombrero on my head and spoon-feeding me as they did so. Not being able to eat ice cream myself, as it very unfortunately tends to make me violently ill, I passed my dessert around for everyone to share. One unlucky hiker ended up with a face full of ice cream. It was a festive evening that ended in a bonfire, as any hiker's birthday should, and I fell asleep feeling happy and loved, even in this community of near-strangers. I was sure that 34 was going to be a great year.

In the morning, after a hearty breakfast of eggs, biscuits, and coffee, we all had one last shower and packed up our gear,

ready for the shuttle to take us back to the trail. Hiawassee had
been an incredible introduction to trail town life, accommodating
and quaint, but I was ready to get back to the forest where I
belonged. As we mulled over our plan for the day, Wintergreen
piped up, concerned. He'd been watching the forecast, and a
powerful rainstorm was expected that afternoon. He was worried
that if we tried to push on too far, we'd miss out on space in a
shelter. Unconvinced that our tents would stand up well in the
heavy rain to come, he recommended that we hike just four miles
to Plum Orchard Gap Shelter and settle in for the evening. That
seemed reasonable, so we agreed.

I was happy with the decision as my knees had been
aching from all the steep ups and downs that Georgia had been
throwing our way, so I figured they could use the extra rest. Years
of running had done a number on them, and they didn't seem to
appreciate the weight of my pack. This was my first of only two
nights spent sleeping in a shelter for the entire trail. I much
preferred the privacy of my tent, but his panic over the weather
forecast gave me enough pause to give shelter life a try.

Pre-rain, it was a gorgeous day, warm and muggy. Upon
arriving at the shelter, my body very much wanted to keep on
going. I rationalized, however, that Wintergreen was right. Staying
put to wait out the oncoming storm was the smart thing to do. But I
was restless for the remainder of the day, even taking a nap to calm
my irritable energy. When I awoke, it was raining, and the rest of
the tramily was hanging on the porch of the shelter talking with a
fascinating, charismatic couple from Atlanta: Dragon's Breath, a
retired Green Beret and physician, and his wife Honey Badger, a
nurse. They'd retired early, selling all of their possessions and
telling their young adult children that they'd need to find their own
housing from there on out. They were done with a life of
conformity; they wanted to live as vagabonds for a while.

I wasn't feeling particularly social, so I stepped away from the group and joined Girl Scout in the loft of the shelter. The two of us chatted and giggled for hours, eventually joined by Max, a long-legged, bespectacled college junior with a lustrous mane down to his shoulders. I asked him for all of his hair secrets. "How the heck do you keep your hair so beautiful in the woods?" I demanded. The guy belonged in a Vidal Sassoon commercial.

Max was happy to spill. His secret, he explained, was that he never washed it. And I don't mean that he sometimes washed it. I mean he *never* washed it. In addition, he chopped it all off every two years on his birthday, only to grow it out again and restart the cycle. It broke his mother's heart every time he cut it short.

In addition to having incredible hair, Max was also a talented song and short story writer. Girl Scout and I, now joined by Jamie, were smitten with him. I spoke to him as if he were a delicate bird; I didn't want to frighten him away. He slowly went from speaking shyly to us from the floor to the ladder just below us. Before long, he was sprawled in between us. After enough delighted begging, he agreed to read one of his short stories aloud. And by this time, his blue-eyed, curly-haired best friend Bay, whom he had met working at a summer camp in North Carolina years before, and Natalie, had climbed into the loft as well. We listened, enthralled, until it was time for bed. Our tramily men were not impressed, but we talked and giggled about these two for weeks. We dubbed them "the Striders" because of their long spider legs and they made our lazy day at Plum Orchard Gap Shelter worth it ten times over.

The next day, on fresh legs, we hiked into North Carolina. Leaving Georgia behind, we checked off our first of 14 states. Michael hiked just behind me as I reached the border between the two states, so we stopped to let out a whoop of excitement and to have a little photo shoot. As we turned a corner just past the border, the warmth of the day turned to cool fog, and I hustled forward to try and build some heat.

I also hustled to get away from Michael. After so much social time in town and at the shelter, I was ready for some alone time. Michael had done about a quarter of the trail two years before, forced off the trail at Partnership Shelter in Virginia due to a stress fracture in his foot, and he was back again to give it another go. We weren't completely sure why he was there though. While the rest of the tramily was intensely excited about living this new, free life, Michael seemed bogged down by it. My theory was that the AT was his white whale. Having failed his first thru-hike attempt, he had returned to conquer it. Michael meant well, but at this moment I needed some quiet time, so I rushed unsuccessfully from both the cold and him.

I was starting to become frustrated with just how social the trail was. While I loved meeting new people every day and hanging out at camp with friends at the end of the day, I struggled to find alone time with my thoughts. Alone time is a necessity for my mental health, so the lack of it at this point in the trail was difficult for me. The beginnings of the trail were crowded, and having a tramily of eight made it that much harder. I was one of the slower hikers in my group as well, so outrunning most of them to find some quiet wasn't an option.

I ended up ducking into a patch of trees and hanging out for a few minutes to lose Michael. This method of escaping company on the trail would become known in my tramily as the old "hike and hide." Just as I tiptoed out of the woods and back to the trail, Natalie came strolling along. Natalie was one of the few people on trail whom I never really needed time away from. Despite wanting to be alone, I didn't mind her presence. It was easy with her, and she calmed me. As we hiked together through the very southern tip of North Carolina, we became mesmerized by the greenery that appeared around us, seemingly out of nowhere.

Apart from the flora of Hiawassee, we'd barely seen any color
aside from the dull grays and beiges of winter since beginning the
trek. Suddenly, there were lush mosses of various shapes and hues
in every direction. Spring was beginning.

Girl Scout caught up with us a couple of miles from Deep
Gap campsite, our home for the night, then Jamie shortly behind
her. As I was preparing an early dinner of macaroni and cheese at
camp, a couple around my age appeared with a cooler full of
sodas, PBRs, cantaloupe, and oranges. Pretzel, who had thru-hiked
a few years prior, brought his girlfriend and their dog out to the
trail for some trail magic and camped out with us for the night.
Dragon's Breath, named so for his ability to make roaring
campfires, was true to his name and built an impressive one. He
also regaled us with thrilling tales of his time as a Green Beret—
speaking of a time he had to dive past enemy lines. After a hard
day of hiking, this was all more than I could ask for. I was content
once again.

Rumor had it there would be a massive trail magic set up
at Deep Gap in the morning. It was Easter weekend, and the
church group putting it on came out each year to do so. We were
all drooling at the idea of a hot breakfast and had not yet learned
that the promise of trail magic wasn't a sure one. After a slow
morning waiting for its arrival, we decided to push on just as some
men in trucks pulled up to begin setting up. We found out it
wouldn't be ready until lunchtime, and we were too antsy to wait
around that long, even for food.

All was not lost, however. Pretzel and Company made our
day once again by inviting us to join them for some hot chocolate
and home-cooked oatmeal, which was loaded with fruit, nuts, and
chocolate. We had our fill then said our goodbyes, thankful both to
have met them and to have been fed by them. We were also told by
the guys setting up the other trail magic that they'd be doing it

again tomorrow, 20 miles ahead of where we stood. Suddenly, we felt extremely motivated to make it those 20 miles by lunchtime the next day.

It was a beautiful day in North Carolina, 60 degrees and sunny without a cloud in the sky. Though the mountains seemed taller than those in Georgia, the trail was more forgiving, with longer and gentler switchbacks. I had a lovely morning hiking with Girl Scout, enjoying both her company and the sunshine. But as was beginning to become the norm, we were joined after a while by a large chunk of the tramily. With so many big personalities in one place, I felt drowned out. The tramily had only just begun, and already I was questioning whether forming it had been the right decision. I liked everyone individually, but all together, it was becoming too much for me even just a few days in.

We stopped for lunch at a sunny campsite and Dragon and Honey Badger showed up and joined us along with the rest of the tramily. It was a nice rest—my body was tired from our long day of hiking the day before, and I gobbled up whole wheat tortillas with cheddar cheese, chocolate Pop-Tarts, and carrots that a volunteer from the Nantahala Hiking Club had given me as an Easter treat that morning. The carrots were delicious—crisp and sweet. The trail diet was a huge shift from my norm, and I was having a hard time adjusting to eating processed foods every day, so any produce was a real gift.

I was quiet at lunch, still annoyed at the group walk when what I really wanted was to continue my peaceful walk with Girl Scout, but things soon improved. I hiked with Dragon for a long while, and we bonded over having similar back injuries. He entertained me with stories of his time in combat, which included helicopter crashes, diving missions, and other high-adrenaline pursuits. He had at some point or another broken just about every bone in his body. He had my single injury beat, that was for sure. And after all of that, he was still well enough to hike long distances. He helped me to cross a huge fallen tree that was blocking the trail, then encouraged me forward, deciding he'd better wait for his wife.

I couldn't blame him. The tree was so colossal in diameter that I could easily imagine slipping off and finding myself tumbling down the cliff below it. Best for him to wait.

That night, the tramily and I camped at Betty Creek, a lovely little campsite nestled deep in a rhododendron grove with a babbling brook running through it. This was the first time I fell asleep to the sound of moving water, something I'd come to absolutely adore doing on the trail because it helped to drown out the crackling sounds of the forest that sometimes kept me awake. And that day, as the North Carolina mountains began to challenge us, they also began to offer us some incredible views. We began to find, as we escaped the dreary, overcast weather of Georgia, that the Blue Ridge Mountains did, in fact, look blue.

Bright and early the next morning, on Easter Sunday, we climbed Albert Mountain, a beast in its own right, to reach our first major milestone: mile marker 100. From here, we had only 2,100 miles to go! One full day of hiking later, we would make it to Winding Stair Gap, where we'd jump off the trail and catch a shuttle to Franklin, North Carolina. There, we'd take our first "zero day," a full day of rest where we didn't hike at all.

CHAPTER 8

The town of Franklin, North Carolina, openly declares that it wants to be the favorite trail town among AT thru-hikers, and does a fantastic job of marketing itself. It has everything you could want in a small town: a charming historic town center, quaint locally owned shop fronts that dot the main street, two breweries, the crystal clear Little Tennessee River flowing through it, and the stunning Blue Ridge Mountains framing it. If ever a town belonged on a postcard, it's Franklin.

In addition, I found many of its people to be incomparably kind. As we waited for our shuttle to take us to town from the parking lot at Winding Stair Gap, at least five cars stopped to offer us rides. Another local sat in the parking lot with a truck full of free snacks for the hikers passing through, and she insisted that we fit as many treats as we could into our packs. The Baptist church in town is famous for offering free pancake breakfasts to hikers each day of the high hiker season every single year, complete with homemade jams and jellies of multiple varieties, juice, and bacon. The church folks will pick you up at your hotel, insist that you eat your fill, provide you with the supplies to write a letter home to your family, mail it for you, drive you back to your hotel, and invite you to come again the next day. And they ask nothing in return.

When we arrived at Winding Stair Gap, there was no trail magic to be found, despite what we had been told the previous day.

We pulled a rookie move by calling a shuttle to pick us up when we could have easily hitchhiked into town. We spent about 45 minutes waiting for our shuttle—precious minutes that we could have spent gorging ourselves on town food. As we waited, Michael decided to ditch us to get his own ride to town. A former thru-hiker-turned-hostel-owner named Zen had shown up at the gap with bribes of snacks, sodas, and the promise of a free ride to town if hikers would stay at his hostel. We declined as we already had reservations at the Budget Inn, but Michael, impatient, accepted Zen's offer. Calling the shuttle though, however inconvenient, turned out to be a phenomenal decision, because it allowed us to spend the entire ride to town with a local celebrity.

After chilling out on the pavement and scarfing down more than our fair share of Goldfish, potato chips, and honey buns, a short bus finally rolled up, making a beeline for us. It was driven by local legend Ron Haven, who runs a free daily hiker shuttle.

There are certain people famous within the trail community, who all thru-hikers aspire to meet. Ron is one of them, for good reason. Ron Haven is a character in the absolute best way possible. The man wears many hats and was more than happy to tell us about all of them in his thick Southern accent as he drove the bus along. He chattered on for the entire 10-mile shuttle to town, and we listened, absolutely enthralled. He hiked the AT back in the 1970s, owned Baltimore Jack's Place Hostel in Franklin, and was a local politician. At one time, he was also a semi-professional wrestler, which he told us about in detail. He seemed to know everything and everyone in Franklin and was happy to share his knowledge. He was incredibly welcoming and made us feel completely at ease, though there was an indefinable quality about him that made me think he belonged at a used car lot. As he dropped us off at the Budget Inn, our second of the trail so far, I asked him where we could purchase some shampoo. He told us that if we switched over to his hostel across the street, he'd throw in the shampoo for free. We politely declined as the four of us gals were not looking to share a bathroom with any other smelly hikers.

Franklin is a place I'd be proud to call home. But as we explored the town the next day, it became clear that despite its charm, it had a seedy side too. We walked past a strip featuring a pawnshop, a gun shop, and warehouses littered with trash. Fast food restaurants like McDonald's and Hardee's dominated the outskirts of town. And as we strolled down the sidewalk in the late afternoon, returning to the motel after a trip to the Dollar General, a young man of probably 18 or 19 stalked up behind us, agitated. As he passed by, he made large sweeping motions with his arms, ran then stopped, ran then stopped, almost entirely lost his pants as they fell to his knees, and began to edgily side-eye a cop car driving down the street. My guess was meth, and if it was showing up in public in broad daylight, I guessed there was plenty more where that came from. It was an odd disparity to witness—beautiful historic homes on one end of town, the Dollar General and a drugged-out teenager on the other. It reminded me of the area where I grew up, idyllic and quaint, yet lacking in economic opportunity and rife with poverty and addiction.

I was reminded of the radio program that my dad and I had listened to on the way to the airport about the problems afflicting my home region. Thinking about it made me feel dirty. Addiction runs in my family; several of my cousins have been drug addicts. And I was acutely aware that if a few things had gone just a little bit differently, that could have been me as well. Spinal ailments are the number one medical condition associated with opioid addiction, especially failed spinal surgeries. I had two things going for me in this regard though: my spinal surgery was a success, and I never liked being on opioids, even when I needed them to function. They made me feel tired and out of it and they messed with my stomach. A pharmacologist later told me that I'm likely a

slow metabolizer, which is why they didn't agree with me. I got
lucky in a way that so many people don't.

On a lighter note though, the historic downtown was
stunning, the community catered so kindly to hikers, and while
there, we got to spend some time with many of our new friends,
including On Step, the Striders, One Up, and Thumper. All in all,
it was a lovely place to spend a desperately needed zero day. My
knees were killing me, and this little town and its people were a
godsend.

As we sat at a local brewery, as became our tradition in
trail towns, a slightly intoxicated John accepted a trail name that he
would later regret. He'd been skinny all his life and had only
recently been able to put on some weight at the ripe old age of 25.
He was determined not to lose the progress that he'd made, so even
this early on, before real hiker hunger struck, he was eating
ridiculous meals and he was constantly and smoothly convincing
others (me) to donate their extra food to his cause. This practice is
known as yogi-ing, as in the bear that is always stealing the picnic
baskets of unsuspecting campers. His lunches regularly consisted
of tortillas wrapped around peanut butter, Nutella, and crushed-up
candy. He'd pack out butter and put it on everything, including in
his morning coffee. And so, he became Butters, which would
evolve into Butterstuff. Later on, he'd swap out this name for
Topper, another food-related name. His mother was a nutritionist
and apparently wouldn't let him have full bowls of sugary cereal
when he was a child. Instead, he'd get healthy cereal topped with
something sugary, which they'd refer to as the "topper." He didn't
know until adulthood that this wasn't normal practice. And so, he
became Topper, though I never knew him as such.

Meanwhile, Erik was back at the Budget Inn, cryptically
dealing with some legal matter over his taxes. His ex-girlfriend
was a lawyer, and he was putting it all in her hands. In our few
days together, I had not yet begun to figure out who Erik was. He

was kind and friendly, but also a bit guarded. I got the impression that he was full of secrets. Of everyone in the tramily, he intimidated me the most. I just wasn't sure what to ask him to learn who he was. I was certain it was going to take some work and some time.

As the rest of the gang headed off to brewery number two, I decided to stay behind at the Budget Inn to get some much-needed alone time. I meandered uptown to get some takeout then settled into the girls-only hotel room for a quiet evening. I was sound asleep when the others returned noisily hours later. If the stumbling hadn't tipped me off, I could tell Girl Scout had partaken in a few too many as she loudly proclaimed in a much thicker-than-usual Minnesota accent that she was "so sorry" for the disturbance. I was unflustered, though anxious to get back to sleep. Unfortunately, another of Girl Scout's tells was a bout of ear-splitting snoring that lasted the night through. She was lucky I liked her so much.

The next morning, after a nearly sleepless night, I stayed behind at the Budget Inn as the rest of the tramily caught the shuttle to the Baptist church for round two of their famous pancake breakfast. I wanted a few last precious moments of shuteye and one more shower, which trumped the pancakes. Once the gals returned from breakfast, we sprinted to catch Ron Haven's shuttle. This time, he drove us to the forest. His shuttle ran twice per morning, at 9:00 am and 11:00 am. The guys missed the first shuttle, so they promised over text message to catch us later in the afternoon. It was a beautiful day for a hike. I huffed and puffed my way up into the mountains for a large chunk of the day, but thankfully, I was rewarded for my efforts with absolutely stunning views of the mountains surrounding us and the valleys below.

I hiked with Girl Scout for most of the day, resting on a log with her for almost an hour on our way up Wayah Bald and making small talk with every hiker who passed by. The guys had yet to catch up, being two hours behind, so we weren't in any rush. When we finally got a move on, making the final push up to the stone tower of Wayah Bald, we found Natalie taking a catnap in the sun, with her hideous floppy sun hat half covering her face. It was a hat made for a middle-aged dad, not for a lovely little pixie person, but she insistently wore it anyway because she's literally allergic to the sun. We roused her from her slumber to climb the tower with us. We wanted to get a view of the mountains that lay ahead. They were gorgeous and blue, jagged and intimidating. We mused excitedly about what the next section of trail might bring. We tried to guess where the Smokies, the most hyped-up part of the trail yet, might be.

Eventually, we decided it was time to move on. The wind was picking up and chilling us to our bones, despite the day's bright sunshine. We had another mile down to Wayah Bald Shelter, where we intended to stay the night. When we arrived though, we found that the tent sites were sloped and crowded. We hung around for several minutes, hoping the rest of the group would catch up so we could decide whether to stay or move on. A few moments later, Wintergreen came down the trail. We made an executive decision to continue on another mile or so to Licklog Gap, where there was a water source and multiple tent sites.

As I meandered down the trail with Natalie, Floyd, the gentle giant from Georgia with whom we'd camped outside Neels Gap, caught up, jovially recounting the last several days since we'd last seen him. There was not a single gap in conversation until we reached Licklog Gap. That's the thing with thru-hikers; friendships and relationships form quickly and deeply on the trail. If you don't see a friend in real life for a few months, it's treated as nothing. But if you don't see a hiker friend for several days, it's all cheers, claps on the back, and hugs as if this is a long-lost friend that you haven't seen in *years*. It's quite charming. Floyd was on a mission to catch some friends who were another five miles up the trail, for which we did not envy him, so he bid us a fond farewell once we reached the campsite. He charged up the trail, and Natalie and I set up, having our pick of the wide, flat tent sites. We began to cook dinner as we waited for the rest of the crew to show up.

Wintergreen, after carrying several cans of beer up and down the mountains all day long, was suddenly in a generous mood. He cracked one open and passed his extras out to the tramily, not wanting to have to lug them around again the next day. I gratefully accepted one, and we all sat, sipping beers and passing around candy to share, content to once again be together at camp. As was becoming custom in those early days, Natalie ate her dinner along with half of mine. Hiker hunger had yet to catch me, but she seemed to have been born with the metabolism of a teenage boy. She's tiny but the girl can eat! Being naturally curvy, I truly envy her for that.

Afterward, Girl Scout and I went off to hang our bear bags together, which had become our evening ritual. I usually watched as she wrapped one of our ropes around a tree limb. Then, we'd both pitch in to haul the hefty food bags up into the tree. I was grateful to her for taking on this activity with me most nights, because I am generally hopeless when it comes to throwing sports of any kind, very much including bear bagging.

A golden evening turned into a stormy night, and I was awakened by the thunderous whirring of the wind through the trees and the bright orange flash of lightning. Suddenly, the trees within our campsite seemed much less secure than when I'd been sitting pleasantly beneath them hours before. The one directly above my tent seemed particularly unstable, wobbling this way and that. I covered my head with my sleeping bag, hoping for the best as I drifted back off into a fitful sleep.

I awoke the next morning, tent and self both miraculously still intact, to find that the temperature had dropped nearly 20 degrees overnight. The perfect spring day that we'd had the day

before had turned into a foggy, freezing morning. I ate breakfast
wrapped in my sleeping bag, and Natalie, Girl Scout, and I got an
early start, anxious to get our blood pumping.
A few miles in, we passed a group of three women. Being
that only about 25 percent or so of thru-hikers are female, it was
rare to see so many together in a group, our tramily being an
exception. So I knew immediately who they were. These were the
"Tennessee Girls," as Dragon affectionately called them, later to
be known as the "Tennessee Trio." They were three 20-something
friends from Tennessee who started the trail together, intending to
go all the way as a group. They were friendly, funny, and self-
deprecating. I could see why Dragon liked them so much. Natalie,
Girl Scout, and I chatted with them for a few minutes until the chill
set in again and then we pushed onward. I was tired, stopping
every couple of miles to stuff some candy into my face for the
quick sugar. Cold and gloom have a way of zapping my energy.
        As the day wore on though, blue sky replaced gray, and
spirits were quickly restored. To make things even better, about
halfway through the day, we stopped for a little rest where the trail
met a dirt road, and a family on spring break from Michigan made
small talk with us, dismayed that we were attempting to thru-hike
the entire trail. Unplanned, they invited us to join in their picnic.
They brought out bags and bags full of Easter ham, several
different types of cheeses, fresh fruit, veggies and dip, and snacks
of many varieties. It was an extremely kind gesture and the food
was fantastic. We ducked out only when several more hikers came
from behind to join in this impromptu trail magic. I'm afraid that
this family didn't quite know what they were getting into when
they offered for us to join. I imagine the hikers that followed
quickly ate them out of house and home.
        This was one of the most enchanting days on trail yet. The
day had begun in a drab haze but was replaced by spring splendor.
Fiddlehead ferns, bleeding hearts, and yellow violets began to

burst from the mountainsides, songbirds whistled prettily to us as we passed by, and we strolled, mesmerized, through the most incredibly beautiful burnt black forest, which was springing to life once again through new sparkling gold and green growth. We'd gotten trail magic, and were able to lay in the sun together atop Wesser Bald observation tower. It was a strenuous day, but lovely.

Until it wasn't. We'd planned to stop about 10 miles into the day at Wesser Bald Shelter. But before I knew it, we had pressed on, as Wintergreen insistently created a reason as to why the group shouldn't and couldn't stop there. I didn't understand; it looked like a perfectly reasonable place to stay for the night to me. But this would become his M.O., and it would be something we'd fight about for states to come. I didn't know that yet though, as I reluctantly pressed past Wesser Bald.

In total that day, we marched almost 15 miles over some of the most arduous terrain we'd seen yet. I nearly ate my entire stash of candy trying to drag myself the rest of the way to camp. By the time I arrived, I was so tired and frustrated that I couldn't even talk to Natalie and Girl Scout, giving them the cold shoulder instead. I would have stopped sooner and ditched the group, but there had been no water to be found for miles after Wesser Bald Shelter; we were too high up in the mountains. Two weeks into the trail and only a week into living as a tramily, and it was time for my first good old-fashioned temper tantrum.

Forming the tramily was more than I had bargained for. I missed the freedom of traveling only with Natalie and Girl Scout, making our own plans and living on our own schedule. I hadn't quit my job and come out to the wilderness to follow someone else's orders, and I was angry that I had somewhat passively allowed someone else to take command of my itinerary. In short, I was pissed.

I pitched my tent about as far from everyone else in the tramily as I could, setting up near a quiet older Swedish couple. They commiserated that the terrain that day had been brutal, and said they were planning to take it easy the next day to make up for it. I went to the stream to collect water then began to cook next to them around a barren fire pit, still ignoring the tramily, lest some unkind words fall out of my mouth.

Natalie hollered cordially to me, asking if I was going to join her and Girl Scout for dinner. I growled back that I was sick of being on Wintergreen's schedule and was not entirely sure about the whole tramily thing. Natalie, not being one for confrontation, let me be. Girl Scout gave me a few minutes to cool off, then tiptoed over, timidly asking if I was okay and what she could do to help. She let me air my grievances, responded empathetically, and said she'd let me have my alone time, though of course, I was welcome to come join her and Natalie whenever I was ready. She promised we'd take a more active role in planning our days from then on.

I ate my macaroni and cheese in a huff. To make matters worse, I poured an entire small packet of crushed red pepper that I'd obtained from the Domino's in town into it. I'm not one for super spicy foods, and I quickly realized my mistake. It was so hot that it was almost painful to eat; my mouth was on fire. At that point on the trail, I'd never finished a dinner myself, always pushing my leftovers onto an all-too-willing Natalie. But since I wasn't speaking to her on this particular evening, I was forced to finish my way-too-spicy, way-too-large dinner myself. By the time I was done, I was both angry *and* uncomfortably full, and I thought my taste buds might never recover. I crawled into my tent, too distraught and exhausted to even journal.

I awoke the next morning in much better form. We had only a mile downhill to get to the Nantahala Outdoor Center (NOC), where there was a store full of snacks waiting in addition to a restaurant overlooking the river, where we would have lunch. I hiked the entire way down in step with Girl Scout and Natalie. We debriefed about the day before, and I vented my frustrations. Natalie agreed that she had been overworked and overtired as well, and she was almost certain the rest of the tramily, with the exception of Wintergreen, had felt the same way, though they'd been perhaps a bit less expressive about it. Even Erik, the most long-legged and arguably the fittest of the group, had been spent by the end of the day.

If we continued to be unhappy with the tramily plan, Natalie conceded, we could break out on our own. We weren't locked into anything, she promised, though she'd like to stay if we could, as she really liked traveling as a group. Girl Scout nodded in agreement, saying that as much as she loved the tramily and wanted it to stay together, ultimately, she was loyal to us and wanted us all to be happy. That made me feel much better.

While we hiked, I animatedly described my macaroni and cheese blunder from the evening prior while the gals cracked up at my folly. It was all good—we were friends again. Natalie was bummed though that my rotten mood had spoiled her chances for extra rations, especially because she loves spicy foods. I promised I wouldn't let it happen again.

As we made our descent to the NOC, the rush of the river below became louder and louder, clueing us in that we were getting close. We took our time, stopping to inspect the spring flowers dotting the trail. Once we arrived, we dilly-dallied around the NOC for hours, exploring the outdoor outfitter, snack shop, and restaurant, and taking advantage of the impressive line of lounge chairs that faced the river.

While we rifled through the "hiker box," a box of freebies that other hikers had left behind, a short, muscular, almost manic man named Napoleon came up behind us and introduced himself.

He chatted animatedly as he scored a new sleeping bag from the hiker box, having damaged his own somehow. I was certain he must be fueled by uppers of a variety stronger than coffee. *I could use some of his energy*, I thought.

Later, as we were seated in the lounge chairs by the river, he offered us all a beer, having bought a case of PBRs at the snack shop. It appeared that he was going to post up there for the day, which was a little surprising given his high energy level. I had assumed that he'd be pushing on, up the miles-long hill past the NOC, but apparently not. We learned that he had already completed the Triple Crown, meaning he'd successfully thru-hiked all three of America's most famous long trails: the AT, the PCT, and the Continental Divide Trail (CDT). He'd traded a high-paying, high-stress corporate job years earlier to live the life of a ramblin' man. He didn't even own a bed. In the hiking off-season, he slept on his sleeping pad in a tiny studio apartment somewhere. He lived for the trails, and he was planning to yo-yo the AT this year, first hiking north to Katahdin, then turning around and hiking all the way back to Springer Mountain. As we got to New England months later, I watched for him, expecting him to bound down the trail on his way back to Georgia. I never did see him again past Tennessee though.

Natalie and I both turned down Napoleon's beer offer, as the climb out of the NOC is notoriously difficult and seemingly never-ending. Instead, we simply chilled out in those lounge chairs by the river, soaking in the sunny spring day, watching the crystal clear water rush past us, and enjoying the company of Playmaker, a sportscaster from North Dakota, Napoleon, Honey Badger, and Dragon, who had once again caught up to us. I complained that I suddenly found myself with two numb big toes, and Dragon genially showed me how to leave a free box around my toes with my shoelaces in order to take the pressure off. "It will take a week to 10 days," he explained. "But the feeling will come back."

Michael, who we hadn't seen since he ditched us at Winding Stair Gap, showed up around lunchtime and stopped by to say hello. In just the few days since we'd seen him, he seemed to transform somehow. He seemed wilder, freer, and happier. Perhaps the break from the tramily had done him some good. Butterstuff showed up later in the day, initially hustling past us then returning to let us know that he was knackered and intended to stay the night in the NOC's bunkhouse. We thought he'd been rushing to keep going up the trail, when actually he'd been rushing to secure a bed. After we'd toiled at least half the day away, the tramily decided we'd best get a move on.

Before we left, Natalie asked if I'd like to split a bottle of red wine at camp with her that night. "I'll carry it!" she promised, if I'd split the cost. I happily agreed. She was much faster than me on ascents, and the trail wound uphill for the rest of the day. I didn't feel a bit of guilt about allowing her to add a couple of pounds to her pack. I'd get to drink the wine *and* it might slow her down a little bit!

Though the day before had been a doozy, I was energized by the perfect blue sky and the spirit of camaraderie bridged by simply *being* with other thru-hikers beyond the tramily for the morning. It was nice to just relax by the water. We had about seven miles to go to get to camp, which was only half of what we'd done the day before, but we had to climb 3,000 feet, which felt like a huge amount of elevation gain in those early days.

It was a tough day, but I felt much clearer and stronger than I had the day before. I'd been involved in this plan to hike to A. Rufus Morgan Shelter, so hiking these miles didn't feel like a chore that someone else had laid upon me. It simply felt like what needed to be done. And after such a lovely morning, I felt re-energized. I spent a good deal of the day hiking with Girl Scout and Jukebox, as Jamie was now known for her penchant for making up colorful tunes about thru-hiker life. Together, we

watched hawks search for prey, passed the Tennessee Girls, and
dumped cold spring water over our heads to cool off.

When I finally arrived at camp, just before dark, Natalie
was waiting with the wine. She and I camped on top of a hill with
Wintergreen while the others camped down below near the shelter.
As she poured me a glass of cabernet, she happily bragged that
she'd kept up with Head Chef all day. She told me that they'd
arrived about an hour before me, Girl Scout, and Jukebox. Head
Chef was Erik's new moniker; he was named for the whole steaks
and chickens that he'd pack out on trail, hoping to hold onto the
muscle mass that he'd worked so hard to build as an amateur
bodybuilder.

But as Natalie served me Triscuits with squares of cheese,
I couldn't even be irritated with her for being so much faster than
me; her enthusiasm was too infectious. The snacks also didn't hurt.
As we sat together in the dark, we glanced up at the moon,
listening to the boisterous hoots of owls calling to each other. I
imagined they had some exciting news to share, the way they were
popping off so loudly and frequently. Natalie and I giggled the
evening away, reinforcing how happy we were to be there. We
were living our dream and buzzed on red wine. The night couldn't
have been any better. It was the antithesis of the night before.

CHAPTER 9

A few cold, rainy, chilled-to-the-bone days later, we very thankfully found ourselves standing at NC 28, a paved road featuring a parking lot with restrooms, a pay phone, and a soda machine, where we could call for a shuttle that would take us into Fontana Dam, North Carolina. As Girl Scout, Natalie, and I burst from the forest, probably looking like drowned rats, we found Kevin, our friend from Massachusetts, waiting. Though he was 20 years older than us, carried gear from the 1980s, and would often go on about how "slow" he was, he always seemed to keep up.

I made a beeline for the soda machine. Even in cold weather, I found myself constantly craving cold drinks, and already I was facing a low-grade addiction to Coca-Cola Classic, something I *never* drank at home. The machine only took change, and I found I only had 50 of the 75 cents needed to pay for it. Seeing my hangdog expression, Kevin took pity on me, handing me his last quarter. I whooped in victory, stuck my coins into the machine, and pressed the button for the Coke expectantly. Nothing happened.

"What?!" I cried as I pressed the button again a little harder. And then I pressed it again, forcefully this time. Still, nothing happened. My hangdog expression returned. Suddenly, it became fiercely important that we get on the very next shuttle to Fontana Dam.

"Let's wait by the road!" I suggested, ushering the others to the far side of the parking lot. We needed to get as close to the shuttle pickup point as possible. A hot shower and a cold soda were waiting for me, and I was beyond ready.

It had rained cats and dogs the evening before, and I had lain in my tent, finishing my entire stash of candy while hatching a plan to get a touch of civilization and a day of rest. The mountains of North Carolina had begun to tease us with hints of spring as Mayapples drilled out of the ground like bats wrapped inside their wings, trilliums of deep red burst to bloom, and little green plants sprouted up everywhere. But they were also rugged, and their weather was bipolar, draining my energy. I'd be prancing along on a perfect sunny spring morning then turn a corner into cold, dark fog without any warning. One moment I'd be trotting along on a perfectly reasonable portion of trail, then suddenly the trail would turn and drive me directly up and over the top of a mountain, seemingly just to be cruel. I had experienced this very thing the day before at Jacob's Ladder. "They," as in the trail collective, say it takes four weeks to get your trail legs. We arrived in Fontana Dam over a week shy of this milestone. My entire body was stiff, and I felt like if I didn't find a hot tub pronto, I might die of hypothermia. From my tent, I called and reserved a room for the four of us gals at Fontana Resort.

Fontana Dam is an interesting place. They call it a village, but it's really just a resort, featuring a hotel, cabins, swimming pools, fire pits, restaurants, and a mini-golf course in the middle of nowhere, just a couple of miles from the southern border of the Great Smoky Mountains National Park. The closest town, I was told, is 40 minutes away by car. It very much reminded me of the resort that the Housemans stayed at for the summer in "Dirty Dancing"—with a large wooden lodge, plenty of outdoor space, and an ice cream parlor. It seemed like it would be a marvelous place to stay in a warmer season, perfect for families that were coming to visit the Smokies.

In the off-season, the place was occupied by only thru-hikers. Even those who chose to forego the price of a room and stay at the Fontana 'Hilton'—a well-kept shelter overlooking the Fontana Reservoir and featuring an unheated shower house—had come by to pay a visit to the resort's restaurants and grab a quick resupply. The Fontana Village General Store, with its limited and overpriced supply of camp foods, was the only resupply point until the jump-off point for Gatlinburg more than 50 miles away. Luckily, The Grill, the more casual of the resort's two open restaurants, was a thru-hiker's dream, its menu featuring pizza, burgers, fries, beer, and desserts.

When I wasn't filling my belly, I was soaking in the luxury of the resort. I took a long, hot shower and a bath on the same day. Jukebox generously volunteered to do our laundry in the one working washer in the entire resort while I beat Natalie, who was now known as Ibex for her ability to push up the steepest of hills quickly, at checkers. I called my parents to check in for the first time since leaving New York for Georgia.

The tramily had initially planned to stay at Fontana for just one night, but I decided that regardless of what they did, I would stay behind for a second night. My body was shot; my tight legs ached just walking up and down the stairs of the lodge and my knees were irritated again. I needed the rest, and I was willing to stay behind alone to get it if I had to, especially since the climb up into the Smokies is notoriously difficult. Luckily, it didn't take any convincing whatsoever to get the rest of the tramily to stay the extra night. I simply mentioned, adamantly, that regardless of their plan, I was going to stay behind. I had already informed reception that I'd be needing my room for an extra night. They quickly agreed to stay as well, citing how bitter cold it was outside, and taking note of the snow that was piling up in the Smokies from the window.

A local volunteer who helped care for the trail told us that the road from the Smokies down into Gatlinburg had closed the day before due to snow.

However, not to make the day in Fontana a total hiking loss, we agreed that we'd "slackpack," or hike without our heavy gear, the 1.2 miles from NC 28 to the Fontana "Hilton" to cut off that short bit of mileage from our journey the next day when we'd make the long and arduous climb into the Smokies. We could do this easily by using the resort shuttle system. As we were readying ourselves to catch the shuttle back to NC 28 in the lodge common area, Dragon and Honey Badger strolled in. We said a quick hello and explained our plan to slackpack, inviting them along. They enthusiastically agreed to join us. While the entire tramily didn't generally hike together due to varying paces, we did that day, jovially bouncing up the trail, free from the deadweight of our packs. Honey Badger, like Ibex and I, was a total nature nerd, so she'd point out birds and plants that she knew as we walked.

We finished up our small hike at the Fontana "Hilton," which gave us a chance to check out the fancy shelter that we were missing out on by staying at the resort. Admittedly, it was amazing for an AT shelter, well-built and well-kept. It looked almost brand new. But those resort rooms, with their bathtubs and heat, were unbeatable for tending off the cold of the day. While chilling out at the shelter as we waited for our shuttle back to the resort, Napoleon appeared, offering us each a chocolate chip cookie. A kind local brought them by and left them at the shelter for the hikers, he told us. I laid contentedly on the grass munching on my cookie, listening only vaguely to his exuberant dialogue with another hiker, when I heard the word "Adderall." *Aha—I knew it!* I suddenly felt better about my lack of energy compared to his.

We had a relaxing afternoon following our pleasant stroll through the forest, and Dragon and Honey Badger joined us for dinner at The Grill that evening. We hung out there, chatting away, until a well-known party crew showed up. This group of hikers was notorious on trail for their heavy drinking, and we heard that norovirus was already passing through their ranks. We decided to make ourselves scarce, mostly hanging out in our rooms. However, at one point in the evening, Wintergreen did the rounds around the lodge to gift each of us some packets of Indomie, an instant ramen noodle brand from Indonesia. I had already done a full resupply and was afraid that I might have unintentionally picked up enough food to last me at least two weeks, so I tried to decline.

"I don't want this," I said. "I'm sure it's not vegetarian." He grabbed a packet out of my hand and turned it over, scanning the ingredient list. "Nope, it's vegetarian!" he said brightly. "And everyone in the tramily gets four!" I sighed, unsure how I was going to fit them in my backpack. A moment later, Kevin came strolling down the hallway, eyeing the packages in my hands.

"Oh what are those?" he asked curiously.

"Fancy ramen! Wintergreen swears by them!" I replied. "Want to try one?!"

"Oh no," he said politely. "I couldn't take your food from you!"

"I insist!" I said, shoving one into his hand. "I have way too much food anyway." I practically jogged down the hallway toward my room, not giving him the option to hand it back.

CHAPTER 10

The next morning, the tramily planned to meet and catch the shuttle back to the trail together. However, just as had occurred in Franklin, the guys didn't get themselves ready and packed up in time. Instead, Ibex, Jukebox, Girl Scout, and I caught the shuttle back to the Fontana "Hilton" with Kevin. Since he knew we had a tough day ahead, our friendly driver, who had a bit of a theatrical flair to his personality, invited us to request any song that we'd like as he offered us a package of mini powdered donuts. I didn't even have to think about it.

"Eye of the Tiger!" I exclaimed while accepting a donut. "Eye of the Tiger" by Survivor had been made popular by the movie "Rocky," starring a young Sylvester Stallone. He played an underdog boxer from Philadelphia trying to make it big. The song played as he trained, running up a grand staircase leading to the Philadelphia Museum of Art. It seemed appropriate. And so, "Eye of the Tiger" it was. We danced, with both excitement and trepidation, in our seats the entire drive back to the trail. Even Kevin joined in.

I had some unfinished business with the Great Smoky Mountains so this was a big day for me. As I previously mentioned, years earlier, I briefly worked at a summer camp in Tennessee. My then-boyfriend and I had been planning to spend some time that summer exploring the Smokies. We'd been hearing the entire time that we were there about how spectacularly beautiful the mountains were, with their breathtaking views, striking waterfalls, and synchronous fireflies. However, because things fell as they did, we ended up unexpectedly rushing out of the state without getting the chance to visit the Smokies. Here was my chance to turn back time in a way, to finally experience the area on my terms. I was ready for it.

As our driver dropped us off, the five of us walked across the picturesque Fontana Dam together. On one side of the dam, a man-made lake sits with a backdrop of mountains. On the other, a steep spillway leads to a river. Eyeing the river, I was suddenly reminded that hellbenders, rare, massive salamanders that live for decades, are supposed to live in the Smokies. I was jazzed. I'd only ever seen hellbenders in fish tanks before, and perhaps this was my chance to see one in the wild. In addition, I remembered reading that a large variety of average-sized salamanders also live in the Smokies. I was beside myself.

As we neared the edge of the forest, we pulled our printed permits out of our packs. This was one of just a couple of areas on the AT that you need a permit to hike through, and the only place where the permit cost money. We were able to pay our $20 fee on the Smokies website and print out our permits for $1 each at Ron Haven's hostel in Franklin. As we entered the park, we each split our papers in half, keeping one part handy in our packs in case rangers asked to see them, and dropping the other in a wooden box labeled "permits." We were allotted eight days to hike the 71.6 miles through the park. Immediately, we started climbing.

Inside the Great Smoky Mountains National Park, unlike the vast majority of the trail, hikers are not allowed to "stealth camp," or stay at undesignated camping spots. We initially planned to hike only 6.5 miles on that first day to the Birch Spring Gap campsite, but we'd heard while at Fontana Lodge that our planned stopping point was closed because of a naughty bear. Instead, we were forced to hike almost 12 miles to Mollies Ridge Shelter.

Because we'd be climbing for most of the day with newly
resupplied packs, I expected it to be brutal. I was pleasantly
surprised to find that whoever built the trail in the park very much
believed in switchbacks, and it was a quite reasonable, gradual
climb. And even though my food bag was embarrassingly
overstuffed, adding unnecessary weight to my pack, the day off
from hiking had done me wonders. I was feeling good!

We slipped and slid in the mud as we climbed through
thick fog for most of the day, unable to see the mountains that
surrounded us as we ascended higher and higher. I prayed silently
to the trail gods to bring us better views tomorrow. Head Chef
finally caught up as we were about three miles from the shelter.
Shortly after, we found a dead piglet lying directly in the middle of
the trail with two puncture wounds, one of which looked to go
straight into its heart. It was adorable and serene; it looked as if it
was at peace. I looked around in the woods, wondering what killed
it and if it was still near, as Head Chef checked to see if it was still
warm, curious as to how long it had been there. It was cold.

Head Chef hiked ahead, so Ibex, Girl Scout and I hiked
with Kevin for the last few miles of the day. The more we got to
know him, the more we liked him. We learned that he had been
married for 19 years and when it didn't work out and his son went
off to college, he joined the Peace Corps. He was sent to South
Africa to be a schoolteacher for two years. Back home in
Massachusetts, he bought a three-family home. He lives in a small
corner of it with his pug and rents the rest out, allowing him to still
make an income while he takes off on adventures. As the four of
us walked in step, Ibex, being a bit of an expert on the topic,
pointed out some mushrooms that she knew while I identified
some of the tree species that I was familiar with.

Once I arrived at camp, I immediately changed into all of
my warmest clothes and set up in the shelter. In addition to
requiring a permit to hike through the park, the National Park

Service also insists on being difficult by requiring thru-hikers to sleep in designated shelters rather than their tents unless the shelters are completely full. What makes this rule worse is that section hikers can rent out spots in the shelters. If a thru-hiker is set up in a shelter and a section hiker with a reservation comes along, at any hour of the day or night, they can kick the thru-hiker out of the shelter.

So, the shelter it was, for only my second and final time on trail. Even with all of my clothes on, I was still chilly, so I found myself feeling a bit antisocial and sulky. The rest of the tramily arrived a short time later. Some of them debated moving on three more miles up the trail to the next shelter. Having already changed and set up, I was staying put.

After much debate, they decided to settle down at Mollies Ridge Shelter as well. As we ate dinner together at the shelter food preparation area, I began to shiver. Girl Scout could tell something was amiss and got me moving, helping me to hang my bear bag on the bear cables near camp. I began to feel better as my blood got pumping. If this was how the weather in the Smokies was going to be, I feared it would be rough going.

Once I had hung my bear bag and warmed up a little, I rejoined the tramily at the shelter picnic table. Ibex came bursting out of the shelter.

"I've got it!" she proclaimed. "Your trail name! I don't know if you're going to like it though...."

"Oooh tell me!" I demanded, excitedly.

"Glowstick!" she said. "Because you found that glow stick in your tent on Springer, and you're getting off the trail for a music festival!" I had plans to take a short break from the trail to join my D.C. friends at the Bonnaroo Music Festival in June. "It's perfect! You're Glowstick!"

It felt right. That was me; I was Glowstick. Henceforth, that was what everyone called me.

CHAPTER 11

I woke up the next morning to an incredible blue sky. The frigid evening had turned into a beautiful morning, and as the sun warmed the day, I estimated that the air temperature had settled in the mid-50s. This was an absolute luxury compared to the day before.

The sun energized me, and as I cruised through thick deciduous forest, I considered that I might finally be getting my trail legs. Until this point, my body had been constantly sore, with tight legs and aching knees. But I stayed ahead of the rest of the tramily for a good part of the day, and even as I passed through steep climbs, I felt there was nothing I couldn't handle.

A few hours into the morning, I stumbled upon a lovely golden meadow. I found Ibex basking in the sun, her goofy hat flopped over her face, but I stopped only for a quick chat as I was feeling energized and wanted to push on. Maybe a half mile or so up the trail, I found the Tennessee Girls—Keeper, Bliss, and Roast—chilling out on a little hill of golden grass. I thought Ibex might come along soon, so decided to take a little break after all, learning their story and how the three came to hike the trail together. Two had just finished a master's degree in psychology together and the third was a college friend who dreamed of opening a bed and breakfast.

It was a worthwhile break, but my body urged me to continue, and Rocky Top was waiting. I climbed to the top without stopping and thanked the trail gods as I reached the summit. There, the panoramic views I had yearned for the day before unfolded in front of me. The Tennessee Girls followed shortly behind and played the "Rocky Top" song on one of their phones. We danced along, cheering. By now it was lunchtime, so I decided to picnic in this scenic spot as I waited for the tramily. Just as I was finishing up, they began to arrive, one by one.

I learned that they'd all paused where I'd last seen Ibex. While basking in the sun, they collectively decided that we were now members of an elite cult called "The Children of the Field," led by Girl Scout. Henceforth, we regularly referred to her as "Leader," often discussing the need to develop our "literature." Wintergreen persistently lobbied for the position of second in command, offering to take over if anything were to happen to Girl Scout. However, she dismissed his aspirations, citing this strong desire to lead as the reason he would be considered dead last in line for the throne.

Seizing the perfect day and the breathtaking views, we took the opportunity to take our first tramily photo. We were only missing Butterstuff. Once again, he'd decided to stay behind for an extended period of rest, sleeping the day away in the Fontana "Hilton" while the rest of us ascended into the Smokies. Driven by a surge of energy in the middle of the night though, he hiked through the dark, greeting us at Mollie's Ridge in the morning. He'd missed us, he explained, and wanted to test himself with some night hiking. After another lengthy nap, he planned to try to catch us later in the day. Unfortunately, he had not arrived in time to join the photo opp.

From here, we finished up the last five miles of the day, climbing steadily uphill, then making camp at Derrick Knob Shelter. We decided to take our chances and set up our tents rather than hunker down in the half-full shelter, despite the rules. Luckily, no ranger came by to enforce them.

The next day proved to be even more beautiful. Though the morning was frigid, the sun warmed us quickly and there wasn't a cloud in the sky all day long. I hiked the majority of the day with Girl Scout and Ibex, and we found ourselves passing through the most enchanting pine forest covered in vibrant green moss. It was a stark contrast from Georgia, where miles of brown forest beneath gloomy gray skies dominated our views. *This* was the Appalachian Trail that I had envisioned for so many years. We faced a considerable amount of uphill throughout the day, but my legs and lungs refrained from screaming at me. Whereas I'd often had to stop on previous climbs, hugging trees to catch my breath and grab a quick rest, I began to find that I no longer needed to do that. While I would get a bit winded, I could keep on going. Climbing through leafless deciduous forests, golden grasslands, and bright mossy pine forests, I felt increasingly energized. Even during the long ascent to Clingmans Dome, the highest point on the AT and the third highest mountain east of the Mississippi at 6,643 feet, I stopped only to snap a few quick photos, otherwise charging on. Girl Scout and I even kept up with Ibex pretty much the entire way to the top, further proof that we were getting stronger.

When we finally reached the summit of Clingmans Dome, we found a peculiar UFO-like concrete structure at the top. While we had enjoyed incredible views of the pine-covered mountains during our ascent, there was no natural overlook showcasing the Smokies' splendor once we reached the top of Clingmans Dome. Instead, there was a 45-foot-high observation tower, built by the National Park Service in 1959, awaiting us. After climbing up the long, winding ramp, we were rewarded with a 360-degree view of the Smokies, including Mount Mitchell, the highest point east of the Mississippi. From the summit, we could also see Fontana Dam, where we'd begun our journey into the Smokies only two days before, and Gatlinburg, the famed carnival-like town where we'd head the next day. On a clear day, it's said you can see 100 miles away, although this is often limited due to air pollution. We found Kevin at the top, so we snapped a group photo with him, took a moment to appreciate our surroundings, and then hurried back down to the ground to escape the frigid air at the top.

As we ate our lunch below the tower, Kevin entertained us with stories of his spunky pug, whom he missed dearly, while inquisitive vacationers stopped to chat with us. Most of them had hiked just a half mile up from the parking lot, so seeing our large packs—and likely our wild, unshowered appearances—they were curious as to where we were headed. One by one, they were blown away when we would enthusiastically reply, "To Maine!" Many had never heard of the Appalachian Trail, and those who had were surprised to learn it was so close by. Several asked us if we were in college, unable to fathom how we'd have the time for this sort of thing if we had already entered the workforce. "We're making the time!" we responded cheerfully. It was fun to enlighten them about our plans; many seemed delighted, albeit a bit skeptical, and wished us lots of luck and good fortune.

From Clingmans Dome, we had just three easy miles left to camp, but after our arduous climb earlier in the day followed by a long break, it was a bit more difficult to get going than it should have been. We managed though. Girl Scout and I, ambling through the forest, stopped for a photo and a quick celebration at the 200-mile marker. Though we had almost 2,000 miles to go, this felt huge. The first 100 miles had been so difficult and slow going. The second 100 miles had passed by much quicker.

Rebel Yell, a sweet, charming man with long blonde hair and an artist's soul from South Carolina, joined us for the evening. He was named due to his signature Southern whoop, loud and bellowing, which you could hear, and recognize, from miles away. Butterstuff also caught up, completing the tramily again. This was one of the last times we'd see him though. Soon, he would decide that he wanted to stretch his young legs and push himself to do bigger miles. And at that time, he would leave us behind in the dust. Michael also joined us for the evening, though he would be getting off the trail in Gatlinburg for a couple of days to visit his uncle.

We made camp at Mount Collins Shelter, nestled deep in a thick, enchanted pine forest. When I woke up the next morning, my eyes were nearly swollen shut and I had an annoying tickle deep in my throat. Putting my contacts in proved extremely challenging because my eyes resisted opening wide enough to get them in. I surmised that I must be allergic to the soft pine floor that I had set my tent upon. This was news to me.

I tried not to let the allergy symptoms or the fact that the tightness in my legs had returned affect me too much as we rushed off to Newfound Gap, where we knew we'd find a shuttle waiting to take us to Gatlinburg. Upon arriving at the gap, we not only found the shuttle but also that the local Baptist church that ran the shuttle had set up an impressive spread of trail magic. They encouraged us to sign their guestbook and to take as many snacks as we'd like. There were cold sodas, chocolate bars, cookies, almonds, bananas, oranges, apples, fruit snacks, and more. Of course, we indulged. It was heaven.

As we sat on the grass amongst our comrades, chomping down on our newly acquired goodies, I hoped that I wouldn't be one of the few hikers to gain weight during my thru-hike. Things I'd never considered putting into my body in "normal" life were now a part of my regular diet. My diet back home was full of fresh fruits and vegetables, whole grains, and beans. But I'd eaten more processed foods in three weeks on trail than I probably had in the last three years at home. It was unnerving, but my body seemed willing to take any sort of sustenance that it could get. Though I'd yet to lose any weight, my body was craving more and more food all the time, and being way less picky than usual about what it wanted. Sugar was the number one ingredient that it seemed to want, and I found myself craving sodas and candy regularly. Luckily, most trail angels were happy to oblige, always seeming to bring plenty of sugary snacks along to trail magic setups.

Once we'd had our fill of the snacks, the church folks drove us the 15 miles to Gatlinburg, free of charge. As the road wound down toward the valley, I watched out the window as the mountains we had worked so hard to climb passed by in the distance. It had taken so much effort, so much power, to get to where we were, and yet here we were moving through the mountains in a motor vehicle as if it were no distance at all.

The town of Gatlinburg, which sits at the bottom of the mountains directly outside of the Great Smoky Mountains National Park, was a bit of a culture shock. The town is a hub of chaotic energy, full of fast food, arcades, bright lights, loud noises, vacationing families, and hokey attractions. It was hard to imagine coming to visit the Smokies, a park full of high peaks and remote wilderness, and staying in Gatlinburg. It didn't make any sense to me. But then again, a lot of things about American culture don't make any sense to me, which is probably how I ended up on the AT in the first place.

As we arrived in town, we stopped at the local outdoor outfitter, where I was able to replace my canister of fuel, then headed to Five Guys for lunch. I got a veggie sandwich with cheese, fries, and a Diet Coke with a splash of cherry. Rebel Yell somehow convinced the workers to allow him to get on the loudspeaker. He proceeded to tell the patrons on the patio that they smelled terribly and must vacate the premises immediately. It was us; we were the patrons on the patio. We were tickled.

Since we suddenly found ourselves in Vacation Town USA, we thought it only right to experience a bit of Tennessee culture before ascending back into the forest. After all, we had hiked 200 miles and passed over the highest point on the AT, and therefore deserved a celebration. This took place in the form of a moonshine tasting at Old Smokey's down the street, where the lot of us, including Rebel Yell and Michael, lined up against the long wooden bar. A handsome 20-something in blue overalls served us all 10 flavors, one after the other, which included apple pie, raspberry, coffee and more, along with a repertoire of jokes, all for just $5 apiece. After we finished our tasting, Ibex, Girl Scout, Michael, and I went to grab an iced coffee at Starbucks so that we could charge our electronics for a few minutes. The others, without even so much as a wave goodbye, proceeded down the street to hitch back into the park.

This left the three of us ladies to fend for ourselves for our first hitchhiking experience, as Michael was staying in town to await his uncle, who was putting him up for the night in nearby Pigeon Forge. Naturally, we put Girl Scout in charge, since she was the least shy and most blonde. After about 20 minutes on the road with no luck, we ordered an Uber, though it was going to be a 24-minute wait. Soon after, a pickup truck screeched to a halt in front of us, circling back around and parking directly in front of where we stood. The driver, a large man with a thick Tennessee accent named AJ, was on his way to a casino past Newfound Gap. He invited us to pile inside as he effortlessly tossed our heavy bags into the bed of the truck. We canceled our Uber and hopped in. AJ was an absolute sweetheart, and living a life completely different from our own. He was only a couple of years older than me, but already a grandfather. He was impressed that we were out here hiking the trail, especially being women, and he couldn't wait to tell his seven-year-old daughter, Maddie, who loved nature, about us. He thought she could be just like us one day.

The ride was full of good conversation and lots of laughs all around, and as the truck climbed higher into the Smokies, we hit our first "bear jam." A group of tourists had stopped their cars in the middle of the road while they stood outside, cameras in hand, snapping photos of a small bear in the forest nearby. Our first bear sighting! Even if it was from the inside of a truck, we couldn't wait to brag about it to the rest of the tramily. We were a little bitter that they had ditched us in Gatlinburg without saying a word. Missing the bear was surely their punishment. As AJ dropped us off, he insisted on getting a photo with us to show to his daughter, and he exchanged numbers with Ibex, asking her to send along some photos of mountain flowers to share with Maddie.

We said our goodbyes, wishing AJ the best of luck at the casino and thanking him for his kindness, and then we bounded off toward the trail. Though the trip to Gatlinburg was fun, even a few hours away from the AT felt wrong in a way. It had already become home. We arrived at Icewater Spring Shelter, about 2.5 easy miles up the trail, to find a crowded campsite and an incredible view of the mountains beyond. Having had a decent-sized lunch at Five Guys, I decided that this would be the night to try the Indomie, the fancy ramen that Wintergreen had forced upon me. To my surprise, it was incredible. Unlike the more typical packaged ramens that you can get at the grocery store, which generally include just one dry flavor packet, the Indomie included multiple dry and liquid flavor packets. And boy did they make a difference. The flavor was so much richer and more complex than my normal Top Ramen. I immediately wanted more. As much as it pained me to admit it, I had been so wrong about Indomie. This was a trail delicacy!

That night, we were afforded a vibrant pink and orange sunset followed by a clear view of the stars, a pleasant change from the usual clouded-in or treed-in view. I was nearly forced out of my tent by Jukebox at 6:05 the next morning to catch the rising sun, for which I was grateful. I emerged, halfway out of my tent and still warmly tucked inside my sleeping bag, just in time to watch as it rose over the mountains. This was my first of very few sunrises on the trail.

The Smokies continued to treat us splendidly until we left her majestic peaks behind. Our days were full of sunshine, blue skies, amazing views, and fairly easy terrain. I fell so hard in love with her forests. I still hadn't spotted a salamander, or any other large animal aside from the road bear, though I did stop in a few streams to turn over some rocks, just in case. I later learned from a Ph.D. student at Virginia Tech that the best time and place to find salamanders is actually within the leaf litter after a rainfall. But since there hadn't been any rain and I didn't know that yet, I was, so far, out of luck.

On our second to last day in the park, Chef took up the rear for the entire day. It wasn't unlike him to leave camp last because he liked to sleep in and, being the fastest hiker in our group, he knew he could always catch up. However, by the time I arrived at camp on this particular day, he was still missing in action. The rest of the tramily set up our tents, cooked dinner, and made small talk with the other campers there. Still, there was no Chef to be found. As nightfall approached, he finally rushed into camp, exhausted but smiling. "I made it!" he proclaimed proudly. He explained that he'd taken a wrong turn much earlier in the day while talking on the phone with an ex-girlfriend and had hiked a full five miles *one way* in the wrong direction. This meant that he had hiked a full 10 extra miles, bringing his mileage for the day to over 20 miles. His first 20-plus mile hiking day was a complete accident! He was in much better spirits than I would have been, promising himself that he would pay better attention in the future.

Meanwhile, in Chef's absence, we got to meet a trail celebrity. Since our first day at Amicalola Falls, we'd been hearing about a specific ridgerunner, an Appalachian Trail Conservancy seasonal worker who hikes up and down the trail to pick up trash, speak with hikers, and generally make sure people are following leave no trace principles and that things are going smoothly in the woods. This ridgerunner, named Chloe, was trail famous for having survived a near-bear attack. She had been bluff-charged by a black bear, which stopped only inches from her face, as she stood shaking in terror. Bears sometimes bluff charge in an attempt to intimidate or scare threats. A bear will puff itself up to look bigger, then run toward a threat, only stopping or veering off at the last minute. Luckily, in Chloe's case, the bear took off back into the woods after the charge. As it did so, she ran away, getting as far away from the bear and the situation as possible. But the bear later returned, tearing her tent and all of her belongings to shreds.

The story was used as a way to warn hikers of the interactions that can happen between wildlife and people and to encourage hikers to properly store food and use good judgment. While we certainly appreciated the education, what this tale really did was make us want to meet Chloe and hear her story firsthand. We were fascinated! We had been hoping throughout the Smokies that we would run into her. And finally, on one of our last days in the park, she appeared. We excitedly barraged her with questions, which she cheerfully answered, laughing at our enthusiasm. She even allowed me to take a photo with her. We were star-struck.

As we neared the end of the Smokies, we began to hear of an impending storm that was on its way to the park. It was supposed to be so significant that meteorologists gave it a name: Winter Storm Xanto. This was the last thing I wanted to hear after my magical jaunt through the Smokies. A return to winter might have been all it took to give me a nervous breakdown. The weather forecasters were calling for a rain-soaked day complete with tornado and flash flood warnings, followed by temperatures that would plunge below freezing, and then finally, a snowstorm. To me, this meant that we'd be soaked to the bone along with all of our gear, which would freeze solid, and then we'd slip on ice on the trail all day while being pelted with snow. This, I could not handle. I called in reinforcements.

Jessica, a college roommate and one of my best friends in the entire world, lived only about an hour away from Davenport Gap, where we'd descend out of the Smokies, in Asheville, North Carolina. Jessica and I were so close that she had come on many of my family vacations, and she was the first person I'd call when I needed a sounding board. I had initially planned to meet up with her for a day when I arrived in Hot Springs, but the plan had to change. I called her from the top of a mountain, my phone crackling and cutting out, begging her to come rescue me from Xanto.

"I can't do it, Jessica," I said. "My life is in your hands. I'll freeze and die and you'll never see me again if you don't come get me. You'll have to explain to my parents what happened to me!"

"Audge," she said calmly. "It's fine. I don't mind coming to get you for a day or two. Just text me when and where I need to be, and I'll come pick you up once I'm out of work."

"Okay, but I need to bring my friend Ibex too!"

"That's fine, you goof," she said. "Bring whoever you want. But remember that I have a small car."

This was a not uncommon dynamic for our friendship, especially when we were younger. I'd call her in some hyper-emotional state, begging her to help fix whatever was wrong in my world. I'm not typically a vulnerable person, but there is something about Jessica that allows me to be completely open and completely myself. Perhaps it is her endless sense of humor, zest for life, maternal nature, and the fact that I've known her my entire adult life that allows me to put my life and heart directly into her hands. She's probably seen, or at least heard via a phone call, me cry more than any other person on the planet. She's been there during my best and darkest times and has been a consistent and compassionate voice as I've weathered breakups, fallouts, and failures. And now, she was coming to rescue me from a literal storm.

Though I would have loved to bring the entire tramily with me, I unfortunately knew that I couldn't ask Jessica to take seven smelly hikers into her cozy two-bedroom apartment. I calculated that three of us would fit in her car with our packs, and Ibex and I discussed in depth whether we should bring Girl Scout with us or not. We desperately wanted to; she'd been with us from the beginning and it felt wrong to leave her behind. But it also felt cruel to take only her and not Jukebox, and I didn't feel comfortable asking Jessica to bring that many people along, especially since I didn't see how we would all fit in her tiny sedan. After much debate about what we should do, Ibex and I approached Girl Scout, imploring her to decide for us.

"We want to bring you," we told her. I'd even already texted Jessica to ask if it would be alright, and of course she agreed. "But we don't know what to do about Jukebox. That's going to look bad to leave her behind with just the guys. We don't want to hurt her feelings, but we can't bring both of you."

Girl Scout made it easy on us. She told us she'd miss us, of course, but it was only right that she stay behind with the group and that she'd be totally fine. I knew she wanted to come with us, but that's how she was, always looking out for the feelings of other people, rather than what was best for herself. In the end, it was Ibex and I who got emotional about leaving her, rather than the other way around.

We tried to convince the rest of the tramily to call a shuttle to take them to Asheville rather than fight the storm on the trail.

"There's a hostel there," I told them. "I've already looked it up and they have space! Think of the brunches, the breweries.... You don't want to be out in that storm!"

They were almost convinced, but the shuttle was going to cost them 75 dollars each way. Personally, having seen the weather

report, I didn't think that was too much to ask divided by five
people. Especially considering I'd seen them drop double that on
town meals without blinking an eye. But they found a hostel only a
few miles from Davenport Gap and planned instead to hustle there
before the rainstorm hit to post up there for a day or two depending
on the weather. We all planned to meet back up in Hot Springs in a
few days.

And so, on our last evening in the Smokies, the tramily set
up camp as Ibex and I cooked dinner at Davenport Gap Shelter.
They would camp there for the night and then head for Standing
Bear Farm Hostel in the morning. Ibex and I were slated to get
picked up by Jessica at Davenport Gap, only a mile down the trail,
once she finished a birthday dinner for her mother. As we were
waiting, Ibex and I picked wild ramps, green, leafy onion-like
plants, to add to our suppers. As I was hunched over plucking the
ramp leaves from the ground, I suddenly heard Ibex whoop in glee.
In addition to the ramps, or wild leeks as we call them back home,
she had found a morel mushroom near the stream. Lucky! Chef
had found one a few days prior and let us all try a piece. It was the
most delectable morsel of food that I'd ever tasted in my life. It
was rich, meaty, and buttery. From the moment it hit my lips, I
wanted more. I'd been on the lookout for them for the past few
days, but I hadn't had any luck, and now Ibex had beat me to it.
The entire tramily searched the perimeter in hopes of finding more,
but this morel was unfortunately a loner. In the process of looking
for more though, Ibex also discovered a red-backed salamander. I
was overjoyed.

After supper, Ibex and I said a prolonged goodbye to the
tramily. Things had been going much smoother between all of us
within the Smokies, possibly because many of our stressors, such
as poor weather, tough climbs, and long days, had diminished.
While we did plan to reconvene in Hot Springs, we couldn't be
sure of what would happen. Eventually, they told us to get out of

there so they could finally miss us, and we obliged, grabbing our bags and turning toward the trail.

That last mile down to the gap was an easy one, and Ibex and I hiked there slowly and casually together. We chatted excitedly about all the fun things that we were going to do in Asheville and talked about how much we had fallen in love with the Smokies. We were sad to leave the park behind, but proud of ourselves for all we had accomplished so far. We arrived at Davenport Gap just as dusk began to turn to night. Soon after we threw down our packs and had a seat on top of them to wait, a white car rounded a bend and inched slowly toward us. Its driver rolled down her window.

"You bitches need a ride?!" Jessica hollered. We certainly did.

CHAPTER 12

It was so familiar yet so strange to suddenly be sitting casually in the car of the one and only Jessica Monroe. I'd been in her car a million times before, riding in the backseat with the window down as my college friends chain-smoked cigarettes around me, giggling about some ridiculous thing or another as we headed to Wegmans, Tim Hortons, or the local beach on Lake Ontario. Just three weeks into trail life, I felt like I was living in a completely different world. My life before the trail was just a memory. So to have someone from my past pop up, especially someone who knows me so well, just as we exited the woods, was a surreal experience. I felt a little bit guilty about leaving—as if I was showing weakness by running from the incoming storm—but not guilty enough to stay and find out just how bad it would be.

Though Jessica had been nervous about driving out into the middle of nowhere to find us, she was in high spirits when she arrived. As we rode back to her place, she questioned us about our trail experiences so far, asked us to describe all our other tramily members in detail so she'd know who we were talking about, and chatted about all the things we could do in Asheville. Once we arrived at her place about an hour later, she had chips, salsa, and fresh towels waiting for us.

Colonel Mustard, Jessica's chubby orange tabby cat, greeted us at the door, demanding to be petted. Her skittish dog, Watson, eyed us nervously from across the room. It was clear we were welcomed by only two of the three residents of the house. The Colonel had a bad reputation for being a bit of a bully, but he was on his best behavior while we were there, snuggling with each of us and even curling up in bed with me each night.

After a quick shower, Ibex and I headed to bed. We were used to going down with the sun, and it was way past hiker midnight. When we awoke the next morning, Jessica had already left for work. I'd slept so hard in her guest bed that I hadn't even woken up as she'd shuffled around getting ready that morning. She'd hoped to get at least one of the two days off that we'd be staying with her, but since it was so last minute, she was unable to. We were on our own for the day.

We figured that since we were living the high life in town for a couple of days, we might as well each take a second shower. We put our laundry in the washer, praying the smell would come out, before ordering an Uber to Biscuit Head, allegedly Asheville's best brunch location. It was a cold, rainy morning, and as our ride pulled up to the restaurant, we noted the long line of people standing out front with umbrellas. Sigh. It was Sunday. Our driver offered to take us elsewhere, but we figured we had nowhere else to be, and we were used to getting wet by that point, so we took our chances with the line.

As we joined the queue, a host brought us a big black umbrella and a menu to share. We had to wait almost 45 minutes to get inside, but it took us nearly that long to decide what we wanted to eat. Biscuit Head was named as such for its "cat head"-sized biscuits. They had a long list of fancy biscuit sandwiches and side dishes to choose from, and it was way past hiker breakfast time. Inside, we found a jam bar with at least 20 different kinds of homemade jams.

Ibex and I each ordered a coffee along with a small shared pitcher of peach Bellinis and a biscuit to start. We had each decided on a biscuit sandwich, but we needed the extra biscuit to try all the jams. I ordered an Asheville biscuit, a veggie hollandaise dish with kale salad and cream cheese, plus a side of vegetarian chorizo. Ibex got a fried catfish biscuit. Everything was incredible. Throughout brunch, our guilt over having escaped the trail faded away and turned slowly to glee. The Bellinis certainly helped. When I stood up to use the restroom after finishing my meal, I was surprised to find I was tipsy!

Trader Joe's, our next stop, was only two miles away, so we decided to walk and do some sightseeing rather than ordering another car. We thought it wise to walk off our buzzes a bit considering it was only noon. The Bellini-fueled wander through town was lovely, and the trip to Trader Joe's was a treat. As full as our stomachs were after our oversized brunch, you would have been hard-pressed to find two people more excited to be in a grocery store. We strolled up every single aisle, and some aisles twice, eyeing all the wonderful things that we could buy ourselves to eat and hunting for the specific requests from our tramily. Whether it was the booze, the hiker hunger, or the fact that we'd been out of civilization for several weeks by that point, I'm not sure, but we came out of there with bags upon bags upon bags of food, forgetting that we'd still have to carry it up and down mountains on our backs.

After what seemed like hours, we finally got out of there, and Jessica called to say that she was on her way home from work. We grabbed another Uber since we couldn't possibly carry all these groceries ourselves, and met her at Burial, her favorite brewery in the city, mostly because dogs were allowed on the patio and she could bring Watson along. From there, we headed to the Funkatorium, a request by Ibex, famous for her favorite type of beer: sours. We each had two flights, trying at least half the beers on the menu. If our morning buzz had left us in Trader Joe's, an afternoon one quickly took its place. We felt like we were on vacation and couldn't stop giggling about how bad we were to have escaped the storm.

From there, we headed back to Jessica's house to drop Watson at home. I'd somehow convinced Jessica that what we needed to do next was to go bowling. She and I, along with our roommates, had gone frequently while in college because the town bowling alley offered a dirt-cheap college night: games for a dollar and pitchers for just two dollars. She hadn't been bowling since, but I was determined that this was the time to relive our glory days. Having missed half the day's fun, she was game. While we bowled, we ordered about every fried snack product on the menu. I again wondered if I was going to gain weight on the trail. Ibex was a bad influence; she was always hungry. But the concern was not strong enough to stop myself from digging greedily into all the snacks.

The next day, our second full zero day in Asheville, Ibex and I headed to the community yoga center for a much needed vinyasa class. Even with the day off from hiking the day before, our leg muscles were extremely tense. The teacher was positive, friendly, and mellow—exactly the vibe that we were looking for. We stretched and contorted our bodies for a glorious hour and a half, rewarding our sore muscles for all their hard work over the previous weeks, then went on our way, refreshed and renewed. Next, we went on the hunt to find a pharmacy to grab a couple of things, passing a picturesque little lake along the way.

We found ourselves being pulled, almost as if by a magnetic force, into a fancy natural foods store, even though we already had more food than we could carry. As we perused the aisles, looking for nothing in particular, we felt as if we were under a spell. Everything looked incredible, and we were sure our eyes were as wide as saucers. We browsed those aisles for hours. Finally, we somehow found the strength to pull ourselves out of there with only a few packets of almond butter and some items from the olive bar, which we promptly scarfed down upon exiting the store.

We continued toward Asheville's downtown, stopping at a double-decker coffee bus for lavender honey lattes, visiting the famous pinball museum and playing the arcade games of our childhoods, buying homemade caramel apples at a local candy shop, and then meeting Jessica at an Indian street food restaurant, Chai Pani, for an incredible dinner of paneer tikka rolls and okra fries. That night, after an extended period trying to fit all of our newly acquired food items into our packs and putting our still-smelly laundry in for a second wash, we curled up with a quirky Netflix rom-com and indulged in some wine, cheese, and crackers.

We had a marvelous time playing tourist in this artistic, eclectic city, but alas, the next morning it was time to return to the trail. We had a couple of quick stops to make first though, at the grocery store for a breakfast of egg, cheese, and biscuit sandwiches and at the local post office to lighten our food bags. We sent along half of our newly acquired Trader Joe's treasures, including the tramily requests and a case of Indomie that we'd ordered from Amazon, up the trail to Hot Springs, where we planned to meet the tramily in a few days. We were happier and fatter than when Jessica had picked us up only a couple of days prior, and while we'd had snow and freezing temperatures the previous day, spring had reappeared in Asheville overnight. I wore my shorts rather than my hiking pants back to the trail; the sun was shining bright and the highs were slated to be in the mid-60s.

I gave Jessica a huge hug and thanked her for her generosity as she dropped us back off at Davenport Gap. I reflected on how lucky I was to have her in my life, then bounded up the trail after Ibex, happy to be "home." We began to notice new green plants and colorful flowers everywhere, including a jack-in-the-pulpit and some wild irises. There wasn't a smidge of evidence left on the trail pointing to the wintery conditions of the previous two days.

Almost immediately, we arrived at a road gap where some trail angels were cooking out on a grill. They called us over, offering us hotdogs and cold sodas. As much as we hated to turn them down, our bellies and packs were already practically bursting at the seams. They insisted that we take some snacks to go. We thanked them profusely but declined as we all but ran back toward the trail to avoid putting even more weight onto our town-spoiled backs.

Despite a couple of attempts via text message to ask how they were faring during the storm, we hadn't heard from the tramily since we'd left them in the Smokies. We briefly wondered if they'd decided to carry on north without us, but we couldn't imagine Girl Scout leaving us behind.

We quickly discovered that taking two straight days off from hiking coupled with eating and drinking everything in sight was a less-than-ideal training regimen for a thru-hike. We had about 3,000 feet to climb over five miles on our first day back, and boy did we feel it. We'd initially intended to hike a bigger day to catch the tramily sooner rather than later, but we made it just over 10 miles, huffing and puffing the entire way. We made camp on a perfectly flat tent site next to a trickling stream at Groundhog Creek Shelter, both deciding it was our favorite campsite yet. It was a quieter-than-usual evening in the woods without the rest of our crew, but it was pleasantly warm. We hung out outside our tents, each cooking up some noodles with our newly acquired variety of cheeses, sun dried tomatoes, and fresh spinach, and we went to bed happy and full.

I was harassed by my first mouse that night, an adorably furry yet decidedly vicious little thing that ran circles over and over and over the mesh of my tent. It did not know that my fancy cheese stash was hanging safely in a tree several feet away. I shook

my tent gently multiple times, hoping to scare him away, but by
about the fifth time he woke me up, my half-asleep, knee-jerk
reaction was to slam my open hand toward the thunderous rustling
above my head. I made contact and I can only imagine Mr. Mouse
went flying. Ibex confirmed the next morning that he'd been
terrorizing her as well. One could hardly blame him though, given
the oversized haul of delicious snacks that we'd brought out to the
woods from Asheville.

As we sipped on coffee, exchanging war stories, Michael
appeared, rushing toward our tents. "Glowstick, is that you?!" he
asked excitedly.

"Sure is!" I replied.

"What are you guys doing here? Where's the rest of the
crew?" he asked. "I thought you would be way ahead by now!"

I described our great escape from the storm, mentioning
the radio silence from the tramily and how we intended to catch
them in Hot Springs. Michael seemed oddly flustered, and I asked
what was ailing him.

"My filter," he said. "I think it must have frozen in the
night and now I can't get it to work. I don't know what I'm going
to do. I can't make it to Hot Springs without filtering water."

I had a few emergency water purification tablets in my
pack, so I handed them over. He seemed grateful, but still entirely
distracted. We were anxious not to pick up a third wheel, wanting
a bit of quiet time before rejoining the tramily, so we wished him
well and were on our way, telling him we'd likely see him in Hot
Springs if not before.

It was another beautiful, sunny day on the trail, with
picturesque creek crossings, trilliums in white, red, and yellow
guiding our way, and more trail magic, which this time, we
accepted. A retired folks' social hiking club out of Asheville, of
which there were probably 50 attendees, sweetly handed us Ziploc
bags full of homemade cookies. The ladies passing them out told

us that they did this each year, and they looked forward to it more than Halloween. The cookies were incredible.

Though there was plenty of elevation gain, there was also plenty of reward as we went up and over Max Patch, a bald with far-reaching views of the Blue Ridge Mountains and a favorite local picnic spot. Ibex, having raced ahead of me earlier in the day, was lounging in the sun at the top when I arrived. I joined her for a little thru-hiker picnic and a barefoot skip across the top of the bald.

We made camp a few miles down the trail at Walnut Mountain Shelter. A calm evening turned into a vicious night, with the wind howling insanely through the trees. I found myself holding down the corners of my tent with all my might in the night, terrified it might blow away. I desperately had to pee, but I didn't dare leave the tent behind unweighted, so I was forced to hold my bladder all night long as I protected my little home. A huge branch, which couldn't have been more than 30 feet away from where I tried, unsuccessfully, to sleep, came crashing to the ground around 2:00 am. My fear that my tent would blow away turned to fear that a tree was about to impale me. Ibex slept through the entire thing. *This is it, game over*, I thought.

Miraculously, I made it through the night unscathed, and we pressed on. Two days later, we found ourselves following the trail straight through the tree-lined main street of Hot Springs, North Carolina. This town, with its charming little main street, old-fashioned railroad, flowering trees, and historic old homes, was the definition of southern charm. From any point in town, you had a clear view of the mountains, and it boasted a huge, crystal-clear river flowing through it.

We snagged the last available room in town at the quaint little Iron Horse Station, an inn that was built in 1929 and boasted comfortable, historic rooms with skeleton key doors. We hadn't been planning to come into town until the following day, but we arrived just outside of town by noon, so figured we might as well get a nice meal and a hot shower, especially as the previous couple of days had been dreary and cold.

We decided not to tell the tramily quite yet that we were in town, as we were both in the mood for a relaxing, quiet afternoon and evening. We still hadn't made a full recovery from our vacation in Asheville, so we weren't exactly anxious for a party that night. Instead, we showered, attempted to clean our clothes at the local laundromat, though every washer in the place was broken except for one, and then explored the town and grabbed dinner at the local tavern. Throughout our meal, Ibex and I each continually cast paranoid glances at the door, worried that the tramily might show up and bust us for being so cryptic.

Rather than partying with the crowd of thru-hikers in town for the evening, we opted to wash our clothes by hand in the shower because we couldn't seem to get access to the working washer, then settled into the common room of our inn. Ibex put "Ru Paul's Drag Race" on the TV and a tall, attractive Norwegian hiker named Bookie joined us. Though we insisted he was most welcome to change the channel, he declined, happy just to have the company and laughing along at the ridiculousness of the show. We chatted with him for a good while before heading to bed, content with our decision to stay in for the evening.

Upon waking in the morning, we realized it was April 20. We had survived our first month on the trail. We texted the tramily to let them know that we'd arrived in town, then headed to the general store to buy ourselves vegan ice cream treats for breakfast in celebration. A trail anniversary, or "trailiversary," after all, was no time for a normal trail breakfast. We then headed to the post office to pick up the package we'd sent ourselves in Asheville as well as some packages from friends and family. My cousin Katie had sent me a box full of goodies, including some delicious homemade chocolate chip cookies, which I began passing out to every thru-hiker that I knew since I couldn't carry all of them out to the trail. Ibex received not one, but three packages, and I wondered where she was going to fit all of those extra goodies. As we made friends with the casually dressed and overly chummy postal service worker, our tramily members marched in one by one. Jukebox and Girl Scout both squealed, rushing to embrace us as they came in through the door, followed by a barely recognizable Wintergreen. He'd shaved off his facial hair the day before, and with his rounded face now much more visible, he looked like a completely different person. Chef followed close behind, and the group convinced us to join them for a second breakfast at the local diner before we headed out of town. We were in no rush, and were keen to celebrate our trailiversary with the whole tramily having had a nice break from socialization over the past few days, so we allowed them to lead the way.

Chef, who was normally very down to finish everyone else's food if they couldn't finish it themselves, began to act strangely quiet at breakfast. Girl Scout offered him her plate of home fries, and he rejected them, a look of disgust on his face. This was extremely out of character. He was usually our garbage disposal. And he did not even polish off his own plate of food, which was concerning.

After taking some group photos and ducking into a local shop, where half the crew got milkshakes to go, we headed across town to return to the woods as a cohesive unit. As we exited town, we walked past multiple gorgeous campsites along the river. I stared at them regretfully, noting that if I'd known of their existence, I would have happily held onto my half of the hotel fee from the previous night. Chef fell behind, soon texting us that he was feeling out of sorts and would catch up in a day or two.

The rest of us only ended up hiking about four miles onward, though it was mainly uphill. Upon reaching a gorgeous grassy knoll with a killer view of the mountains, we couldn't resist staying put for the evening, even though it was next to a dirt road. For safety reasons, camping next to roads was not my favorite thing, but this camping spot was stunning enough to make it worth the risk. The closest water source was another half mile down the trail, so Jukebox and I volunteered to go ahead and fill everyone's bottles if it meant we could stay.

The group of us gathered downed wood for a fire. Wintergreen began to pile green wood around the fire ring. I had grown up camping in Western New York and regularly having bonfires at my parents' rural homestead. My dad had taught me how to choose pieces of wood that would burn rather than smoke, and to leave the green or wet bits behind. Wintergreen had been an Eagle Scout, so I was confused about his choices, but he didn't seem to want my opinion on the matter. *I guess a little smoke won't hurt*, I thought.

As we got the fire going and gathered around it, three other hikers—Peter Pan Squatch, Captain Jack, and Johnny Appleseed—walked up. They intended to stop only for a short hello, but our excitement over our gorgeous and unplanned campsite, complete with an incredible orange sunset, convinced them to stay. I was happy to have their company. Johnny Appleseed, a guy in his mid-twenties, was handsome, quiet, and mysterious. Peter Pan Squatch, who I guessed was around 50, was a friendly, sweet ball of nervous energy. He told us that he was on the trail to save his own life and missed his wife dearly. Despite being just out of town, he had run out of fuel, so I gave him my extra half canister. He couldn't believe his luck and was over the moon about it. He tried to give me some money for it, but instead, I insisted he simply pay it forward if the opportunity arose. "The trail provides," I said.

In addition to being our one-month trailiversary, it was also the national holiday of stoners everywhere, so the guys passed around a joint. I did not partake—weed makes me anxious and antisocial—but Ibex and I had bought a bottle of red wine in town to split. We got roped into passing the bottle around the fire as well. I did not get the wine buzz that I'd anticipated, but the sunset and the company gave me enough of a natural high that I didn't miss it. As dusk fell upon us, a loud whirring noise came from the woods nearby. It sounded like a car alarm, but we hadn't passed any cars along our way, even as the trail had followed the dirt road. The shrill siren repeated several times, seeming to get closer and closer to us. We couldn't imagine what it could be, and we were all a bit freaked out, already on edge from setting up next to the road. Taking a long shot, I Googled "car alarm in the woods" and discovered, shocked, that the sound was coming from a bird. This was the call of the Eastern whip-or-will, an elusive, camouflaged nocturnal bird that regularly sings into the night in a boisterous quest for love. While we found the idea of the bird charming, its song was less so, and we hoped it wouldn't stick around past hiker midnight.

Shortly before bed, a white pickup truck went flying down the road in front of us. Then, it turned around, driving back and forth in front of our makeshift camp several times. While the extra number of hikers with us that evening did make me feel a little more secure, it still scared me. I tried to put it out of my mind as I lay in my sleeping bag, but between the presence of the truck and the call of the lonely whip-or-will, I found myself tossing and turning late into the night when I usually fell asleep quickly and easily.

CHAPTER 13

We planned to make up a few miles the next day as part of our bargain with Wintergreen to stay at the grassy knoll. We had two things working in our favor that day: perfect spring weather and the knowledge that there was a "country store" open several miles ahead. I was counting on an iced cold Coca-Cola to push me through the last few miles of the day. Unlike in the few days past Asheville where I'd been feeling sluggish, I was finally back to feeling as energetic as I had in the Smokies. I stayed ahead of everyone, including Ibex and Wintergreen, who were *always* ahead of me, thoroughly enjoying myself as I raced up the trail.

Upon arriving at the so-called country store, I timidly crept inside. Not so much a "store," it was more of a dilapidated old shack along a busy highway with the words "country store" sloppily spray-painted in large letters on the side of the building. Inside, there was a bunch of old, musty-smelling furniture and a table piled with snacks, a refrigerator full of drinks, and a small freezer holding frozen convenience foods, none of which were vegetarian, unfortunately. I chatted with the friendly owner, who explained in a thick southern accent that he'd built the store with his dad when he was a kid, and now he kept it open in remembrance of his parents. He'd placed a small shrine dedicated to them in the corner. I could only imagine the store must have been in better shape when they'd been alive. But I didn't discriminate when it came to snacks and I was grateful that he kept

it open, despite its shoddy appearance, so I helped myself to a
Gatorade, a small bag of Doritos, and a Coke. I paid in cash and
then headed out the door to enjoy my treats in the sun. As I headed
back up the trail, all of the liquids I'd just consumed sloshed
around in my stomach noisily.

The next few days passed somewhat unremarkably, save
for a few things. Chef had yet to catch up, as he'd come down with
a sinus infection and stayed behind, camping at the river for a full
two days. Girl Scout's foot pain, which had begun in the Smokies,
was now so intense that she couldn't stand to hobble around on it
any longer. She called a shuttle to pick her up and take her to
Erwin, Tennessee, a good 30-plus miles ahead of where we were
currently, so that she could rest. And, we experienced another
insanely windy, thundering night at Bald Mountain Shelter, in
which my tent nearly collapsed. After being blown halfway off the
mountain en route, I arrived at the shelter just as night was falling,
hoping to sleep inside for once. But the entire thing, save for only a
couple of spaces which included one that Jukebox had cajoled
Wintergreen into giving her, was taken by a large church group,
there on spring break. I popped a Benadryl and, for only the
second time, shoved a pair of earplugs into my ears that
Wintergreen had given me at Plum Orchard Shelter. This was the
only way I felt I could make it through the night without having a
panic attack.

In the morning, from the mountaintop, I called ahead to
Uncle Johnny's Nolichucky Hostel & Outfitter in Erwin,
Tennessee, to book us a place to dry our things and lay our heads. I
snagged the last available accommodations at the hostel. We'd be
staying in "Grandma's Cabin" just 16.8 trail miles ahead. After a
long, wet, soggy, cold day tramping through the Tennessee forest,
I finally arrived, ahead of Jukebox but behind Wintergreen and
Ibex. They'd caught the day's last shuttle to town, so promised to
bring us back dinner and treats. Being alone for the moment and

expecting Jukebox at any time, I greedily rushed into the shower, anxious to wash the mud from the last couple days off of my skin and to regain the heat I'd lost to the day's rain. Grandma's Cabin was spectacular. We were pretty sure it had literally been Grandma's cabin before she'd passed away. It was decorated in mismatched 1970s furniture and the closets were full of old lady clothes with explicit instructions not to touch them. We would try to keep our hands off them. Erwin, on the other hand, was not one of the many adorable, walkable towns of the south. It was more like a standard American suburb—too spread out and inconvenient to walk anywhere. But Uncle Johnny's was directly off the trail and shuttles were readily available for a fee, so it worked just fine for our purposes.

Once Jukebox arrived, we put our orders in with Ibex for the local Mexican joint. Girl Scout, having arrived ahead of us, had a private cabin across the lawn and came to hang out with us as we waited, hangrily, for the others to return. When they finally got back, Ibex had just half of my food order. She'd brought shrimp fajitas for Jukebox and a sad, single cheese enchilada for me, rather than the enchilada dinner that I'd been hoping for. Ibex is known for being a bit of a space cadet. I internally berated myself for entrusting her with something as important as town dinner. Jukebox generously offered me the sides that came with her dinner, and I huffily got out the menu for the local delivery pizza place. After a 19-mile day followed by an almost 17-mile day over some pretty tough terrain, I was starving and cranky. A single tiny cheese enchilada simply wasn't going to cut it.

The five of us spent the evening eating, drinking, taking turns choosing the most ridiculous songs that we could think of, and playing card games, including classics such as Fuck the Dealer and Horse Races along with some Minnesota specials, courtesy of Girl Scout. Jukebox was nitpicking at me for some reason. She was picking on me for being too girly, so in retaliation, I named my

Horse Races horse "Fairy Dancer." She rolled her eyes and groaned loudly. I just laughed. I had a happy little wine buzz going, we had Girl Scout back, there was cheesecake, and Ibex was getting laughably and cheerfully drunk. Over and over, she sang "Rock Lobster," a classic B-52s song about, well, a lobster. Wintergreen claimed to hate the song, though he couldn't help cracking up over her enthusiasm for it.

As the drinks flowed, we all attempted to mimic Girl Scout's thickening Minnesota accent, which morphed into Scottish accents, then into Irish accents. The night continued on gaily until an Uncle Johnny's staff member came over to sternly remind us that quiet hours had begun some time ago. And at that, we sheepishly slinked off to our beds, with Girl Scout going back to her cabin across the way, Ibex and I sharing a double bed in our single bedroom, and Jukebox and Wintergreen each taking a couch in the living room.

The next morning, we cooked breakfast as a group with supplies that Ibex had brought back from her town run. This consisted of cheesy eggs, avocado toast, cinnamon donuts, and instant coffee. We then called a local shuttle driver named Doug for a ride to the laundromat. As was becoming the norm in these trail towns, we discovered that the laundromats both at Uncle Johnny's and in town were closed. But Doug had the inside scoop and took us out to a large, working laundromat in a neighboring town, telling us to call as soon as we were done and he'd come back to get us. Since Ibex and I always split doing laundry, I volunteered to go, wanting to spend some extra time with Girl Scout since she'd been away from us and hoping to get to know Wintergreen a little better in a small group. I'd had such a positive first impression of him, and though we'd been traveling in the same group for weeks, I felt like I'd never talked with him one on one. More often than not, I was irritated at him for taking leadership of the group and how many miles we'd push each day. I thought I should make an effort if we were going to stick together.

I brought a book in case I got bored waiting for the laundry to finish, but it turned out that I didn't need it. Girl Scout, Wintergreen, another hiker named Brian who was a journalist from Florida, and I hung out at the diner next door, chatting away and having many laughs as we waited for our clothes to get clean. By the time Doug came back to get us, I was having such a great time that I regretted that our clothes were already done.

That evening, we caught the Uncle Johnny's shuttle into town to grab dinner and resupply our food stashes. Ibex, Wintergreen, Girl Scout, and I dined at the Mexican restaurant beforehand, which was in the same plaza as a Walmart. Wintergreen and I split a pitcher of margaritas and Girl Scout made a joke about how we should just stick our straws into the pitcher as if we were on a cute date, which made us both blush.

Jukebox skipped dinner, which was out of character. She was the most social among us, and always in the thick of things. She was feeling a bit out of sorts so went next door to resupply at Walmart alone instead.

Once we returned to Uncle Johnny's, Girl Scout hunted down a VCR so we could take advantage of a couple of the many VHS tapes that adorned the cabin. We found an old electric razor under the bathroom sink, and Ibex begged me to shave her head as we sipped sparkling wine with blueberry pomegranate juice. I agreed, facetiously spouting off about my artistic talent while giving her a trendy little European-style faux hawk.

We'd also all picked up skincare face masks at Walmart, with me grabbing an extra for Wintergreen, sure that he wouldn't buy his own. We laughed raucously at "Wet Hot American Summer" on the TV as we exfoliated our pores, certain that Chef would be sad to have missed this. I sat between Ibex and Wintergreen during the movie, and I could swear he was flirting with me, finding little excuses to touch me, offering me his last Kit Kat, making eye contact as we laughed at the movie's jokes, and sitting a little closer to me on the couch than he needed to.

Jukebox, meanwhile, spent the evening in the bathroom, sick as a dog. We were all confused—though she'd been drinking with the lot of us the night before, she hadn't seemed intoxicated in the slightest. She'd been fine. But she'd been feeling under the weather all day and now here she was, holed up in front of the toilet, vomiting profusely.

In the morning, we found Jukebox lying on the bathroom floor—even sicker than she'd been the night before. This wasn't a hangover; this was food poisoning. We were scheduled to check out of Uncle Johnny's that day but called the front desk to see if perhaps it would be an option to stay another night. With Jukebox feeling deathly ill, Girl Scout's foot still aching, and Chef still behind, it seemed like it might be our best option. But alas, Grandma's Cabin, as well as the rest of the compound, was already booked for the night. If we wanted to stay in town, we'd have to find alternative accommodations.

Ibex and I were keen to get back to the trail. One zero day was great, but we'd learned our lesson in Asheville and weren't ready to make the mistake of the double zero again anytime soon. Chef caught us as we were packing up and joined us for a breakfast of cinnamon rolls and coffee. Then, he called a shuttle to drive him to a hotel in town. He promised to take just the rest of the day off and then catch us as soon as he could. He took Jukebox with him, escorting her and carrying her pack so that she could book her own hotel room and get some rest. She was in rough shape, and we were all glad that she wouldn't have to make the trip down the highway alone. Girl Scout, having booked her private cabin for the entire week, gave us each a hug and promised to skip over the section she'd missed and catch us as soon as her foot felt better.

Wintergreen seemed paralyzed with indecision. It was supposed to rain during the afternoon, and there was nothing he hated more than rain. He'd been banking on us staying at Grandma's Cabin one more night, so when it became clear that wasn't an option, he wasn't sure what to do. Reluctantly, he followed behind Ibex and I, agreeing that it would be better to get some miles in.

The morning was beautiful, sunny and warm, but in the afternoon, things took a turn for the worse and a torrential downpour rolled in. I was in high spirits. I felt well-rested after the day in Erwin, well-accomplished with the resupply and finished laundry, and ready to hit the trail. Wintergreen, on the other hand, was having a meltdown about the rain. About 10 miles in, we reached a field called Beauty Spot, which is supposedly quite stunning during agreeable weather. As we passed by though, we found it shrouded in fog. I was feeling good and wanted to push a few more miles to the next shelter, but Wintergreen demanded that we stop and set up camp, so Ibex and I obliged. This was different; Wintergreen was usually the one hounding us to do more miles, and here he was wanting to stop short. Once we had set up, we sat in our tents, Ibex happily drinking the can of wine that she'd brought along, me cheerfully chowing down on my stash of candy, and Wintergreen stewing about the weather and his decision to come back out to the trail. He realized that not only did he have to deal with the rain, but there was also some big sports event happening on television that night that he was missing.

Despite Wintergreen's foul mood, I was excited to be out on trail with just the three of us for a little while. I'd had such a good time with him in Erwin; here was my chance to get to know him better in a smaller group. It would likely only be a few days until the others caught up and we were back together, so I wanted to take advantage of the time we had.

Though we awoke to chilly temperatures, a slick, muddy trail, and a thick fog that made the forest look like the set of a horror movie, the day improved quickly. Ibex ran out of camp early, and I found her around lunchtime, posted up at a shelter with a small but hot fire that had been built by a section hiker named Richard Cranium. As I sat down, his companion, a fluffy, dark gray, curly-haired pup with a cowlick, curled up on my lap. Her name was Bernie Sanders.

"She's a socialist," Richard Cranium told me. "She doesn't discriminate—she'll take treats from anyone!"

While Ibex and I sat huddled together by the fire, sharing our snacks with our new friend Bernie, we met and chatted with a young, blond-haired, blue-eyed Finnish couple named Snickers and Alma. Snickers, a rail-thin, smiley 19-year-old, was named for his penchant for eating up to 12 Snickers candy bars per day. Alma, his 20-year-old girlfriend, was the spunky one, sporting a bleach-blonde pixie cut and prone to giving Snickers the side-eye.

"I don't even consider them to be candy anymore," he told us about his namesake. "It's just food to me now!"

As we sat, enjoying the warmth of the fire as well as the company, the sun peeked out from behind the clouds and the fog began to clear. We stayed for almost two hours, with Wintergreen eventually catching up, and continued on into a completely different forest than when we'd arrived only a short time before.

I was again quite enjoying the day, happy to be on the trail once more and feeling rather energetic, when out of nowhere, my left ankle began to throb. I hadn't done a thing to it—I hadn't fallen or twisted it. But suddenly pain was shooting up my leg and it cracked painfully as I rolled it from side to side. When it began, I was only about a mile from the shelter where I planned to meet Ibex and Wintergreen, so I hobbled up the trail, mildly panicked. I couldn't believe my luck. Just as I'd finally started to feel strong, it looked like I might have to take a break and stay behind.

When I finally arrived at the shelter, I threw my pack down in front of Ibex, almost in tears. I told her what had happened, asking her to carry my pack over to the tent site for me. She reluctantly agreed, sighing loudly as she picked it up and lugged it to the site next to hers. Clearly, she did not see this as the emergency that it was. Using my trekking poles for support, I hobbled after her dramatically. Preacher, another thru-hiker whom I had not yet met, followed me, offering advice. He'd had ankle issues on another hike and he had an extra compression brace and a small container of icy hot that he lent to me for the evening. His best guess was that it was just a muscle spasm, and he recommended I go ice it in the stream for a while.

Though there was a steep incline down to the water, I needed to refill my bottles anyway. I was desperate to take any advice available, so did as he suggested, sitting glumly on a rock with my foot in the stream for some time. Luckily, I had some cell service, a luxury on trail, so I was able to do a quick Google search on my phone. I learned that it was likely tendonitis from walking in the slippery mud all day. That was good news; though it was painful, it wouldn't be debilitating. I'd take it as easy as I could, popping Ibuprofen until I could get to town and rest and ice it.

Once I'd had enough of icing it in the stream, I hobbled back up the incline and joined the others around a roaring fire. There was a full crew at the shelter that evening, with many new faces, including the Finns, whom we'd met earlier, Tab, a quirky but friendly older guy, and Bear Box and French Toast, a 20-something female duo, who I immediately liked and felt at ease around.

The next morning, I was overjoyed to find that my ankle felt much better. On top of that, Bear Box let me know that she'd found a roll of KT Tape left in the shelter, perfect for taping up injuries. The trail provides. Ibex and I looked up how to tape an ankle for tendonitis, and she helped me do so before we headed up the trail. I still had some pain in my ankle, but it was not the spastic, shooting pain of the day before so much as a dull ache. *I can do this*, I told myself.

That day turned into one of my very favorites on trail. I hiked the first couple of miles with Wintergreen, chatting away and watching as he almost stepped on a huge brown snake. We discussed our hope for trail magic as it was a sunny Saturday—the most likely recipe for it to appear. And sure enough, as we rounded a corner at the base of Roan Mountain, a group of enthusiastic young adults called us down to their campsite, where they had multiple chairs, a grill, and a hammock set up, as well as piles of food. They were led by Silver Linings, a former thru-hiker from Raleigh, North Carolina, who had brought his friends out for the weekend to set up a "hiker diner," complete with pancakes, hot dogs, cans of beer and soda, packs of gummies, pieces of fruit, vegetables with dip, and more. They invited us, rather enthusiastically, to take a seat in their camp chairs while they served us pancakes. The group felt like old friends, and we hung around with them for a couple of hours, eventually dragging ourselves up from our camp chairs. At the insistence of Silver Linings, we each packed out a beer for the road. I would have loved to stay there all day, but we had a big old mountain that we needed to climb.

Knowing I'd be behind on the climb, I persuaded Ibex and Wintergreen to wait for me at the top so we could drink our beers together. I climbed, mesmerized, through the thick spruce forest, dry despite the buckets of rain that had come down only two days prior. At the summit, I was greeted by a golden meadow that was sparkling in the sun, with views of the mountains ahead and remnants of an old hotel within. As promised, I found Ibex and Wintergreen sprawled out in the sun at the top, waiting for my arrival to crack open their beers. "Cheers!" we said in unison, clinking our cans together. We sipped our drinks, soaking in the glorious spring day.

Shortly after, as we continued, the trail became a stream full of slick, golf ball-sized rocks. The unstable ground forced my throbbing ankle this way and that, sending pain shooting up and down my leg. In the thick of this, however, a group of middle-aged men in flannels and baseball caps passed by going southbound, stopping to let me know there was a huge trail magic setup only a couple of miles ahead at Carvers Gap. This knowledge pushed me forward through the discomfort, as I knew that there would be a place for me to sit and if I was lucky, some ice for the taking.

Two painful miles later, I finally arrived at Carvers Gap. There, I was greeted by several ragtag 20- and 30-somethings, who insisted I take a seat and, when I asked if they had any ice to spare, immediately wrapped some up in a plastic baggie for me and handed me a Gatorade. They were a tramily of about 10 who had thru-hiked the year before, and one guy specifically came over to talk with me about my ankle.

"The same thing happened to me last year," he said. "Only three weeks before the end of the trail."

He shared that upon calling his doctor and explaining the situation, the doctor diagnosed him with tendonitis and told him that to get through the hike, it was perfectly acceptable to live off ibuprofens for the remainder of the trail, with explicit instructions to stop the drugs immediately past the finish line. He was able to finish his hike without any lasting damage. It was a relief to know he'd gone through it and made it to the other side, unscathed. This cheered me up.

As was normal in the South and with trail magic, there weren't any vegetarian dinner options, despite the fact that one of the trail angels was named Little Veggie for her tiny stature and vegetarian diet. Hot dogs and burgers were the normal fare of choice. So while Wintergreen and Ibex wolfed down cheeseburgers, I helped myself to about half a pan of brownies. The Finns were there as well, on their third or fourth beer each when I arrived, giggling up a storm. As Europeans, they were used to being able to buy alcohol on their own at home. But since they were underage in the States, they took every opportunity to indulge when someone was generous enough to share it with them.

This group of trail angels was a rowdy, fun crew who I was sure would be a blast to party with, but we decided after an hour or so that we'd better get a move on if we were going to make it to Overmountain Shelter, our intended campsite, before dark. We'd already spent a good chunk of the day with Silver Linings and crew, and we still had over six miles to go, so we didn't have as much time to spare as we would have liked. After saying our thank yous and goodbyes, we got on with it. The Finns promised they'd be close behind, intending to camp with us for the night. But given their buzzed state, we expected it would be another day or so until we saw them again.

Onward from Carvers Gap, we passed through what was probably the most beautiful part of the trail to that point. We were led up and over two golden balds, surrounded by deep valleys and sapphire mountains as far as the eye could see. It reminded me of the mountains of New Zealand, "Lord of the Rings" country.

After losing Ibex, as I stopped to take one too many photos, I found myself fighting to follow the exceptionally slim trail through a thick patch of rhododendrons. Once I finally pulled myself free, I found that I was now on top of a third bald, unable to find a white blaze anywhere. Multiple trails were crossing each other atop the bald, and I must have tried all of them, searching in vain for the AT. There were multiple tent sites atop, and a few were full, which was unsurprising since it was Saturday.

After my second or third time hiking across the bald, I stopped to ask a camper if he could tell me where the AT was. He confidently pointed me back across the bald the other way and to the left. Upon arriving at the exact spot that he had pointed to, there was still not a single white blaze to be found. I passed a mother and her two preteen daughters for the third time, and she awkwardly suggested I camp at a tent site over yonder.

"Oh," I stammered, taken aback by her coldness. "I'm just lost—I'm looking for my friends and not sure where they've gone. They were ahead of me."

Relief immediately crossed her face. "Oh! You're with friends–that's great!" she said. "I hope you find them!" I gave her a tight smile, then turned back the opposite way that I'd come, frustrated. I eventually stumbled upon a young couple walking a tiny golden retriever puppy.

"Excuse me," I said. "Do you happen to know how to get to the Appalachian Trail? I'm a thru-hiker and have lost my way. I can't find it anywhere!" They pointed me back down the bald, giving me explicit instructions as to where I'd find it. I'd gotten off trail when I followed the narrow corridor to the top of the bald. After a few moments of tramping back through the rhododendrons, I finally spotted a white blaze. I was overcome with relief. There was no way I was going back up that bald to ask directions again. It turned out that the trail had taken a sharp left, and I had completely missed it, continuing straight up the bald mistakenly. Luckily, I was now back on track.

I had wasted at least a half hour up on Grassy Bald, so once back on the trail, I knew I'd have to book it to catch Ibex and Wintergreen before dark. Overmountain Shelter was one of the most famous on the trail, and I didn't want to miss out on staying there. Luckily, the terrain was easy and cruisey. I hiked through the evening and into twilight when the setting sun began to cast a golden light on the lush green of the forest. I passed a herd of deer chomping down on fresh spring plants, and I stopped for a moment, quietly reflecting on the fact that I was a visitor in their home. This was only my second time seeing deer on the trail so far. The first had been during the eerie beginnings of a thunderstorm, so this felt special. They stared back at me for a second, then returned to their meals, unfazed.

I made it to Overmountain Shelter just in time to catch the sunset. The shelter itself was a large, mouse-filled red barn with a huge field on the side for tents that overlooked the mountains. The view was incredible. I was told the barn and the land under it had been donated to the AT community by a farmer some years ago.

"What happened to you?" Ibex demanded. I told her about the day's misadventure and asked if she'd seen the Finns anywhere. I was sure they would have passed me while I was up on Grassy Bald, but in my race up the trail to catch Ibex and Wintergreen, I hadn't seen them.

"Nope!" she said. "It's just us and Tab. I think all these other people are weekenders." Tab was another thru-hiker that we'd been hiking around in recent days. The campsite was teeming with large tents and dogs. It was definitely the weekend. We didn't mind though—we were all in high spirits from the tremendous day.

I set my tent up next to Wintergreen's and began to cook dinner. I figured I had better eat some real food after a breakfast of pancakes followed by a lunch of brownies. I still had some spinach and sundried tomatoes left from our stop in Erwin, so I poured a generous portion into my macaroni and cheese, enjoying the last remnants of the sunset as I chowed down. Ibex hit the hay early, leaving me to hang out with Wintergreen as I finished my supper and sipped on the beer that the Carvers Gap crew had thrust into my hands when I said my goodbyes earlier. He smoked a joint that someone had given him at the trail magic as we sat together, chatting about nothing in particular and gazing up at the full moon.

Once I had finished the dregs of my beer, I went off to my tent to hunker down for the night. It had been a wonderful, but long, day. Despite our many breaks, we still managed to push 17 miles. Between that and the junk food and beers that I'd lived on that day, I was feeling lethargic and ready for some sleep. Washington, D.C. is a big drinking city, and I had been determined when I left the city to also leave that part of my life behind. I had grown out of it. As it turned out, though, the AT had a big drinking culture as well. Free beers were a regular aspect of trail magic, and most trail towns had at least one brewery that everyone wanted to visit. Ibex once described our hike through the south as one big brewery crawl. Luckily for us, hangovers were much less of a thing when you were moving your body all day every day, so it did not feel like a big deal to indulge. We'd get a little buzz and wake up the next day feeling perfectly fine and ready to crank out some miles. The beers seemed to burn right through us. It did not have the same effect on my body in normal life.

The beautiful day turned into a cold, blustery night and I barely slept a wink. I awoke to Ibex rushing out of camp early. She tended to do that when we'd had crappy weather overnight. I had run out of water the night before, so I had to gather some from the frigid creek first thing that morning before I could even have my coffee or brush my teeth. I'd been too spent to do it the night before.

The day's scenery was unreal. I couldn't believe this was Tennessee; it felt like we were in some incredible foreign land. The terrain was tough though. The trail was slick with deep mud and the climbs were steep as we went up and over two more golden balds. On the other side of the balds, though, was the exit point for the town of Roan Mountain, Tennessee, where we'd find Mountain Harbor Hostel, rumored to have the best breakfast on the AT.

I took my time so as to not annoy my ankle more than necessary, and when I finally arrived at Mountain Harbor, I found Wintergreen seated on a picnic bench outside a large farmhouse.

"You okay?" he asked, handing me his beer. "Need a drink?" I gratefully took a sip and then dropped my pack down on the ground.

"It could have been worse," I said. "At least this part of the trail is incredible." I went inside, paid for a bed in their four-person loft, then ordered lunch from the onsite food truck. I had a grilled cheese sandwich, fries, and a salad, which I ate at the picnic table while Wintergreen finished his beer. Ibex was showering, he told me.

As we sat, basking in the sun, a pickup truck pulled into the hostel driveway. Silver Linings energetically slid out of the driver's seat. "Hey guys!" he called. "Long time no see!"

He was on his way home to Raleigh, having finished up the weekend camping trip with his friends, and was keen to unload the copious amount of leftover hiker snacks filling the backseat of his truck. Of course, we volunteered to help him out. "We'll make sure these get to the right people!" we promised.

He filled the entire picnic table with various kinds of Pop-Tarts, bags of gummies, pouches of Capri Sun, rolls of toilet paper, and more. We thanked him profusely for his kindness, then said our goodbyes once again. Wintergreen and I both agreed that we'd like to have been friends with him if he had been hiking the trail this year. He was aptly named Silver Linings—it was obvious that he saw the good in people and situations and he was a lot of fun to be around.

Once I had taken my pick of the snacks, I stuffed them into my pack and shouldered it, heading to the loft, our home for the night. It was a neat place. There was a guesthouse that was used as a bed-and-breakfast—for the fancier customers, I supposed. The hiker hostel was on the top two floors of a converted barn, with the general store, which sold camping supplies and hiker snacks, on the bottom floor. It was cozy and relaxing. The property was lovely and had a cold stream running through it, perfect for icing my aching ankle. And the owners had several pet dogs on site, all of whom were friendly and used to people. I happily obliged when they each came by looking to be petted.

A bit later, after putting in some laundry and catching up on some journaling, we hired the owner to shuttle us down to the local grocery store. We'd been hoping to visit a local bakery and wood-fired pizza shop that we'd heard was to die for, but this was a Sunday in the South so it was, unfortunately but not unsurprisingly, closed. We had to settle for grocery store subs instead.

Fisher, a 40-something-year-old army veteran who was hiking with his sweet, well-behaved service dog named Forrest, joined us. Most dogs that we met on the trail obviously weren't meant for the thru-hiking lifestyle. They were either poorly behaved, injured, exhausted, or all of the above. But not Forrest. He was well taken care of and seemed healthy and happy. And he never left Fisher's side.

When we returned to Mountain Harbor after our errands, it was still sunny and warm, so we sat outside to dine together. As we were doing so, the Finns finally showed up, ecstatic to have caught up to us. They filled us in on what had happened to them the previous night. They'd made the same mistake that I had by missing the tight turn on the trail and going up Grassy Bald. They'd been a tad intoxicated at the time, and it had taken them much longer than I to find their way back to the AT. They ended up camping elsewhere as a result and making up the miles on this day.

We had a jovial night together, all of us in a social mood, chatting with the few others who showed up at the hostel. At one point in the night, I glanced at Wintergreen out of the corner of my eye and found him watching me. We'd been spending a lot more time together since it had just been him, Ibex, and I, and I was starting to think there might be something growing between us.

The breakfast the next morning did not disappoint. It cost
$12 per person, was all-you-can-eat, and was well worth the
money. The vegetarian version consisted of eggs, potatoes, hash
brown casserole, a raspberry and cream pastry, an oversized
pancake, and a biscuit with butter and jam. I was in heaven. I
would have loved to go back for seconds on all of it, but I knew
that I had 17 miles to hike out that day, so as delicious as it all was,
I couldn't risk the stomach cramps that seconds would surely
cause.

It was another incredible sunny day, and the trail was
much more forgiving than it had been during the few days prior.
We followed alongside a rushing river for a spell, then passed by
multiple bubbling brooks, two large, rushing waterfalls, and fields
full of wildflowers. We also passed by the 400-mile marker, where
we stopped to get a group photo before carrying on through the
forest. We had descended almost 3,000 feet the previous day, so
we were out of the pines and back in a more varied deciduous
forest. It was an endlessly charming day on the trail.

Tab stayed with us that night, in a sandy tent site within a
rhododendron grove. He talked to himself non-stop as he set up his
hammock. He was a nice guy, and fun to have around, but
eccentric. Ibex, Wintergreen, and I, unable to find a proper tree in
which to hang our food bags among the rhododendrons, decided to
set them high up on a natural shelf created by a fallen log.

"You're leaving those there?!" Tab asked in disbelief. "I'd
call that a bear pantry!" We did not heed his warnings,
unconvinced that there were bears in these young woods. But when
I climbed out of my tent in the morning and went to retrieve them,
they were gone. *Oh my god,* I thought, white-faced and panicked.
*Tab was right. We shouldn't have been so careless. What are we
going to do?!*

I tried to remember if I'd left any snacks with my pack. It
is inadvisable to do so since it defeats the purpose of hanging your

food bag to keep the smell of food away from your tent, but sometimes I'd forget to take the snacks out of my hip belt pockets. That could be my lifeline. I didn't know where the next town jump-off would be, but I hoped I had enough food to get me there.

I glumly walked back to the campsite to find Tab holding our food bags.

"Picked these up for you!" he said cheerfully. "Guess there were no bears around after all!"

CHAPTER 14

The week continued this way—it was sunny and beautiful and colorful wildflowers and butterflies were emerging left and right from their winter slumbers. I felt energized and happy. My ankle still hurt a small bit, but it wasn't the frightening pain that I had experienced the first day; it was more of a dull ache. I also began to notice that my feet were getting swollen daily from the bigger miles that we were pushing. Neither of these things dimmed my enthusiasm though. Spring had sprung, and nothing could keep me down.

The day we arrived in Hampton, Tennessee, for our next resupply, I felt so good that I passed both Ibex and Wintergreen on the trail. They were both baffled. Wintergreen sped up his pace, not wanting to be left in the dirt by the slowest of the group.

I ran into Prince Charmin, a hiker we'd met back in Georgia, as I stopped to take in a beautiful meadow. Within it, there was a dilapidated wooden shelter sitting on the bank of a pond, and we stopped together to see if the frogs had yet emerged from their hibernation, having been encouraged by the sight of all the butterflies. We saw and heard several, and I was so grateful at that moment for the change in the season.

From the meadow, the trail meandered over wooden foot bridges that crossed a rushing, clear creek surrounded by budding trees, through crumbling rock walls, and then on to the most gorgeous waterfall I'd seen on the trail yet. This was Laurel Falls, a

40-foot high, 50-foot-wide waterfall in the middle of the Pond Mountain Wilderness, and we had it all to ourselves except for a sole hammocker who set up so that he was jutting out over the stream. As we stopped to have a snack, we took the opportunity to wash our dirt-caked arms and faces in the cool water. Floyd and Butcher, friends we hadn't seen in at least 200 miles, came shortly behind us. We caught up for a bit as we enjoyed the scenery.

From here, we marched on along an easy, flat path along the creek, stashing our packs behind a tree before taking the side trail to Hampton. To this point, we'd been fairly spoiled by delightfully idyllic little trail towns. And we'd already had a wildly charming day, so couldn't help but expect the trend to continue.

Our expectations were not met, however. In stark contrast to the stunning patch of forest that we'd passed through to get there, in Hampton, garbage lined the streets, half the buildings in town were run down and boarded up, and "Problem with addiction? Call this number" posters were tacked onto every telephone pole in town. And the town was hot and dusty. I later learned that Hampton sits right smack in the middle of one of the worst areas of the country for opioid addiction.

I walked into Brown's Grocery Store, excited for the chance to momentarily escape the heat, to find half-empty shelves covered in dust, and very few decent resupply options. A sign on the side of the building read, "If we don't have it, they probably don't sell it." This was the only shop in town, so I guessed that was true. No one else in Hampton was selling what I was looking for, either. As I stepped up to the cash register to pay, the greasy, acned teenage cashier ignored me in favor of her phone and a side conversation with a fellow worker. I asked if I could use the store restroom, but she refused me in her thick southern drawl, telling me I could probably use the one at the McDonald's across town. She then promptly returned her attention to her phone.

Not having had much luck in the "grocery store," I sauntered across the parking lot to the food truck parked at its edge. The only vegetarian option on the menu was a grilled cheese sandwich and steak fries, so that's what I ordered, adding in a 30-cent Sun Drop from the soda machine outside the store. The "grilled cheese" was a warm hamburger bun topped with melted American cheese and mushy tomatoes. It was not the tastiest meal I'd ever eaten, but since I was a hungry thru-hiker, I ate it anyway. At the very least, it was cheap.

Ibex ran to the post office while Wintergreen and I sat on the side of Brown's, in the only tiny patch of shade that we could find, surrounded by litter and dog poop that careless owners had not bothered to pick up. We got to work planning our next town stop, which would be Damascus, Virginia, in just a few days. Wintergreen called and got our hostel booked, and as soon as Ibex returned, we high-tailed it back to the trail, keen to escape the grittiness of Hampton as soon as possible. Our moods were dampened by this side excursion but began to lighten as soon as we got back on trail. We had almost three miles to hike uphill to reach camp, and the climb was brutal in the heat of the day. I turned on a podcast and popped in my headphones to get out of the Hampton headspace, and the miles flew quickly by.

Ibex stayed behind at the creek for a few minutes as Wintergreen and I headed up the trail, and once she caught up with us at camp, told us that we had just missed Chef. He'd been working to catch up to us and nearly had, but he was feeling all of the big miles that he'd been pushing and was going to stay down by the creek for the night, taking the rest of the day off. He hoped to rejoin us by Damascus.

On the way up to camp, I met Energizer, a blond, 20-something thru-hiker with an accent I couldn't quite place. He told me that he was from Ohio and claimed to be Amish, though he was in street clothes and carrying a smartphone. My immediate impression was that he was friendly but overly chatty, laying out his entire life story and how important he was back home in his community, completely unprompted. I was also not sure that I believed he was Amish. There were some Amish communities where I grew up in Western New York, and as far as I could tell, they were not carrying around cell phones or wearing street clothes, even when they did go into civilization like the grocery store.

Early in the evening, Energizer stopped to make camp with us at Pond Flats campsite. He'd already told both me and Wintergreen separately that he'd been "crushing miles" and planned to go much further than us that day. Yet here he was. He loudly announced himself as he arrived at camp, and Wintergreen told me that he'd had to give Energizer half his water on the way up our 1,700-foot climb because he had run out. There had been a stream at the bottom of the hill before the climb started, but even in 80-degree heat, Energizer didn't see the sense in carrying water that he probably wouldn't need.

I had initially been excited to meet someone new around our age, but as I was setting up my tent, he loudly announced, in response to nothing in particular, that he wished all American scientists would be sent to India. When Wintergreen asked why, he responded "To get them as far away from me as possible, of course!"

Ibex is a microbiologist. I am a science communicator with an environmental science degree. We were not impressed by this attitude.

The evening continued in this same fashion. Energizer plopped himself down in the middle of our crew, telling us what we were sure were tall tales about his life, bragging about how great of an employee he was, how he took care of all the youth in his community, how wolves are horrible animals because they hunt in packs.... He mentioned several more times that he was Amish, but when I asked him pointed questions about his culture, he skirted around them.

On the bright side, in order to escape Energizer for a bit, I spent a good deal of time gathering firewood, which Wintergreen then used to start a fire. It was a beautiful, warm, clear night, and we hung around the campfire together for hours. As Wintergreen went off to hang his bear bag, he urgently called me over. He'd found a gorgeous black and white spotted salamander. He knew I'd been searching for them. I was ecstatic. "This is the best thing you've done on the trail so far!" I told him. He laughed and agreed it probably was.

The next morning, I hustled out of camp, not wanting to get stuck hiking with Energizer. As I stopped for water just up the trail, a bright green hummingbird began buzzing around next to me in the rhododendrons. I love hummingbirds; I thought this had to be a good omen of what was to come.

We had a long, steep climb down to Watauga Lake, which we knew to have a beach, so I was amped to stop and have a swim. Unfortunately, though the lake was an inviting turquoise blue, the "beach" was polluted with dirty diapers and trash, so I decided to forego the swim and continue hiking instead. It was an easy three-mile walk around the lake, but we didn't dilly-dally because there were rumors of "problem bears" in this area, and signs urging caution—"Don't stop here due to bears"—taped to trees backing up what we had heard

About halfway around the lake, near a shelter that was closed to hikers due to said bear activity, I found Fisher and his dog Forrest perched by a creek. Fisher had decided to "slackpack," meaning hike without all of his heavy gear in his pack, for the day. Here, they were taking a short break. Fisher had lost his glasses and couldn't see well without them, so I stopped to chat and make sure that he knew about the bears. He did, but with Forrest around, he wasn't too worried. Ibex and Wintergreen showed up moments

later, and we hiked on together, taking a short break at the dam at
the lake's edge, just before the trail began to climb back up into the
mountains.

As the day wore on, it became hotter and hotter, which
meant the terrain felt tougher and tougher. We spent most of the
day climbing in the heat, and water sources were scarce. We
stopped for lunch at a lovely little creek, but soon after, Energizer
showed up, followed by Floyd and a sweet girl named Soup Spot.
Though I would have been happy to talk with Floyd and Soup Spot
longer, I didn't stay long, pushing on in hopes of losing Energizer
again.

Podcasts once again got me through the day, and I listened
to a particularly memorable one from Love + Radio about a
woman whose sex life was intimately tied to "The Lord of the
Rings." She had a long-term, serious relationship based on a shared
love of writing and acting out fantasies from the perspectives of
characters from the series. It was fascinating. I immediately shared
this story with anyone who would listen. I'd been thinking about
"Lord of the Rings" a lot on the trail, drawing parallels between
Frodo's journey and my own, so this podcast episode was relevant,
intriguing, and highly entertaining.

We pushed a 19-mile day, and I arrived at Iron Mountain
Shelter completely exhausted. I had just dropped my pack and sat
down to cook dinner with Ibex and Wintergreen when who should
appear? Energizer. I was fuming. I'd only agreed to travel that
distance to get away from him, and suddenly, here he was anyway.
I was much too tired to keep it together if he dared dominate the
evening conversation again, which he surely would. I couldn't take
another night hearing about how great he was and how horrible
scientists were.

But luck was on my side that night. Energizer was amped
up from the day's miles and began bragging that he could totally
go on and hike the seven remaining miles to the next shelter. I

demurely suggested he do so since he obviously had way more energy than us. "Oh wow, I really bet you could do it!" I told him, batting my eyelashes innocently.

"You're so right, I totally could!" he boasted, though I caught a flash of uncertainty cross his face. He waffled back and forth for a few moments, undecided. Then, the next thing we knew, he had taken off down the trail, on his way to Double Springs Shelter. I giggled hysterically in relief, and Wintergreen and Ibex cheered. At least for tonight, we were free.

It was just the three of us at the shelter that evening, and we made another fire, enjoying the gorgeous spring night together. Ibex took a short break to call her boyfriend Zack, who she had learned had been arrested for drug possession. He'd been smoking pot in his car and when he was pulled over for something else, the cop smelled it, warranting a search. She was pretty upset about it, especially because he was supposed to make the interstate trip from New York to hike with her for a spell soon.

After the long day, I was sure I'd sleep soundly that night. And I did, until about 4:00 am, when I awoke to the sounds of snapping twigs and the heavy plodding of what I assumed was a *very large* animal circling the campsite. Whatever it was, it came too close to my tent for comfort, then visited the shelter, which I was happy not to be sleeping in, then ambled over to the tree where our food bags were hanging. I suddenly regretted chasing Energizer off. This was no mouse. I was certain, this was a bear. It *had* to be a bear. And if one of us was going to be eaten, I was certain it was going to be me.

I lay in my sleeping bag, terrified, listening to the bear's every move as it trudged back and forth, back and forth around the campsite. After about half an hour of this, I heard Wintergreen shuffling around in his tent.

"Chet?" I asked, tentatively. I hadn't called him Chet in weeks.

"Yeah?" he responded.

"Do you, um, hear that?" I asked softly.

"Yep!" he replied.

"Well, um, what do you think it is?" I asked.

"Uh, I'm gonna have to say that's a bear," he responded matter-of-factly.

"That's what I thought, too!" I squeaked in terror.

To assuage my fears, he volunteered to peek outside his tent with his flashlight to ascertain that it really *was* a bear. He wasn't able to see anything, even though it still sounded to me like it was quite close. I was thankful that he was awake; at least I wasn't alone in this experience any longer. Ibex, on the other hand, was fast asleep. She could sleep through anything—wind, cold, thunder, bears—completely undisturbed. It was her superpower.

I came close to asking if I could make a mad dash for his tent. I couldn't decide which was safer, staying put in my tent alone, or crawling into his for more protection. Ultimately, I was too frightened to leave my tent to move to his, so I put the hunting knife that my dad had bought for me before I started the trek next to my head. Just in case. In the morning, Wintergreen told me that he'd had the same thought and almost suggested we'd be safer in one tent together. My heart skipped a beat at the thought.

The story seemed much funnier in the light of the day, and Ibex was in hysterics over having slept through the entire thing. She told us that she had heard our voices briefly in the night, but rolled over and went back to sleep, annoyed that we would dare disturb her slumber with our chitchat, none the wiser about the presence of the bear.

It was another sunny day in Tennessee, and it felt even more special than usual, because I was now carrying around the knowledge that I could have been eaten by a bear in the night, but had lived to tell the tale. I was alive!

The shelter didn't have any water. The last water source had been down a steep incline a couple of tenths of a mile south, so I decided to forgo my normal morning coffee in favor of getting an early start and getting away from known bear territory. Only a few miles down the trail, we were met with a wonderful surprise: the best trail magic so far!

Beth and Bernie, a sweet, funny couple from Florida, had set up shop along a dirt road just before the trail crossed through a picturesque little farm. Each year, these two take a little wedding anniversary trip to do trail magic for thru-hikers. They had never hiked the trail themselves but had somehow learned about it and had gotten involved in the culture and community early in their relationship, and they just loved helping and connecting with hikers each year.

As we arrived, they insisted that we take a seat in the camp chairs they'd set up and gave us a tour of the menu. They had brought fresh bread and bagels from the local bakery and pizza shop near Mountain Harbor that had been closed as we passed through. What luck! And to top them, they had a spread of hummus, several kinds of cheese, plump tomatoes, leafy green lettuce, guacamole, egg salad, deli meats, salad with homemade dressing, chips, brownie sundaes, cold sodas, and even a hiker box full of supplies for those who might need them, such as instant coffees, a medical kit, socks, and more.

They laughingly told us they didn't want to be best friends, they just wanted to feed us, but they were some of the nicest, friendliest people I'd ever met. They encouraged us to take seconds, asked us to sign their hiker logbook, and took our pictures while we ate. While we were there, a few other hikers showed up, including our friend Easy Bake, a middle-aged woman from Texas who'd gotten her name because of a penchant for baking muffins over her camp stove. We hadn't seen her since the Smokies.

When we finally rolled ourselves out of the trail magic spot, we crossed a gorgeous meadow through private farmland, then had a fairly easy terrain day. It was all very relaxed, and though we hiked 16 miles, I wasn't exhausted by the end of the day. We camped at Abingdon Gap Shelter, only 10 miles from Damascus, Virginia, and while the trail had been a little lonely lately, save for our evening with Energizer, we found a nice crowd there. There was Smoke, an intelligent 20-something from Virginia who reminded me of my old friend Andrew in both looks and spirit, Magpie, a 30-something veterinarian from Colorado who was crushing miles, and Dog Whisperer, an overly kind retiree from Florida who hung my bear bag for me. We spent the evening seated at a picnic table gabbing with the three of them, in high spirits.

I felt like Wintergreen was flirting with me. He'd repeat things I'd say in a cutesy, mocking way, hold my gaze far longer than was necessary, and he would find little excuses to touch me. I wondered if this was simply how he acted with his friends. Personally, though, my friends don't tend to look that deep in my eyes. Ibex certainly never did! So I suspected it might be more than that. My own emotions were starting to stir. In the time since we left Erwin, the three of us had become a team. It felt less like Wintergreen was bossing us around, and more like he was someone I could count on and looked forward to seeing throughout the day. He was still a miles pusher, but he also made me laugh and I couldn't help noticing the gold flecks in his dark eyes.

The three of us agreed to get up extra early the next morning to bank ourselves extra time in Damascus. Just across the Tennessee border into Virginia, Damascus was widely known as a favorite trail town. We'd spend a day and a half there, resting our weary bones and allowing Chef to catch up to us. I was almost hesitant to leave the woods, as we'd been in such a happy groove lately, but one of the things I'd been most excited about in hiking the AT was visiting the famous trail towns, especially those in the south, and Damascus was not one to miss. I awoke around dawn to the sound that had come to be my morning alarm clock each day: the obnoxious squealing of Ibex's deflating sleeping pad. I groaned but roused myself out of my cozy sleeping bag. We got ready quickly and hit the trail. It was just 10 miles downhill to Damascus, and town food was waiting!

CHAPTER 15

Rushing out of camp at 8:07 am marked a new record for us. Despite our best efforts though, we were among the last to depart, as many of our fellow thru-hikers, particularly the retirees, tended to be early risers. We, on the other hand, were not. The path to Damascus was easy, green, sunny, and picturesque. It was mostly downhill, and we noticed the leaves were really coming in on the trees as we approached town. Up until this point on the trail, there had still been a lot of bare gray and brown in the forest. However, once we hit Virginia, it was like someone had flicked a magic wand, ushering in full-on spring just in time for our arrival. We stopped for a cheer and a photo at the Virginia and Tennessee border then all headed to town together.

A couple of easy miles later, we arrived. We had been told early in the trail that those who made it to Damascus had the stuff to make it all the way to Katahdin. We were sure they were right because just under 500 miles in, we already felt like hiking gods—fit, tan, and hungry.

We stopped at the diner for lunch before even bothering to check into our hostel to drop our bags or take a shower. There, we ran into Thunderbird, an incredibly good-looking, friendly 20-something swim coach from Buffalo, New York, whom we'd met at Uncle Johnny's hostel in Erwin. We sat down at the counter to join him for lunch. He'd stayed behind in Erwin as we hiked out because he'd planned to take an extra zero day. Given his long legs, youth, and level of fitness, we expected him to catch up and pass us despite the extra day off. We never did see him pass by us though, so we were surprised to find him in Damascus. He explained that he'd jumped ahead by 20 miles to get new shoes due to some recurrent foot problems. After picking up his new ones and getting some rest, he'd be going back down south to make up the miles.

Over lunch, we chatted amiably about the many things that had transpired since we last saw him. Namely, I described our run-in with Energizer and how I was confused by the whole "Amish" thing. Thunderbird almost choked on his food, erupting into laughter. "No way that guy's Amish!" he sputtered out. Having bunked with Energizer the night before at a hostel, he'd gotten some intel. Contrary to Energizer's claims, Thunderbird was fairly certain that he hadn't even begun his hike at Springer Mountain. Despite claiming to be a thru-hiker, no one that Thunderbird had talked to could place him until the Smokies, and now, he was planning to catch a bus up to Shenandoah National Park to do some fishing with a friend. Then, he would head home to Ohio. His community needed him. This confirmed my suspicions: the guy was full of it.

After our meal, we headed to the post office, where Wintergreen had a giant package of homemade cookies from an aunt waiting, and I had one full of homemade cookies and Rice Krispy treats from my mom. As soon as we got to the Broken Fiddle, our home for the next 36 hours, we busted those boxes open at lightning speed and began stuffing our faces with treats, despite the fact that we'd just come from lunch.

The Broken Fiddle reminded me of a fraternity house. And believe me, I spent a lot of time in them during college, so I would know. It was disorganized—no one was there to check us in—and it was filthy. We had to wash the sheets on our beds because they'd been left dirty by the previous guests. The couches looked like they'd come from someone's grandma's basement, there was only one bathroom for the entire hostel, and there were a bunch of young people smoking and drinking on the back porch. It did the job though, giving us access to beds and a shower, so we did what we had to do and tried not to spend too much time there.

We spent the day running errands and exploring the town, which was beautiful. The trail marched directly through town, as did the Creeper Trail, a biking path that follows the Old AT along Whitetop Laurel Creek that is popular with locals and tourists alike. There was one main street running through town, lined with cute little shops and huge historic homes, and the flowering trees were blooming in full force. I'd spent a decent amount of time in Virginia during my years living in Washington, D.C., mostly to hike in Shenandoah National Park, and I'd always found it to be stunning and quaint. Damascus was just so, and I was sure I was going to love getting to know this state even more.

That evening, we walked an easy mile down the main street to the Damascus Brewery, continuing our brewery tour of the AT. Ibex and I each ordered a honey mango sour, which was incredible, while Wintergreen ordered an IPA. It was open mic night, and the first band was made up of four older guys playing Johnny Cash. They set up their instruments as we sat on the patio sipping our beers, some of the only people in the place because it was on the early side of the evening, so we chatted with them before their set. As a result, I was given not one, but several personal shout-outs, including a dedication during "Rocky Top," which I found hilarious and charming. Ibex and Wintergreen rolled their eyes as I danced and cheered during "my" songs.

Thunderbird, Floyd, Butcher, Smoke, and a few others showed up and joined us, filling the patio with thru-hikers. Then, the locals began to show up, many of them engaging us and asking questions about the trail. One guy questioned us about his best food truck ideas for the property. The brewery didn't have a kitchen inside, so he was keen to start a side business and wanted it to cater to hikers. We told him any food would do—we didn't discriminate. He then bought us all a round of drinks.

About halfway through the night, Head Chef came trouncing through the patio door, dripping with sweat and smelling like a wild animal. I was so excited to see him that I risked covering myself in the musk and gave him a gigantic hug anyway. One of the first things he told us was that he'd seen a bear—at none other than Iron Mountain Shelter. Wintergreen and I were vindicated.

As the evening came to a close and the brewery issued its last call, the same gentleman who'd bought us a round of drinks offered us a ride home. Accepting it wasn't the smartest thing any of us had ever done, as we knew he'd been drinking, but we did it anyway. It was just a mile up the road, we rationalized. What could go wrong in just a mile? I slipped into the middle seat in the back between Chef and Ibex, and Wintergreen took the passenger's seat up front. As soon as our driver began idling down the street, our recklessness in getting into the car promptly became clear, at least to me. This guy had definitely had one too many. He talked the entire way back to the Broken Fiddle, frequently taking his eyes off the road to do so. The car crept slowly across the double yellow line more than once, and each time, he responded by violently swerving it back to the right side of the road. He stopped at each and every crosswalk that we came to and seemed to speed up and slow down for no reason at all.

"Chef," I whispered. "Put your seatbelt on!"

He hurriedly swung his seatbelt across his body and clicked it into place. Ibex, with her horrible hearing from attending way too many concerts in her younger years, loudly inquired as to what we were whispering about.

"Nothing!" I squeaked.

Our driver began to tell us about how much money he made and how he owned a huge farm, inviting us to come home with him to continue the party and take a ride in his Porsche rather than returning to our hostel. We politely declined, and he slowed the car way down, buying time to try and convince us to change our minds before he got us across town to our destination. As soon as he stopped in front of the Broken Fiddle, we practically jumped out of the car, ran to the back door, and rushed inside. We knew how close we could have just come to death and we were anxious to put space between us and the experience.

Upon stepping inside the gate, we found the entire place crammed with people. Hikers were sleeping in every bed, on each couch, and even set up in the middle of a party on the porch. Wintergreen continued to party with the porch crew while Ibex and I hung out in our room with Chef, gossiping about everything we'd missed by being apart for the last couple of weeks. We'd been separated from him since he'd stayed behind to sleep off his sinus infection in Hot Springs, except for the hour or so that we overlapped in Erwin. That had been almost 200 miles prior, which felt like a huge distance that early on in the trail. Hot Springs laid at mile point 274.5, and we were already up to 470. We had so much to catch up on!

We spent our zero day eating, sleeping, running errands, and hanging out with other thru-hikers, including Thunderbird, Tab, and Floyd. As we sat for breakfast at the diner, a woman from a local church came over to welcome us to her town, and to let us know about all the free happenings and amenities, including showers and laundry, that the church would have available during Trail Days, the annual hiker festival held in Damascus, occurring in just two weeks. As she edged herself into our conversation, she told us that she'd been wanting to come over for several minutes, but we'd been talking with each other so intimately and animatedly that she didn't dare budge in. "You all must really like each other!" she told us.

"We really do!" we agreed, almost in unison.

The next morning, as we hit Mojo's, the local coffee shop, for one last meal before heading back to the trail, we ran into the Finns, Tab, and our friend Kevin, who was now known as Workhorse. As he told everyone, he was slow, but he put in the work and rarely took a day off, so he kept up with everyone else. It fit. We were overjoyed to see him—we had been hearing rumors that he was close behind and hoped he'd catch up and say hello before we left town. He'd had the same thought and asked around town trying to find us. We adored him. We began to refer to him affectionately as our tramily uncle, along with Dragon.

It was raining that morning, but we couldn't justify staying in town any longer considering we'd already been there for a day and a half. We contacted Girl Scout and Jukebox to find out if they were close behind, but they weren't scheduled to get into Damascus for at least another two days. Since falling behind, they'd begun to take their time, giving Girl Scout's foot time to heal and, from what we heard, partying even more than we were.

I found myself feeling a bit grumpy and hungover as I climbed out of town. That was the thing about towns, you always had to descend to get into them, which was marvelous, but that meant you'd have to immediately start climbing to leave, just as you'd resupplied and your bag was at least five pounds heavier than when you'd arrived. It didn't help that our tramily seemed determined to try every brewery along the trail.

I kept to myself for most of the day because of my dark mood. I kept leap-frogging this tall, largely built guy carrying a wooden staff and wearing his Buff like a dew rag over his head. I wanted to be alone and was deeply annoyed that he dared take up space on the trail when I wanted it for myself. I couldn't count the number of times I rolled my eyes as he passed me. However, later

into the afternoon, as we were only a couple easy miles from
camp, I found Wintergreen and Ibex stopped at a beautiful little
pond, talking with him as he set up his tent. I stopped to say hello
as I reached them. It turned out, this guy that I had been fuming
about all day was ridiculously friendly and nice. I can't even
remember what we talked about, but I left our five-minute
conversation thinking this guy was a person that I wanted to know.
As corny as it probably sounds, he radiated positivity. He had an
easy demeanor and, I could already tell, a good heart. And I had
been such a sulky jerk! His name was Jukebox, due to a penchant
for singing '90s songs at the top of his lungs while he hiked. We'd
lost one Jukebox, but we'd found another one. We'll call him
Jukebox 2.

Though I would have been down to stop hiking there, just
11 miles into our day, there wasn't enough space for the four of us
plus Chef, who had stayed behind in town to resupply before
hitting the trail. He promised us that he wouldn't fall behind again,
so we gave Jukebox 2 explicit instructions about where we would
be camping to pass on in case he saw Chef that night.

We passed the Creeper Trail several times throughout the
day, and we camped next to it. While the AT goes up and over
mountains, the Creeper Trail follows along the creek at lower
elevation. The two trails intersect multiple times, and for those
who don't mind "blue blazing," or hiking off the official trail, this
is an opportunity to skip some tough climbs in favor of a cruisier
trail. We couldn't take the easy route though. Ibex was too much
of a purist and would guilt us for missing even a foot of the official
AT. We stopped at a small campsite just off one of these
intersections in front of Little Laurel Creek. I slept soundly that
night to the white noise caused by the rushing of the creek in front
of our tents, content to be in the woods once more.

CHAPTER 16

We didn't get out of camp the next morning until nearly 10:00 am, which was late even for us. I had been up since 7:30 am, so I had no idea where the time had gone. In the middle of the day, one full of steep climbs, I ran into a couple of older men hiking the opposite way.

"There's big trail magic ahead!" they told me.

"Oooh about how far?" I asked excitedly.

"Oh, probably about three hours ahead," one of them told me.

I deflated. As any thru-hiker knows, if you're three hours from trail magic, those trail angels will be eaten out of house and home long before you can get there, even if you book it. That trail magic was not happening for me and I knew it.

We stopped for lunch at a rocky overlook at the top of the steepest hill of the day. Jukebox 2 joined us, and listening to him talk, I got the impression that he's the kind of person who would let anything and everything roll off his back. He just seemed so unbothered by anything and everything. I was in much better spirits than I'd been the day before and merrily stopped to inspect each new wildflower that came across my path, including a lady slipper and a field of bright yellow trout lilies that covered the forest floor.

Chef caught up near the end of our hiking day as we stopped at a trailhead parking lot. There, Jukebox 2 had acquired the last of the trail magic. He handed me a tangerine and a beer. Having only met me the day before, it was a generous offering, and I was thrilled. We hung out in the parking lot with several other thru-hikers and a ridgerunner named Okay, the first we'd seen since meeting Chloe in the Smokies, while watching some colossal gray clouds appear almost out of nowhere. As the thunder began to rumble in the distance, we took that as our cue to get a move on. We had two more miles to hike up to Thomas Knob Shelter and wanted to get there before the rain came in.

I'd been intending to take a side trail half a mile off the AT to summit Mount Rogers, the tallest mountain in Virginia at 5,730 feet, but as I passed by the intersection, I was in a race against time to make it to the shelter before the storm reached me. I rushed as fast as I could as the thunder boomed louder and louder and the lightning flashed much too close for comfort. I was keenly aware that I was carrying two metal rods in my hands in the form of my trekking poles, and I was anxious for some protection from the storm. I'd heard stories of thru-hikers being struck by lightning, and I was not super into that idea for myself. I passed Butcher as he ambled up the trail, seemingly not in a hurry at all. *Surely the lightning would strike this slowpoke rather than me*, I thought.

The minute I stepped into the shelter, the sky opened up and it began to downpour. I'd made it just in time. Inside, I found Wintergreen, Chef, Floyd, Smoke, Soup Spot, and the Finns. Butcher and Ibex were close behind. Though I had a general policy against staying in shelters, since it was raining cats and dogs, I assumed I'd either have to stay or put my tent up in the rain. The shelter was filling up quickly, so I rolled out my sleeping pad and bag on the top floor next to Chef's. Just sitting up there, I already felt like a caged animal beneath the low ceilings. The shelter life was just not for me.

After changing out of my wet clothes, cooking dinner, and chilling with the other hikers for a bit, the rain stopped and we were coaxed out of the shelter by Ibex. She wanted to share the tremendous view of the mountains that she'd discovered behind the shelter while gathering water. As we stood, mesmerized during this spectacular magic hour, a double rainbow appeared over the mountains. The unpredictability of nature and how quickly things could turn around, for better or worse, never ceased to amaze me.

As I returned from gathering water at the stream, I learned that Wintergreen and Ibex had decided to move a few tenths of a mile down the trail to set up their tents. Though I'd already set up my bedding upstairs, I hurriedly stuffed it into my pack and followed them, happy for any excuse to get out of sleeping in a shelter. Chef was already settled into his sleeping bag, so he decided to stay behind in the shelter.

Since the road crossing a couple of miles back down the trail, we had hiked into the Mount Rogers National Recreation Area. This area, along with Grayson Highlands State Park, which we were just outside of, is famed for its population of wild ponies. I'd caught a glimpse of a couple of them in a field as I rushed to Thomas Knob Shelter but hadn't had the time to stop and take too much notice of them as I raced against the storm. However, as we set up camp in a field overlooking the mountains, we began to notice pony poop scattered throughout. *Ponies have been here.*

The ponies have roamed these mountains since the 1940s, according to Smithsonian Magazine. They were initially bred by ranchers to maintain the area's famous balds, originally cleared by logging in the nineteenth century, and they stayed when the state park was designated in 1965. The ponies do not rely on people for food, water, or shelter, but the herds are maintained by the Wilburn Ridge Pony Association, which was formed in 1975. Once per year, the association rounds up the ponies for a health check, taking a few, usually young males, to auction to keep the population size down to a manageable size of about 100.

Once again we simply shelved our food bags high up in a tree near my tent. *Too tall for ponies*, I reasoned, *and why on Earth would there be a bear in pony country?*

Since I'd already eaten dinner at the shelter, I sat with Wintergreen and Ibex as they ate, contentedly staring at the dimming mountains as Venus, that bright yellow vixen planet, became brighter and brighter in the twilight sky. I crawled into my tent, exhausted, as the other two cleaned up from dinner. As I laid my head on my pillow and began to drift off to sleep, I heard a heavy movement off to my right. Wintergreen and Ibex, I knew, were off to my left.

"Uh, guys?" I said, cautiously. "What's that noise?"

"That's just us cleaning our pots," Wintergreen replied.

"Um, are you sure?" I asked.

"OH MY GOD THAT'S A PONY!" he cried, having searched the area with his flashlight after I'd said something.

I grabbed my headlamp and crawled halfway out of my tent, scanning the campsite. Sure enough, there it was: a big, brown, beautiful pony, chomping on the grass just 10 feet away. I watched it excitedly. *This is just like a fairytale*, I thought.

Little did I know, I was about to be terrorized. I fell into a sound sleep, exhausted and happy. Until, that is, the middle of the night, when I was rudely awakened by the sounds of not one, but two large animals chomping extremely loudly just outside of my tiny, fragile tent.

I realized that they were munching on the grass that poked out from under my tent. There was an entire field of grass surrounding us, and yet, they'd had to go for the particular blades of grass directly beneath where I slept. "Go away, ponies!" I yelled, clapping my hands.

Wintergreen started cracking up in his tent. I, however, did not see this as a laughing matter.

"This is how I die!" I cried. "Death by pony!"

More laughter followed. The ponies soon moved over to Wintergreen's tent, and I fell back into my contented slumber. Ibex, once again, slept through the entire encounter.

In the morning, once Chef had joined us for breakfast, we were greeted by a beautiful brown and white momma pony with her adorable little foal. I thought the ponies would be shy with people; they were wild animals after all. But quite the contrary. They charged toward us. While the baby stayed a few feet behind, the momma pony walked straight up to us and began to lick our arms aggressively. She wanted the salt from the dried sweat caking our bodies. The skittish baby pony hid behind its mother. It would only be charmed by Chef, the pony whisperer, who gave each of the ponies full-body pony scratches. As the momma became more aggressive, biting and licking at our shirts in search of the precious salt, I backed away. Cute as they were, I'd always had an irrational fear of being kicked by a horse. I didn't want to be eaten by one, either.

Wintergreen went off to find a tree as nature called, asking Chef to keep an eye on his gear for a moment as he did so. As he marched down the hill, a brown male pony strutted into our campsite. Chef was distracted grooming the mother and baby, and as his back was turned, the male grabbed Wintergreen's trekking pole and made a break for it. Chef chased after it in vain, but it was clear that the pony had some speed on him. In a flash of genius, he stopped, held out his hand, and pretended that he had a treat for the naughty pony. It came running back, and Chef was able to snatch the pole from it. The pole was covered in pony spit and the strap was a bit chewed up, but it was in fine working order.

As Wintergreen returned from down the hill, he eyed his pole in exasperation and amusement. He groaned as he wiped the copious amount of pony spit off it.

As we were packing up, Smoke and another thru-hiker, a tall, handsome former Manhattanite with a slow, sexy southern drawl named Easy, stopped by to ooh and ahh at the ponies. Smoke began to coax them toward him and we giggled, content to have the naughty ponies directed elsewhere. They'd caused quite the ruckus in the shelter during the night, poking their heads into the shelter, stealing a bear bag, biting people's trekking poles, chomping on someone's shoe, and stealing a gaiter. Easy's food bag, containing all of his cookware, had been stolen in the night, though he wasn't sure what had stolen it. He'd properly hung it, so didn't think it could have been a pony, but it was long gone when he woke up. He was heading down to the closest road gap to hitch his way into town to replace all of his supplies. Despite this, he seemed to be in high spirits. We breathed a sigh of relief that our bags had still been there in the morning, especially considering we'd been so careless with them once again.

As we marched on from camp, leaving Smoke and Easy to deal with the ponies, we officially hit the 500-mile mark. We were almost a quarter of the way into our journey.

CHAPTER 17

They tell you to keep your cold weather gear until
Damascus, and then it's fairly safe to leave it behind and lighten
your pack. I mailed my four-pound, zero-degree sleeping bag back
to New York while I was in Damascus, picking up a much lighter
55-degree summer bag at an outfitter there. It cost me a pretty
penny, but I was happy to pay it if it meant shedding a few pounds.
I'm a cold sleeper so I knew it was a little risky, but luckily the
gorgeous spring weather continued as we hiked north into
Virginia. Green leaves filled in the trees, and the rhododendrons
and mountain laurel that I had been impatiently waiting for finally
began to bloom, decorating the forest in white, pale pink, and
fuschia. Along with the ponies, the flowers added to the fairytale-
esque atmosphere.

Jukebox 2 continued to hike around us and camp with us
each night. He was upfront that he was doing his own thing and
maybe he'd see us or maybe he wouldn't, but he'd chat for a while
on trail each day, and I'd often hear him crooning in the distance
even when I couldn't see him. One day, I was looking at my
AWOL guide and found that there was a hostel just a quarter mile
off trail, rumored to sell snacks and sodas. I convinced
Wintergreen that we should drop our packs and go check it out. He
agreed. The hostel was in a big, beautiful, historic house with a
well-manicured lawn and gorgeous views of the countryside and
mountains. In the front yard was a huge old grandpa tree with two

hammock chairs swinging from it. I thought it would be the perfect place for a treehouse.

Inside, we met Tina, the owner, and her adorable dog Hazelnut. We cooked up some frozen pizzas in the toaster oven, slurping down sodas as we waited for them to finish baking. Just as we were about to move to the front porch to enjoy them in the sun, Jukebox 2 showed up and joined us. We had a leisurely two-hour lunch and said hello to Easy Bake and her hiking partner, Wingman, as they arrived to stay the night, then headed back to the trail. "You're really leaving?" Tina asked. I regrettably told her that our friends were waiting back on the trail. We found Ibex and Chef having lunch in the meadow where we left our packs, wondering where we had gotten off to.

As we got back on trail, it began to wind through a farm, where cattle watched us curiously as we wandered by. Thunder began to clatter and a few scarce raindrops began to fall. We hiked along a lovely creek for a bit, and obstacles sprung up in the form of cow gates that we had to climb over. As the trail narrowed on a hill above the creek, two cows ran onto the path ahead of us, turning to watch us, eyes bulging, as we continued behind them. They must have been wondering why we were following them. A third barreled up from the creek to join them. Safety in numbers, I suppose. Although the woods were damp from the storm earlier that day, Chef made us a fire when we got to camp. Jukebox 2 joined us again.

Hikers worry about Virginia—the trail winds through this one state for over 500 miles, or approximately a quarter of the trail, mainly through the George Washington and Jefferson National Forests. People start to burn out. The novelty of hiking the trail starts to wear off, and they get bored when they're not passing through state line after state line. This is known as the "Virginia Blues." But so far, Virginia had been treating us just fine.

The next day, I hiked with Jukebox 2 pretty much all day, and we really started to get to know each other. He told me that he was burnt out from a decade of working for a government agency as a cartographer and manager in Fort Collins, Colorado, and that he was sick of the snow. He'd quit his job, sold all of his possessions, and was hiking the AT to find his next home. He wouldn't call himself a thru-hiker; he was going to stop hiking when the time felt right. Ibex joined us for the afternoon as well, and we passed Easy Bake on a bridge overlooking a creek as she gazed into the water. She told us excitedly that she'd seen a hellbender in the creek. It was unfortunately long gone though by the time we arrived. I was bummed to have missed it, but encouraged by the sighting. Perhaps I would still see one!

That evening, we made it to the famous Partnership Shelter near Marion. This shelter was well-known for two reasons: there was a shower, sinks, and a clothing line there, and it was located next to the Pat Jennings Visitor Center, the "headquarters and gateway to the Mount Rogers National Recreation Area." The visitor center was cool and all—there was a hellbender in a fish tank inside—but the real reason that people got excited about it was that there was a landline phone attached to the outside of the building where hikers could call the local pizza shop for delivery. You better believe we took advantage. Ibex and I split a large veggie pizza and also got some side salads, mozzarella sticks, slices of tiramisu, and sodas.

I braved the shower while I waited for the pizza to arrive and washed my clothes in the sink. I'd been carrying a travel-sized bottle of shampoo and conditioner from our last town visit for this very thing. The shower was clean and spacious, but the water came straight up from the ground below so it was frigid. I hyperventilated as I attempted to wash my hair. *Deep breaths*, I told myself. I came out much colder and slightly cleaner than when I had gone in.

As we were chowing down on our pizza, I noticed that some itchy red bumps began to form around my ankles. "Poison ivy," someone told me. I had been seeing the notched, three-leafed plants around, but I was surprised. Of all the running around in the woods I'd done over the years, I'd never reacted to poison ivy. And I *knew* that I'd accidentally stumbled through patches of it before. But apparently, the more you are exposed, the more likely it is that your body will react to the oils of the plant. My luck, in that regard, had run out, it seemed.

The next day, we caught the shuttle from the visitor center into Marion for a resupply. People are intimidated by the idea of spending six months in the wilderness during a thru-hike, but it's just a series of hiking for a few days, going into town for a shower, a resupply, and a hot meal, then rinse and repeat. Especially on the AT, you're never that far from civilization, and you never have to carry that much food on your back. In this case, though, the shower had been at the shelter, so we had no reason to stay in town. After the pizza from the night before, we didn't even feel the need to grab town food, especially because we knew that we'd be hiking by a couple of restaurants at a truck stop in Atkins later that day. We dipped into the grocery store and then got back to the trail, hiking on.

I felt sluggish that day. The miles were flat and cruisey, but for some reason, I was struggling and the day was dragging on especially slowly. I fell way behind my tramily, but I couldn't convince my body to speed up any. It was just like this sometimes; my energy would dissipate out of the blue for a day or two, and I would have to fight to push forward, usually drinking some extra caffeine to help me through. Then, my energy levels would return, as quickly as they disappeared. I suspected hormones played a part. In addition, about a year later, I was diagnosed with exercise-induced asthma. I wondered if that had something to do with the lapses in energy as well.

On this particular day, luck was on my side. As I was hiking that afternoon, the trail passed by an old schoolhouse. I would have gone right by it, but Easy Bake was standing on the porch, and she enthusiastically waved me over. "Trail magic!" she called. Inside, there was a refrigerator full of cold sodas and a box of snacks and medical supplies. A local church owned the schoolhouse and set it up for hikers to take a rest and get a snack. I downed a Mr. Pibb Xtra, loaded with caffeine and sugar, and scurried back out to the trail. It helped immensely.

By the time I arrived at the truck stop in Atkins, the guys had already polished off one meal at a burger joint and they were moving on to a second dinner at the Mexican restaurant next door. I followed them over there, where we found Thunderbird and Jukebox 2 seated in a booth. We joined them, and I stared out the window as rain began to fall on the pavement outside. We took our time getting back to the trail, waiting until the last drop fell to get a move on. As we exited the restaurant, bellies full, we grabbed some tallboys of beer from the gas station across the way to take to camp. We had some celebrating to do; we had passed the quarter-way point on the trail, and we were also officially past the point where Michael, now known as Double Stack, had dropped out during his first thru-hike attempt. Though we hadn't seen him since just past the Smokies, we thought of him at this moment, feeling proud of how far we'd come.

Our campsite that night was on the outskirts of a lovely meadow. As night fell, we lay together by our tents, staring up at the sky and watching for shooting stars. Fireflies, or lightning bugs as we called them back home, began to light up the field around us. Wintergreen whooped in excitement. He'd never seen fireflies before.

From here, we'd follow the fireflies and the mountain flowers—azaleas, mountain laurel, and rhododendrons—north with the spring for several states. Later, the flowers and fireflies would be replaced by plump, juicy wild berries—strawberries, huckleberries, black raspberries, and cranberries. It was magical. The days and nights were also much warmer by this point in the trail, and the browns and grays that had surrounded us for our first few weeks were now replaced by bright greens. Our legs were stronger and our spirits higher. We were having fun.

CHAPTER 18

The best part about having Jukebox 2 around was that he was always up for a good time. He was a laid-back guy, and the fact that he wasn't trying to make it all the way to Katahdin made him even more so. He had nowhere to be, so when an opportunity arose for anything fun, he was going to take it. Wintergreen, on the other hand, was always trying to push us to do more miles faster. Ibex and I were not on a tight schedule. I had quit my job, and she had taken a leave of absence from hers; they would take her back when she was ready. Chef was in a similar situation. He wasn't on any sort of schedule but because he was the strongest hiker of the group, he was always willing to do more miles. Wintergreen had been let go from his job so it was not employment that called him back to Montana, but a Labor Day weekend concert with friends. In addition to that, he was always rushing to get to the next town to go to the next restaurant or brewery. "I'm a city mouse," he would tell us.

Ibex and I had no interest in finishing that soon; we were aiming for mid- to late-September. So it was nice to have Jukebox 2 traveling with us to tip the scales in our favor. He was willing and enthusiastic about taking things slower and enjoying the experience more. And his attitude gave us more ammunition to fight back when Wintergreen tried to push us farther up the trail. I wanted to stop and smell all the rhododendrons, and now that spring finally warmed our days, I wanted to swim in every creek as well. With the help of Jukebox 2 and Ibex, I got my chance to do so during the best week of the entire AT, which we fondly dubbed "Creek Week."

Trail Days, the annual hiker festival in Damascus, was just a week away. I had arranged for a former thru-hiker to pick us up in Pearisburg, about 70 trail miles away from where we started the week, and drive us back down to Damascus for the festival. Though 70 miles over a week was a mild pace for us by that point, Wintergreen was adamant that we must hike our first 20-mile day. He'd heard that Girl Scout and Jukebox had already hiked a 20-plus mile day, and soon, we would be reunited with them at Trail Days. He couldn't allow us to show up there and be one-upped by them. We were regularly hiking 15-plus miles per day, so this mandatory 20-mile day meant we *had* to slow down that week to not pass by Pearisburg.

That Saturday morning, we woke up at Lynn Creek Camp, enjoyed our coffee and breakfast together, then headed out. Yellow and black millipedes crawled around the campsite. There are about 7,000 species of millipedes in the world, and about 1,400 of them can be found in Virginia and Maryland. Now that spring had arrived, we were seeing them everywhere. Yellow ones, orange ones, rusty ones… we had to be careful not to sit on them when we stopped for breaks.

Chef had gotten out of camp early that morning to beat the heat, and Wintergreen passed by me shortly after I started hiking down the trail. Three miles into the day, I arrived at Lick Creek, a huge creek with a wooden footbridge built across it. Its cool water called to me; I just couldn't miss another opportunity to take a dip. I had passed by so many streams in the previous few days because life had been about making miles and I hadn't wanted to fall too far behind my tramily. But at Lick Creek, I threw down my pack and began to dig my swimsuit out from the bottom. Just as I was about to look for a tree to duck behind, Ibex came around the corner. "Let's go swimming!" I sang. She enthusiastically agreed. I changed into my suit and then she and I slowly waded in. Once we got to the middle, we each dunked fully underwater. I resurfaced, gasping. It was cold!

With the two fastest hikers of the group ahead of us, and knowing that we didn't have to make any big miles, we decided to take our sweet time splashing around in the creek and searching for crayfish and hellbenders. We would see Chef and Wintergreen later. We moved our gear to a sunny campsite on the far side of the creek and went back and forth between sunbathing and swimming. Soon, Jukebox 2 came by. He originally planned to say a quick hello and keep hiking on, but as he passed by, we cajoled him into the water. Thunderbird showed up shortly after, and we coaxed him in as well. Ibex and I watched, mesmerized, as he pulled off his shirt and dove into the water. He was a swim coach back in his normal life and it showed. The man certainly kept himself in shape. Caroline, a 30-something from the U.K., stopped to chat with us for a few minutes, dangling her feet into the water. As the party got bigger, Jukebox 2 pulled out his phone and began to play '90s music—his favorite. He, Ibex, and I began to dance and sing in the creek. We stayed for hours, enjoying the sunny day and the company. Eventually, though, we knew we had to move on; we still had six more miles to hike, all uphill.

The birds were out in full force that day, and I saw a scarlet tanager—a brilliant red songbird—and an indigo bunting—a small, iridescent turquoise bird. We arrived at our planned stopping point for the day, Chestnut Knob Shelter, to discover a sign advertising trail magic 1.4 miles ahead. We had wanted to stay at that particular locale for some prime star gazing, but we simply couldn't resist the lure of food. So instead, we had a quick snack break on a grassy knoll overlooking the valley below, then headed down to the so-called "hillbilly hiker party." The spread was amazing and included cold sodas, potato salad, fresh fruit, fresh veggies with dip, cake, and more. As the party broke up, we stayed put and set up our tents. We searched the sky for stars as night fell, but the trees blocked our view.

I hardly slept a wink that night. A sweet but quirky 40-something named Hamburglar who followed Jukebox 2 around like a puppy joined us at camp, circling the perimeter at least three times before finally setting his hammock up about three feet from my tent. He turned out to be one of the worst snorers I'd ever heard. His snorting kept me up all night, even after I slipped in my earplugs.

On Sunday, the day before our 20-mile day, luck was on our side. About 3.5 hours and 10 miles into the day, we stumbled upon another creek with the most perfect swimming hole carved into it. We stopped to have lunch there, rinsing our clothes in the water and taking a quick dip, planning to continue up the trail. But Hank Hill, a friendly 30-something from Missouri who Jukebox 2 was already friends with, changed those plans. He came down the trail as we swam, stopping to join us. Before jumping into the water, he pulled a trail luxury out of his pack: a full bottle of bourbon, which he promptly began passing around. We took turns sipping it until we had emptied the bottle. Then, we made an executive decision: we weren't going any further that day. Again, we swam, lay in the sun, and enjoyed the company of those around us.

A little while later, I climbed the hill behind our campsite, hoping to find a bit of cell service. We were in a dead zone, but it was Mother's Day, and I was hoping to get a call through to my mom. With just one bar of service at the top, I settled for a text. On my way back down the hill, I made a quick stop at the shelter to see if Chef had arrived yet. He'd slept in again and was a ways behind us, having missed out on the bourbon.

I did not see Chef at the shelter, but I did find the Finns and Easy Bake there, along with a few others, and I let them know about the creek and the marvelous swimming hole below. They spread the word, and the next thing I knew, a bunch of hikers had joined us, including On Step, who we hadn't seen since Franklin, North Carolina. Floyd came down shortly after, telling us about how he was afraid he'd lost his hiking buddy, Butcher. As I was hiking that morning, I ran into a couple of men standing next to a beat-up pickup truck in the woods. I couldn't put my finger on why, but they had given me a bad vibe. They had not done anything wrong, but there were a bunch of flies buzzing around their truck and something about the way they looked at me just seemed *off*, so much so that I hurried down the trail for the next several miles, freaked out. So when I heard that Butcher was missing, I became slightly concerned. Chef was one thing; he was huge, muscular, and wore a knife hanging from his neck. I was sure that he could take care of himself. Butcher, on the other hand… I wasn't so sure.

On Step sat with me at the water's edge and he laughed at the tan lines circling my knees as we caught up. My knees had been bothering me on and off since Georgia, so I regularly wore braces around one or both knees to help support them. Combined with all of the time I was spending outside, this left me with some interesting tan lines. Overhearing our conversation, Wintergreen came over and grabbed my knee to inspect it, taking a seat on the other side of me. He sat much closer to me than he needed to. I sensed a little jealousy. Butterflies filled my stomach.

The next day, as I finally hiked into cell service, I found that I had missed a nighttime text from On Step. "Want to join me at the creek for a skinny dip?" he'd asked. I laughed, wondering what I would have done if I had seen it in real-time.

This day, though, was all business. After two short, easy days of hiking, Ibex and I knew that Wintergreen wasn't going to allow us to dilly-dally for a third day. I hiked by myself for most of the morning, meeting up with the gang for lunch at the Brushy Mountain Outpost, a deli and burger shop right off the trail. I ordered a veggie burger, fries, and a soda, then joined the others at a booth. Several other hikers came through, and the big topic of discussion was Trail Days, if people planned to go, and how they would get there. While I had arranged a ride for Chef, Wintergreen, Ibex, and me, there unfortunately was no room for Jukebox 2, so he'd have to find his own ride. Though he was undecided if he even wanted to go, I was trying to convince him to come. He was so much fun; I loved having him around and didn't want to lose him as we got off trail for two days for the festival. Ibex and I tried repeatedly to get him to commit to joining our tramily, but every day it was the same thing. "I'm doing my own thing," he'd tell us. "Who knows, you might see me at camp tonight or you might not!" And for those few weeks in Virginia, we always did. Parked in a booth at Brushy's, he began to ask around about possible rides to Trail Days, just in case.

We were all feeling so good at lunchtime, especially with the deli food and sodas providing extra fuel, that we let Wintergreen talk us into this being our 20-mile day. Because of where the shelters and campsites were located on the trail though, it made sense for us to hike a 23-mile day. *I can do this,* I thought. I just had to put my head down and keep trucking. But when I arrived at Jenny Knob Shelter that evening, absolutely exhausted and my feet throbbing, I found Ibex waiting for me, her full pack sitting next to her. This wasn't a good sign; she should have set up by now. I looked around, not seeing the others. "Shelter's full," she told me. "And so are the campsites. We've got to hike another mile down to the next campsite."

I groaned. I did not want to hike anymore that day. The truth was though, that until I turned the bend and saw the shelter, I had thought that I had another mile to go. So truly, no harm no foul. I was past ready to get off my feet, but it was all downhill from here, so I figured another mile wouldn't kill me. Ibex and I were greeted with cheers as we arrived at the next campsite. We had done it, 24 miles in one day!

That night, I awoke to the sounds of what sounded like several clumsy animals moving about our campsite. I swear I even heard at least one of them fall down an embankment next to our tents multiple times. Fear kept me from peeping out of my tent to see what they were, but I wondered if they were bear cubs since they couldn't seem to stay on their feet, or perhaps raccoons. I regretted not peeking out of my tent to investigate.

Compared to that 24-mile day, the rest of the week was a cakewalk. Ibex and I demanded that we stop for funsies whenever the opportunity arose since we were drained from the long day, and we only had 31 miles to hike in three days to get to the jump-off for Pearisburg. About 5.5 miles into the next day, we took a half-mile detour up the road to visit Trent's Grocery. It was really just a gas station, but with pay showers and a small deli in the back. I ordered a grilled cheese, and while I was waiting for my sandwich, an older local man in denim overalls named Bob chatted us up, telling me and Ibex that we were too skinny. "You look like a stiff wind could blow you over!" he told us in his thick Southern accent. "I do alright in the wind," I replied. Jukebox 2 cracked up. "You got the nicest legs I've seen all season though," he said to me. "Those are Tina Turner legs!" He then offered to buy me a popsicle. The guys quickly steered me away from him.

"Don't accept the popsicle!" one of them hissed adamantly.

After we'd had our fill of the gas station delicacies, Chef, Wintergreen, Ibex and I posed for a quick photo outside. It was Girl Scout's birthday, and I sent it to her over text, wishing her a happy birthday and letting her know how much we all missed her and that we couldn't wait to see her at Trail Days.

Another easy 2.5 miles later, we reached a wooden sign pointing down a side trail to Dismal Falls. As we walked up, we found On Step in the water. He called us over to join him. People were jumping off a small cliff into a deep pool below, where he was swimming. Ibex and I climbed up to the top of the waterfall, readying ourselves to cannonball in. As we did so, On Step pointed to a floating woodpile off to the right of where we were about to jump. "There are two snakes in there, and I think they're water moccasins," he told us. "So steer clear." Water moccasins, also known as cottonmouths, are venomous, semiaquatic pit vipers that are found in freshwater habitats in the southeastern U.S. Bites can be deadly if not treated immediately. These two looked harmless to me, but I was not going to take my chances with any venomous snakes, so I stayed as far as possible from that side of the pool. The day was hot and sticky, so the water felt amazingly refreshing.

While we swam, some ominous gray clouds began to move in, and we began to hear thunder in the distance. We decided to set up our tents at a campsite there at Dismal Falls rather than risk getting soaked up the trail. Wintergreen hated getting wet, so we'd sometimes get away with shorter hiking days if he thought there was a danger of rain. Once our tents were up and our gear safely inside, we returned to the water. I forced my tramily, including Jukebox 2, to gather 'round for a photo shoot on a downed log that had fallen across the creek.

While looking at the GutHook trail guide on his phone, Wintergreen discovered a shortcut back to Trent's Grocery. He wouldn't risk getting caught in the rain on trail, but he would risk getting caught in the rain for more beers, especially since we would now be staying at the falls for the afternoon and evening. He convinced Jukebox 2 and Chef to join him, and they took off in search of the shortcut. Meanwhile, Ibex and I chilled by the water until it was too cold to stay in our wet bathing suits any longer. On Step, having had his fill of the water, hiked on toward the trail. The Finns eventually showed up and joined us, taking his place. When the guys returned, the rain began to fall, and Chef built us a fire. This was one of his many trail skills.

Ever since Chef had rejoined us in Damascus, he and I were becoming closer. He made a point to hike with me on occasion, even though he was a much faster hiker than me, and the more I learned about him, the more I wanted to know. He was an electrician by trade, but for fun, he was always getting into some wild thing or another. In addition to being an amateur bodybuilder, one of his favorite hobbies in Hawaii was feral pig hunting. The pigs are an invasive pest species there; they breed quickly and are destroying the rainforests. He also loved to cook and fish, and he wanted to have enough kids to form his own soccer team. Because he was in his early thirties, he was hoping the trail would give him some clarity on who the right person to have a family with was. He had several prospects back in Hawaii and around the world, and he was always talking on the phone with one of them. He'd grown up by the AT in New York and had always had the idea of hiking it in the back of his mind. Now, here he was.

That night, we partied around Chef's fire in the rain. Wintergreen and I, the two in the group who most often heard animal sounds around camp in the night, made a pact that we would start looking outside of our tents to see what was out there. We shook on it, and the "bear pact" was official. I was in such a cheerful mood that evening. I loved these people and I loved trail life. I couldn't imagine being anywhere else.

The pouring rain continued throughout the next day, so we hiked on for about 13 miles before reaching a dirt road that would lead us to Woods Hole Hostel. Though we didn't typically stay in hostels because it was often cheaper and more practical for us to split a hotel room when we went to towns, Woods Hole was

known for being one of the best on the trail, so we had to
experience it. It was a working farm out in the middle of the Blue
Ridge, run by a maternal yogi named Neville. The farm had been
in her family for generations and boasted 100 acres of property, a
huge garden, and ducks, pigs, cows, and goats. It was stunning. I
was grateful for the rain because it made the decision to stop there
and spend the money to sleep indoors that much easier. Jukebox 2
was on the fence about staying, but he followed us over there
anyway, just to check it out.

When we arrived, Neville asked if we'd like to purchase a
strawberry smoothie, which would be delivered to our bunks. We
did not even have to think about it; every single one of us said yes.
She also invited us to choose which meals we'd like to purchase.
"It's all family style, and we expect you to help out in the kitchen,"
she told us. After a shower, we'd be happy to. There were washers
and dryers on site and immaculate showers that looked out onto the
farm. I chose a bed in the bunkhouse, and Wintergreen set his pack
on the bed across from mine. Ibex would have to sleep across the
room, as that was the last open bunk available. The beds were the
most comfortable that I had ever lain upon. I considered staying
there forever. Jukebox 2 was talked into a private room.

Ibex and I helped peel eggs in the kitchen, then I was
given the job of whipping up some egg salad. After I had diligently
mixed everything together, I found a hammock on the porch in
which to rest my weary bones. When it was time for supper,
Neville called us over into a circle on the front lawn of the
farmhouse. She asked us to hold hands, and one by one, to share
something that we were grateful for. That was easy; I was so
incredibly grateful for this life on trail. I was meant to be here.

We moved to the backyard, where we sat at round picnic
tables together, breaking bread and chattering about life on the
trail. The food, stir fry with noodles, homemade bread with butter,
egg salad, homegrown salad with ranch and tahini, and homemade

ice cream, was heavenly. I had seconds. All was right with the world.

Until it wasn't. After supper, I returned to the bunkhouse. When I had initially set my things on my bed, I didn't know who would be in the bunk next to me. We had snagged the last three available beds, so our choices were limited. But now, the dark reality of the situation became clear. I would be sleeping next to none other than Hamburglar, the horrible snorer. *Oh no*! I barely slept a wink. Even with my earplugs in, I could hear the chainsaw revving up Hamburglar's nose all night long.

In the morning, I groggily dragged myself down to the farmhouse for breakfast. Once again, the food was incredible. I considered that Mountain Harbor Hostel in Tennessee may not have the best breakfast on the AT after all, though it was a close second. Woods Hole was the victor. After this final incredible meal, we packed our things and got back to the trail. We had just 11 miles to go to get to the jump-off for Pearisburg, where my friend Dave would pick us up at the local Dairy Queen. This is where we said goodbye to Jukebox 2, still unsure if we'd see him at Trail Days.

I knew Dave from a stint working for an American study abroad program in Australia almost a decade earlier, and I hadn't seen him since. I was an intern while he was a student, but we had hit it off and become friends. The program was based on studying the environment and we lived with a group of about 20 students and a few interns and staff in a rainforest about a 45-minute drive from Cairns. Dave had seen on social media that I was hiking the trail, and since he was living in nearby Blacksburg, studying African birds via a doctorate program at Virginia Tech, he reached out to offer up a shower and a warm bed. He'd discovered his passion for birds in Australia—I remembered him always walking out to explore the forest there with binoculars in hand, trying to identify as many different species as he could. He generously agreed to take in my tramily for the night as well.

Despite having not seen him in several years, I immediately felt comfortable with Dave. At the Dairy Queen, he pulled me in for a huge, warm hug then easily shouldered my backpack, leading us to his car, and offering to make a pit stop at the grocery store on our way to his house. We would stay with him for the night, then catch a ride to Damascus the next day with a former thru-hiker named Swamp who was driving down from Ohio to attend Trail Days.

After we'd showered and loaded up on snacks, Dave took us out for a scrumptious dinner at a local Thai restaurant, then onward to a pool hall where his friends were playing in a foosball tournament. We downed pitchers of beer and had our own darts tournament, periodically saying hello to Dave's friends as they took breaks from their games. Blueberry, a woman from his program who had hiked the AT a few years prior, shared some tips on how to find salamanders. We told her that if she came down to Trail Days, she was welcome to join our crew for the weekend. The night went by in a flash, and I fell fast asleep as soon as my head hit the pillow at 1:00 am. It was way past hiker midnight, after all!

CHAPTER 19

Trail Days was more than we bargained for. While Damascus usually has a population of a few hundred people, it swells to about 20,000 during Trail Days. The festival has been happening since 1987, and it is a popular meeting spot for those in the trail community, including current and former thru-hikers and section hikers, outdoor brands and vendors, trail angels, influencers, and locals. As Swamp dropped us off at Tent City on Friday afternoon, the area where thru-hikers can camp during the festival for just a small fee, Jukebox 2 was there to greet us. He'd caught a ride with the husband of a fellow thru-hiker who'd come for a visit, and he'd already scoped out the best camping spots. Tent City was loud, crowded, and located in an exposed field. But there was a quiet patch of forest behind it, so we marched past the rows of colorful tents and made a beeline for the trees. Jukebox 2's site was already full—he was tenting with Hank Hill and a spunky tattoo artist from Pennsylvania named Wiki. But he showed us to some open spots nearby, which we snatched up.

Once we'd set up, we checked out the vendors that were set up in the festival area. There were several outdoor brands there that would fix your gear for free and many more that were holding giveaways for free gear. We entered as many raffles as we could, under strict instructions to come back either that evening or Saturday evening for the drawing, as you had to be present to win.

I stopped by the Osprey booth to see if it would be possible to shorten my hip belt or switch it out for a smaller size. Though I had barely lost any weight, my body had started to change, and my pack no longer fit around my waist quite as tightly as I'd like. They couldn't do anything there but recommended that I reach out to their customer service via email. Later, when I reached out, the customer service representative recommended that I wear a pool noodle around my waist for the next four months to provide extra padding in the hip belt. I had the smallest size hip belt available for women from the brand, and their size chart said that it should still fit just fine. But it didn't, and it would only get worse. I later heard of multiple women who had the same issue. And yet I was told by Osprey that they did not warranty size and fit issues.

After we'd entered every single contest that we could, we began the long walk into town to grab some beers for the weekend. We passed several hikers that we knew but hadn't seen in weeks. We said hello to Akuna, whom we'd met the first day in Georgia, Double Stack, whom we hadn't seen since North Carolina, One Up, Thumper, and a few more friends. It was like Old Home Week; we were thrilled.

As we returned to Tent City from the Dollar General, I received a text from Girl Scout. She and Jukebox had arrived. We ran to the parking area to find them. As my eyes scanned the vicinity, I suddenly heard a loud squeal. I turned toward the sound, and there they were, in the flesh. I ran to Girl Scout first, wrapping my entire body around her in an embrace. "Finally!" I cried. "Where have you been all my life?!" I hugged Jukebox next. "I heard you replaced me with another Jukebox!" she said accusingly. "Well, we lost one, so we had to find a new one!" I told her, laughing. She exaggeratedly rolled her eyes.

After a quick reunion, Girl Scout and Jukebox let us know they had some errands to run but would catch up with us when they returned. They had been partying through southern Virginia with two gals, Pika and Houdini, and a group of guys, one of whom Girl Scout was now involved with, so they'd be camping with them but would make an effort to spend time with us. Girl Scout apologized for not having caught back up to us. "I miss you guys!" she told me, but they were having fun and enjoying a slower pace than we were.

That night, we found them at the Riff Raff bonfire. Riff Raff is a fraternity of sorts for AT thru-hikers. The group is predominantly male, and they love to party. Each year, they host a huge bonfire in the woods near Tent City at Trail Days, and that's where you can find most attendees. So once night began to fall, we headed over to the bonfire. My friend Andrea was en route from D.C. She was coming to Trail Days for a visit, but she couldn't leave the city to make the six-hour drive until after work on Friday, so she was going to be late, which meant I had a few hours to kill before she arrived. I danced around the fire, stopping to chat as I saw more and more people that I knew. A group of Damascus cops showed up and took people's cans of beer away from them in the name of open container laws. They made me feel like I was a naughty teenager at a high school party.

Andrea finally rolled in around midnight, and after giving her a big hug, I led her to the fire to introduce her to the tramily. She was exhausted after the workday and the long drive though, as was I. We got her tent set up and hit the hay.

The rest of the weekend, it poured in Damascus, and everything got covered in mud. Andrea, Ibex, and I hit up a free pancake breakfast, then visited the festival and the downtown area. The Twelve Tribes, a fundamentalist Christian community that runs a chain of restaurants called the Yellow Deli, had a food truck set up, so we decided to grab lunch there. We were curious about them. The Southern Poverty Law Center describes them as a cult and there were a lot of rumors about them on trail, especially because they run a hiker hostel in Vermont. We were hoping they'd come to chat with us as we sat at the picnic tables outside the food truck having lunch, but they mostly ignored us. The food was incredible though. From there, Andrea and I attended a lecture on wild edibles, then headed over to the community pool, where I got a free shower.

One of the main events at Trail Days is a hiker parade. It starts near MoJo's Trailside Café & Coffee on Douglas Drive near the Creeper Trail and marches onward through town. Appalachian Trail thru-hikers from present and previous years are invited to line up with their classes and participate in the parade. I was planning to walk in the parade with my class of current thru-hikers, but by the time it started, I was seated under an umbrella at MoJo's with Andrea and Jukebox 2, and the rain had picked up again. I wasn't looking to get soaking wet, so I opted out, along with most of my tramily. Ibex was the only one of us to participate, and she ended up both drenched and sunburnt somehow.

Andrea's stomach was bothering her, and the inside of her tent had gotten drenched the night before, so she decided to take off after the parade. She had made the six-hour drive each way to stay for less than 24 hours. But I couldn't blame her. The weather was less than ideal, there was mud sticking to everything, and there were puddles in her tent. I asked if there was any way that the tramily and I could squeeze into her Jeep for a ride back to the trail, but with only two doors, there just wasn't room for all of us plus our packs. I waved goodbye, watching her drive away, and wishing I could get out of there as well.

I took a nap in my tent, and when I awoke and returned to Tent City to look for the crew, I passed several hikers that I knew. Each of them told me that I'd missed hearing my name called at one of the drawings, and that had I been present, I would have won a grand prize of a whole new set of gear from Backpacker Magazine. Chef had missed out on winning the very same grand

prize. We were despondent. We couldn't believe that we had
messed up Trail Days so badly. I had attended the drawings for a
few of the other giveaways, but I had completely forgotten about
that one!

While I had lined up a ride for us on the way to Trail Days,
I had not been able to find one for the way back to Pearisburg. So
on Sunday morning, we packed up and headed back downtown to
try to hitchhike. We stood on a corner in town, arms outstretched,
thumbs up, hoping against hope that someone would pick us up
and we could get out of there. We were all long past ready to get
back to the trail.

Luckily, after about an hour, two brothers in a large pickup
truck who were towing a camper pulled up beside us. "We can take
two!" they told us. Ibex, Chef, Wintergreen, and I stared at each
other. Who gets to go? And who has to stay? As we were trying to
sort that out via a game of rock paper scissors, they took pity on
us. "Actually, we could probably squeeze you all in. You'll just
have to share the back with our dog!" We didn't mind; we loved
dogs. We hopped in. These two brothers had hiked the AT a
couple of decades before and regaled us with stories of their thru-
hike during the two-hour drive to Pearisburg. They even offered to
grill us some hot dogs once we got there, but we were ready to get
back on trail, so we politely declined.

They dropped us off at the grocery store so that we could
resupply before getting back to it. Chef packed out an entire
chicken. He and Wintergreen also stopped by the all-you-can-eat
Chinese buffet, but Ibex and I declined to join. We had an eight-
mile uphill climb to get to Rice Field Shelter where we'd stay the
night, and we didn't think Chinese food would help us get there. I
struggled to get to camp that night, exhausted from the weekend of
festivities. I was so relieved to be back in the woods though. Trail
Days had been loud, crowded, and overwhelming. I wasn't used to

seeing so many people in one place. I felt much cleaner and calmer in the woods. Wintergreen set his tent up about five feet from mine that evening. This was becoming his norm; he was sticking close by. I didn't mind.

The next week, Wintergreen made us pay for having had such a slow, easy week in the days leading up to Trail Days. We hiked 95 miles in six days, followed by a 16-mile slackpack, or hike without our heavy packs, immediately after. We hiked by and climbed up the famous Dragon's Tooth, a tall quartzite spire with incredible views of the mountains beyond. We awoke at 4:00 am to hit McAfee's Knob, allegedly the most photographed place on the entire Appalachian Trail. And we hung our legs over Tinker Cliffs as we stared out into the Blue Ridge. It was a rainy but incredibly beautiful week. The forest had come alive in the weeks since we'd first arrived in Virginia, and there were mountain laurel, rhododendron, and azalea flowers bursting out from their branches everywhere we looked. The green tunnel had become an enchanted path out of a fairytale embellished with magenta, flaming orange, and baby pink.

We had lost Jukebox 2—he didn't appreciate the quick pace and thought it might be time to break back out on his own. But sometime in the middle of the night before our 4:00 am McAfee Knob summit, he showed up and was ready to make the hike up with us in the morning. We all hiked the two miles from camp to the knob together, headlamps on as we took our first night hike. We timed it perfectly, making it to the knob before the sun began to rise. As the morning slowly broke, the sky over the knob transformed from a dull gray to magenta, orange, and purple. It was spectacular.

At the top, Jukebox 2 introduced us to his friend Edward Shitterhands, or Eddie for short. He'd been talking about her for weeks, so it felt like meeting a celebrity. Eddie was a physical therapist from Tennessee who'd gotten her trail name from an unfortunate incident her first night on trail. She crept out of the shelter in the middle of the night, thinking she'd had to number one, but really she'd had to number two. She didn't have her trowel, so tried in vain to cover the surprise in leaves and dirt with her hands, getting some on her hands in the process. The next morning, she told everyone what had happened. And so, Edward Shitterhands was born. Eddie was friendly, intelligent, and beautiful. I liked her immediately.

From McAfee Knob, we had 16 miles of hiking to get to Daleville. Chef and Wintergreen ran ahead, in a hurry to get some town food. I was a little bitter about the quick pace that week and decided to take my time with Jukebox 2 and Ibex. We hung out at the edge of Tinker Cliffs with Eddie for a while, then took a nap by a creek a few miles from Daleville. We found out later that the creek area was infested with snakes, but we hadn't seen them when we lay down for our nap. I shuddered in horror when I found out. Snakes are fine if they're far away, but I certainly don't want them creeping around as I'm napping! Ibex was the first to wake up from her slumber, pushing ahead to town. Jukebox 2 and I stayed together for the afternoon and hiked straight into a Mexican restaurant as we arrived in Daleville. We met up with a couple of other hikers inside and ate, drank, and laughed with them for hours.

My tramily was staying the night for free on the grounds of a local brewery outside of town—the Flying Mouse—while Jukebox 2 booked a room at a cheap motel under the thruway. I was going to have to Uber out to the brewery when I was ready to turn in for the night, but I was irritated about the big miles I'd had to pull that week, so I opted to take my sweet time getting out there. I received a text from Wintergreen around 10:00 pm while I was still at the restaurant. "Where are you, Glow?" My heart melted a little bit. No one had ever shortened my name to "Glow" before. I told him that I was hanging out with Jukebox 2 and would be there later. Jukebox 2 let me take a shower in his hotel room, and even generously offered his second bed. He was a known snorer though and always camped off on his own because of it, so I declined and reluctantly called an Uber.

When I arrived at the brewery, everyone was sound asleep in their tents. I set up my tent under the light of the full moon, with fireflies lighting up the night around me. Aside from the noise that I was making, the world was completely silent. This was *midnight* midnight, not hiker midnight. Way past my bedtime. I left the rainfly off my tent for the first time, content to feel the light breeze running through the mesh, and hoped I wouldn't regret it.

The guys woke me up at dawn the next day, anxious to get started on our day of slackpacking. Wintergreen took off first, practically running down the road. We had about a mile to walk into town to catch our shuttle to the trail, and he speed-walked the entire way. I felt like I was being punished for my fun evening with Jukebox 2. Because we were all taking a shuttle together, I had to throw my gear in my pack and practically run the entire way into town to keep up.

Our slackpack was wonderful though. We made our way up to Harvey Knob, 16 trail miles north, with the help of an older gentleman named Homer who ran paid shuttles in the area. I left my pack at the Super 8, where we'd be staying that night, and used the brain, or the top of the pack, as a fanny pack to carry just the essentials. Ibex and I hiked together for most of the day, and because we were going southbound rather than our usual northbound, we passed and chatted with several hikers that we knew throughout the day, including Eddie and two older guys named Raggedy Crow and One Foot. By the end of the day though, we were done. It had been an exhausting week. It was all we could do to drag ourselves down to the grocery store for some maple syrup, berries, and whipped cream for the next morning. The hotel had a complimentary breakfast with a waffle maker, and it had become our tradition to get all the fixings to pile on top of our waffles anytime a hotel had one of these machines.

The Super 8 was a hiker's dream for one reason: it had a massive outdoor pool. The next morning, we were blessed with a few hours of sun, so Ibex and I took full advantage. We swam, we lay out, we swam again, and we lured Jukebox 2 over from his motel to join us. This was by far mine and Ibex's favorite way to spend a town day. Once it started to rain, Ibex, Jukebox 2, Wintergreen, and I grabbed an Uber to Ballast Point, another local brewery, where we gorged ourselves on bar snacks and challenged each other in cornhole. We finished out the day in our hotel room, watching movies and having some much-needed downtime. We stopped at the grocery store the following morning for a quick resupply, then got back on the trail.

Wintergreen's birthday was just a few days away, and we'd likely be in the woods for it, so while at the store, I picked up some small treats for him. I grabbed a miniature bottle of apple pie Ole Smoky Moonshine, reminiscent of our time in Gatlinburg, a small bottle of Knob Creek bourbon, which we'd drank on our creek day with Hank Hill, and some Red Vine candies, one of his favorites. I love birthdays, and I was immensely excited to celebrate a friend's birthday on trail.

The next few days were especially rainy. It was near the end of May, and during that month in Virginia, it rained 25 out of the 31 days. Nothing ever dried, and my clothes and hair started to smell like mildew. As hikers cross over the James River Footbridge in Central Virginia, many stop halfway across and leap into the waters below. It's illegal and probably unsafe, but people still do it. But it wasn't even an option for us because the river was so high and moving so swiftly. As I walked across the bridge, I noticed full trees floating on top of the water, being pulled downstream by the current.

We started pulling some big miles in this section, both because we were pushed forward by Wintergreen, and because we were uninterested in having hours to spend at camp while it was pouring. My favorite part of the day was hanging out with the tramily at camp in the evenings, but it was no fun when we all had to hide in our separate tents. Here, I got my first blisters of the trail. I got caught in a downpour while crossing a cattle field, and I watched as a stream of water rushed down my legs and straight into my hiking boots. My shoes got wet, and stayed wet for several days, causing enough friction to partially rub the skin off my feet. We lost Jukebox 2 again in this section because he just didn't want to push those kinds of miles.

The night before Wintergreen's birthday, after pulling a 22-mile day and getting to camp just as it was getting dark, I sat in my tent, eating some Kraft macaroni and cheese and writing an article about hiking the AT for American University's alumni magazine. Suddenly, I noticed that I was feeling a little lightheaded. *I'm probably dehydrated from the long day,* I thought. I shut off my phone and curled up in my sleeping bag. My stomach started to burn. I tried to coax myself to sleep. *You're fine, you just need some rest.* But it became quickly apparent that I was indeed not fine, and my dinner was not going to stay put in my stomach.

It was raining cats and dogs, so I swiftly switched on my headlamp and began rifling through my pack for my extra Ziplocs. I found one just in the nick of time. The contents of my stomach came up, and up, and out, filling the contents of my Ziploc. I had just two spare baggies that I wasn't using to protect my gear from the rain, so once they were full, I had to make some moves. I was forced to leave the warmth of my sleeping bag and the safety of my tent to stumble down a muddy bank, across a creek, through a field to the privy. I spent the rest of the night on the privy floor, only moving when I had to hang myself over the toilet and vomit. One of my Ziploc bags, which I'd brought to dump into the privy, leaked and spilled all over my fleece sweatshirt and down my legs. I was an absolute wreck. The one saving grace to the terrible situation was that the privy was brand new. Instead of smelling like poo, it smelled mostly like new wood.

Just before dawn, I began to hear movement around camp, and I knew the privy could no longer be my private escape for long. I inched my way back to my tent, hoping that my stomach would finally calm down. I lay back in my sleeping bag, curling my arms around my stomach, finally falling asleep. I got maybe an hour of shuteye before being awakened by Chef moving around outside. I peeked out of my tent. "I'm dying, Chef," I told him. He tried to coax me into eating half of a bagel. You couldn't have paid me.

Ibex came over to my tent a few minutes later, wondering why I hadn't emerged yet. I explained in detail about my rough night and thrust the gifts that I had for Wintergreen into her hands. I told her that if he thought they had too many germs on them then he could leave them at the bottom of the pond, for all I cared. This was unprompted; no one had suggested anything about germs infecting the gifts. I was feeling immensely sorry for myself and was on the verge of tears. All week, I'd envisioned leaving the gifts outside of his tent as a surprise. Instead, I was a pariah, locked inside my tent.

I called a shuttle driver to come pick me up at the next road crossing and take me to the town of Buena Vista, where I'd book a motel room for myself and have access to a real bathroom. Wintergreen stopped by my tent before I left. "Glow? You feeling pretty bad?" He told me that if I was going to get a room in town to go to the Buena Vista Motel rather than the Budget Inn because there were rumors of bed bugs. Chef continued to try to get me to eat his half of a bagel.

The half-mile hike down to the road was the hardest of the trail. I was dizzy, nauseated, exhausted, and dejected. But I made it. My shuttle driver, Nancy, told me this same thing had happened to a few people in this area. She thought the water must be infected with something bad. I had filtered my water, but filters aren't 100 percent effective against everything. She was probably right.

The $20 that I spent on the shuttle and the $72 that I spent on that seedy motel room were my best purchases on trail so far. As soon as I walked into my room and closed the door, I stripped and hopped into the bathtub. I wanted to wash the vomit from my legs, and I didn't think I had the strength to shower. I could have lain in that hot bath for the rest of my life.

I napped, cleaned my dishes, gear, and clothes the best that I could in the sink and shower, and settled in for a marathon viewing of "The Office" on TV. I was feeling a little bit better, but suddenly terribly alone. Chef, Ibex, and Wintergreen had hiked 11 miles beyond where I had exited the trail, and were supposed to be coming into Buena Vista to celebrate Wintergreen's birthday. I had been so excited for his celebration, and I was missing the entire thing.

Ibex promised to drop by with some conditioner and Gatorade for me, but she never showed up until 9:00 pm. They'd also done laundry and hadn't asked if they could wash anything for me. They hadn't checked on me all day, even via text. So I called my dad, which I hadn't done since Fontana Dam. I didn't have the energy for a long conversation, but it was still nice to hear his voice and check in. Our talk made me feel a little better.

In the morning, I got a small resupply of foods that I thought would be easy to digest, like crackers, plain donuts, tortillas, and Smarties candies. Chef agreed to drop a package off at the post office for me, and I sent my thermals, my last bit of cold-weather gear that I was willing to part with, on their way home to New York. Summer was coming, and I didn't think I needed to carry them any longer. I lay around in bed until the others were ready to head back to the trail.

Luckily, we stayed put until check-out time at 11:00 am because they'd had a wild night celebrating Wintergreen's birthday. I couldn't blame them, but I felt left out. Jason, a local who the guys had met the day before, gave us a ride back to the trail in the back of his pickup truck for free. Knowing that I was going to make slow miles and not wanting to fall too far behind, I chose to get dropped off with the tramily, where they'd left the trail the day before, 11 miles north of my exit point. I vowed to come back and finish those 11 miles another time.

The coming days were rough. My energy levels were at an all-time low, I had a difficult time eating, and it rained almost nonstop. We barely got any time to hang out together at camp, and it was hard to chat while hiking when we were just sort of putting our heads down and pushing on. The guys would wait for me to show up at lunch, then immediately take off because they would have already taken an hour break. Chef took pity on me and gathered water for me a couple of times. I'm sure he could tell I still wasn't feeling 100 percent. While we did continue hiking, the gang took it easy on me and didn't push any big-mile days, which I appreciated, but I still would have liked to have been going slower. I suspected that they might be a little hungover from the birthday celebration, which I believe helped my cause. I heard something about rounds and rounds of tequila shots.

We learned shortly thereafter that this had been the wettest May on record in Central Virginia, and the gloomy weather was beginning to take a toll on me. I ran into Workhorse during this time and told him how I was feeling. He offered to let me join him if I ever decided to ditch the tramily to go at my own pace. He also encouraged me to think about stopping to wait for Girl Scout and Jukebox instead of rushing on with the guys. I told him that I would consider it, and I meant it.

CHAPTER 20

It's tradition to stop at the Priest Shelter and confess your trail sins in the logbook. As I read through it one day during lunchtime, I noted that most of the confessions were about not burying poop properly, masturbating in inappropriate places, and the like. I confessed that I'd skipped those 11 miles of trail, because I was sick and because I was mad at the AT for making me so.

It was pouring again, and Chef and Wintergreen decided they were going to stay behind at the shelter and take a nap in hopes that the weather would improve. Ibex and I pushed on, through mud and past swollen creeks, because we knew we'd be hitting the jump-off for Devil's Backbone Brewery in Charlottesville, Virginia, the next day, and we wanted to get there fairly early in the day.

Five miles past The Priest, at the bottom of a slippery, slick, muddy hill, we struck gold: trail magic! It had been a while since we'd had some really good trail magic. After my illness and several days straight of rain, it was just the thing I needed to lift my spirits. Sparky, a former thru-hiker, had a couple of big tents set up. One for sitting and one for cooking. He had eggs, toast, cheese, bacon, beers, fruit, and oatmeal cream pies. We sat for two hours having our fill, chatting with other hikers, and staying out of the rain. The food went down easy for the first time since I'd gotten sick. I practically wolfed it down. I was relieved, knowing the ability to eat normally was going to make everything else easier.

We'd been hearing for weeks that there was another Wintergreen on the trail, and while we were chilling at the trail magic, she finally showed up. She was a jolly, charismatic middle-aged German woman, and she was a delight. We had to get a selfie with her, of course. Wintergreen needed to know that if he got out of line, or pushed us too far too fast, we could easily replace him with this other Wintergreen.

After a couple of hours, we finally peeled ourselves away from the trail magic. We still had a few miles to hike until camp, but luckily it was mostly downhill. My tent filled with condensation that night and water dripped from my tent ceiling down onto my sleeping bag, dampening it. I was looking forward to drying things out at Devil's Backbone Brewery, which owns a huge campus out in the middle of the Blue Ridge Mountains with restaurants, bars, a stage for music, and a campground where they let thru-hikers camp for free. They also serve hikers breakfast for just $5 apiece, and let you pick a gift from their hiker box: a t-shirt, snap bracelet, or koozie. We were excited to check it out.

Ibex and I got up and at 'em early the next morning. The guys never showed up the night before, and we didn't want to give them the pleasure of beating us to the brewery after their extended stay at The Priest. All of my gear was absolutely soaked, including my sleeping pad, and caked in mud so I wasn't super keen to hang around camp any longer anyway. Before ducking out of camp, I tried my best to wash the mud off my ground cloth and tent in the creek. It was already drenched, so I figured I couldn't make things worse. Then, we had eight miles to hike to get to the road where we'd hitch down to Devil's Backbone. The first four miles were straight up the side of a mountain. The woods were covered in chilly haze and fog and the trail was muddy and slick. I was ready for a break.

After a tough morning of hiking, we finally made it to the road and stuck out our thumbs. Only a few cars passed by, so we were waiting there for much longer than we would have liked. Finally, two kind ladies on their way to a massage parlor stopped and offered to take us halfway down the mountain. They couldn't take us the full way or they'd be late for their appointment, but they wanted to help. They were bubbly, fun, and sweet, and they didn't even fault us for getting their creamy, white leather seats a little muddy. The driver, a dentist, even offered me some money, though of course I didn't take it. They were angels. As we got out of their car and started walking downhill to the brewery, a Devil's Backbone pickup truck pulled over to the side of the road. Fred, a nice but curmudgeonly man, offered us a ride the rest of the way, which of course we accepted. Our first order of business was to order everything on the menu. Ibex was always starving anyway, and finally, my hunger had returned with a vengeance after barely eating for several days. Our second order of business was to get out of our soggy wet clothes. And lastly, we needed to consume copious amounts of coffee and perhaps a little beer.

By the time I cleaned myself up and changed my clothes, Chef and Wintergreen had arrived and were seated at our picnic table with a new, young, early 20-something friend named Chandler, who was from Minnesota and California. Chandler was his real name; he figured with a name that no one would forget, why take on a trail name? We became fast friends, despite our age difference, and he spent the entire day with us, eating, drinking beers, and playing cornhole. That's the thing about trail friendships. They come easily, and age doesn't matter. I made so many friends on the AT of all different ages. Some were as young as 18, and some were in their 60s. It was a real gift.

Later in the day, we tore ourselves away from the cornhole boards long enough to set up our tents at the campground across the campus. As I crawled out of my tent after laying out my sleeping pad and sleeping bag, Chef appeared with a bottle of silver rum that he had purchased from the distillery on site. He proceeded to peer pressure us into taking some shots. I tried not to vomit as I conceded.

That evening, we perched ourselves up at the bar inside, snacking on pickled beets and mindlessly glancing at the sports games on TV. Wintergreen and I were the last two hikers at the bar. I announced that it was time for me to hit the hay, and Wintergreen said that he'd walk with me back to camp. There were more fireflies here than anywhere else that we'd seen on trail. They filled up the fields around us with their blinking yellow lights. Since Wintergreen had never seen fireflies before coming to the East Coast for the trail, I suggested we try to catch one. We passed by the tent sites in favor of getting closer to an especially sparkly field. It was incredible. They were everywhere.

As I stared out into the night, wondering which way we should go to get close to them, I suddenly felt Wintergreen's hand on my shoulder. It moved up to my neck, and the next thing I knew, his lips were on mine. His hands moved to my waist and he wrapped his arms around me. My heart began to beat out of my chest as I leaned into him.

"This has been a long time coming," he told me. "I've been hoping for something to happen between us before you leave for Bonnaroo." I agreed, I wanted that too. "You drive me crazy," I said. "In a good way?" he asked. "Both ways," I laughed. He kissed me passionately.

My whole body was on fire. I couldn't believe this was happening, and on such a perfect night. He gently pulled me to the ground, and the next thing I knew, my top was off, and then everything was off. And then we were tangled up in each other on the dirt road that circled the campground.

Once we finally stood up, a little disoriented, we walked back to camp, hand in hand. He stopped me just before we got back to the tent sites, pushing me against a tree and kissing me hungrily one more time. I smelled his neck. The tramily had been talking just a couple of days prior about how smell determines compatibility, and we'd all been joking about smelling each other's necks. Now, I was actually doing it, and I liked what I smelled. With one last lingering glance, we let our hands fall apart and retreated to our tents. He texted me goodnight. I squealed silently, hugging my pillow. I was over the moon, and excitedly texted my friend Katie back in D.C. to tell her what had happened. As my feelings for Wintergreen had begun to develop around the border of Tennessee and Virginia, I had been keeping her updated. And this was huge! I drifted off into a contented sleep.

I was a ball of anxiety the next morning. Now sober, I was much more self-conscious about what had happened. I didn't regret it; I was smitten, actually. And I was proud of myself for falling for someone so *nice*, that I was friends with before anything else. I didn't have the best track record with choosing men, so this felt like a victory. I just didn't quite know how to act in front of the tramily. When Wintergreen made eye contact with me at breakfast, I had to look away to prevent my face from getting too red. I thought Chef and Ibex were going to be able to read in my face what had happened, and I wasn't ready to share just yet.

We made our way back to the trail and stopped at Paul C. Wolfe Shelter just five miles from Waynesboro, the gateway to the Shenandoah National Park. In just two days, I'd be hopping off the trail for the weekend for the Bonnaroo Music Festival in Tennessee. I turned in early that night, having barely slept the night before at Devil's Backbone. We hiked into the Shenandoah the next day, where we were met by Wintergreen's parents, who had come out from Montana for a visit.

Mr. and Mrs. Wintergreen were a delight. They were fun to be around, and they catered to our every whim. They set us up at the local Hampton Inn for two nights while slackpacking us through the park, drove us to the laundromat and grocery store, and treated us to dinner and drinks. We crushed a couple of big days of miles while they were there since we didn't have to carry our heavy packs. The only downside was that I never got a moment alone with Wintergreen in the days that followed the magical night at Devil's Backbone. We were either hiking, him usually way ahead of me, or we were in a big group. So we never got to talk about what happened. But each time we piled into the back of their SUV, Wintergreen would squeeze in next to me, and I would get a small thrill feeling the heat of his legs on mine.

They dropped me off at a wayside, which is what they call these combination grills and general stores in the park that are famous for their blackberry ice cream, two days later. I got a hug from each member of the tramily as they told me to hurry back. I felt a jolt of electricity run down my spine as Wintergreen wrapped his arms tightly around me and held on for a moment longer than necessary. He held my gaze for a minute before walking back to his parents' vehicle.

And then, they drove away and I sat at a picnic table, waiting for my friend Kelsey to pull up and whisk me away.

CHAPTER 21

About an hour later, I was awakened from a daydream when Kelsey pulled up in her black SUV, honking the horn and waving emphatically. Kelsey is one of my best friends from D.C., a soul sister. We bonded while playing together on a recreational soccer team, and then she promptly moved into the basement apartment below my group house. We loved a lot of the same things: soccer, Taylor Swift, hiking, Sweet Green, and traveling. We injured our backs around the same time, and we had our hearts broken by long-term boyfriends only weeks apart. She got me into improvisational theater and yoga, and lent me her copy of "Wild," Cheryl Strayed's book about hiking the Pacific Crest Trail. I adore her family. She's the best.

Kelsey wasn't even going to Bonnaroo, she just volunteered to pick me up and take me to D.C. to catch my flight when I couldn't figure out how to get a shuttle from the Shenandoah. I was originally supposed to attend the festival for the entire week, but after actually getting on trail and bonding so hard with my tramily, that became impossible. My brother, Bryan, was joining my friends there, so I couldn't bail completely. Instead, I simply cut my trip a few days short. I'd be off the trail for three days. I figured that my tramily would take one zero day while I was gone, so if they took it easy the other two days, it wouldn't be impossible to catch up. At least I hoped not.

On our way out of the park, Kelsey and I saw a bear sitting near the side of the road. I was delighted. I'd also seen a momma bear and some cubs while I was in a vehicle with Wintergreen's parents, squeezed in the back seat between Chef and Wintergreen. So far, my only bear sightings were from cars, here and in the Smokies. Shenandoah National Park is known for its healthy population of about 300 to 500 black bears, so I was not surprised to see them here, but they kept evading me while I was on trail. Countless times, I'd come around a corner and someone would say, "You just missed a bear!" It seemed like I was cursed; I might never see a bear while actually on the trail.

I spent a lovely evening with Kelsey and her partner, Erick, in D.C., then caught an Uber to the airport before first light. I had a 6:00 am flight to Nashville, and the line at the airline counter at Dulles International Airport was shockingly long. By the time I got to the counter, I was informed that it was too late to check my bag. I'd have to wait for the next flight, hours later. I was infuriated. I had gotten up insanely early, to wait in an hour-long line to check my bag, to be told that I couldn't board my flight. This trip wasn't starting well.

A few hours later, I landed in Nashville. I grabbed a veggie wrap and made my way over to the bus stop, where I would catch a bus to take me the rest of the way to the festival. I finally arrived at the festival grounds five hours later than planned. I dropped my stuff off at my friends' campsite and sprinted to the entrance of the music venue. I found my friends Andrea, Alysha, Allison, Seth, Emily, and my brother, Bryan, at a Sheryl Crow concert. They greeted me with huge hugs and cheers, making the long journey there seem more than worth it.

But only a short time later, I felt a familiar burning in my stomach. *No, it couldn't possibly be*, I thought to myself. Again, I tried to talk myself out of being sick. But the burning continued. I asked if anyone had any Pepto Bismol and Bryan offered to walk me back to camp to raid his stash. I took him up on it, promising my friends that we'd be right back. But that promise was soon broken. By the time we got to Bryan's tent, I felt like I was being stabbed through the abdomen. The stomach bug that I'd had a mere week ago? It was back, and it plagued me all weekend.

I called my mom, a registered nurse, from our campsite. "What's wrong with me?" I asked her in tears. I felt like I was dying.

"Maybe you should smoke a little pot, honey," she responded. I declined her advice and sprawled out on the ground. Marijuana, something I did not even like to use recreationally, was the last thing I wanted when I was lying there violently ill.

I didn't understand. I had washed all my dishes thoroughly in Buena Vista, including my reusable water bottle. I'd thrown my Smartwater bottle in the trash, opting to buy a new one. I had no idea how this could have happened to me twice in a week. I suddenly had serious concerns about my health.

Bryan, the saint, hung out with me for hours at camp while I vomited into a trash bag. "Go listen to the music!" I told him. "I'll be fine!" But he stayed anyway. I was sad that not only was my weekend ruined, but his was as well. But there was nothing I could do about it. Once again, I was a complete disaster.

I had weighed myself at Dave's house the night before Trail Days, just three weeks ago. There, my weight had been 132, just two pounds lighter than when I'd started the trail two months prior. I weighed myself again after Bonnaroo and found that I had lost another 10 pounds. And it wasn't water weight; the weight loss stuck. I was suffering.

I was relieved when Andrea dropped me back off on the trail on Monday evening. I had felt awful all weekend, but felt like I had to put on as brave a face as I possibly could, and go see some music when I was able. The music went on for half the night, the base often booming so loudly that I could feel the vibrations from inside my tent, so my sleep had been restless at best. All I wanted was to crawl into the privacy of my tent in the middle of a quiet forest and finally get some real rest.

It was a foggy, chilly evening as I returned to the trail. It had poured all day during our drive north from Tennessee, and I spent the worst of it in the safety of a minivan. I said goodbye to my friends around 6:45 pm and hiked onward for about two hours before stopping to stealth camp. I slept like a baby that night. My exhaustion continued the next day as I squeezed out 14 miles by the skin of my teeth. I ran into Caroline, who reported that the weather had been absolute shite the day before. She also told me that Easy Bake and Wingman were nearby.

Eleven miles in, I passed a park lodge and stopped for a coffee and a cookie. I was supposed to be making extra miles to catch up with the tramily, but I just couldn't muster the energy. The coffee helped a little, and I was able to push three more miles to the next shelter. Ibex texted to ask how far I'd made it, and when I told her, she began to guilt me. "You'll never catch us at that pace!" she scolded. She was right, but there was nothing I could possibly do to drag myself any further that day.

The next day, I vowed to get up early and try harder. I ran into Workhorse, which was always a pleasant surprise. Just when I'd think he'd fallen too far behind and I wouldn't see him again, he'd pop up. We hiked together for a couple of hours, chatting away. He had run family interventions as a job, owned property, and had been a Peace Corps volunteer in South Africa in his fifties, so he always had interesting stories and a helpful perspective. And he was always so encouraging. Running into him after having such a horrible few days was such a blessing. I waved goodbye as he stopped at a shelter for the night, knowing I needed to push on, but since he was an early bird and I wasn't, we agreed to meet at a wayside for breakfast the next morning. I made it 20 miles that day.

I stealth camped alone again that night. I loved hiking alone, but camping alone was another story. I'd get bored and my mind would start to play tricks on me and make up stories about the most mundane forest noises. I played some Ellie Goulding on repeat to calm my mind, then finally fell asleep, exhausted, and slept the night through until my alarm buzzed in the morning.

As I headed to the wayside to meet up with Workhorse, I ran into him on the trail, and we hiked the rest of the way there together. We were joined there by his friend Amua from Hawaii and Taco, a young 20-something woman whom I had met previously on the trail. We dined on breakfast sandwiches, hash browns, cinnamon rolls, and coffee, and Easy Bake, Wingman, and Caroline showed up about halfway through breakfast to join us. Despite being away from my tramily, I wasn't lonely at all.

Jukebox 2 was only about 10 miles behind me at this point and he considered trying to catch up, but he was waylaid by some pretty incredible trail magic which included a free stay at a huge house with an outdoor pool. I couldn't blame him, but sadly, I didn't see him for the rest of the trail.

I knew I had some big mile days ahead of me, so despite the wonderful time that I was having with this crew, I knew I had to hit the trail. I hiked a 23-mile day, landing at a campsite only .2 miles down the trail from Chef. I would have hiked the extra .2 miles to join him, but he was planning to wake up at midnight to hike a 50-mile day as a personal challenge. Night was falling fast as I arrived at my campsite, and he was trying to get a few hours of shuteye before he started his push. We listened to the same fox calling into the dark night like a pterodactyl as we lay in our tents less than a quarter mile from each other.

Ibex and Wintergreen were another 10 miles up the trail. They would have been further ahead, Ibex suggested, but

Wintergreen had forced them to stop at just five miles one day
while I was gone, allegedly because of the weather. I thought
perhaps it might have had a little something to do with allowing
me to catch up as well. I smiled thinking about it.

The next few days and nights were a blur until I stumbled
into Harpers Ferry later that week. I hiked more than 20 miles each
day and camped alone each night. I hiked through the evenings,
finishing my days alone on the trail as fireflies danced around me
in the dark. I started sleeping with my food because I was too
exhausted to hang it by the time I got to camp. One night, I was
awakened by a large animal just outside of my tent. And it was
close. I clapped as loudly as I could, yelling "Hey! Get out of
here!" And then I heard it tramp off. There was no mistaking it for
my imagination.

I hiked through Sky Meadows State Park in Virginia, a
park I'd been to many times during my years in D.C. During
numerous visits to this lovely place, I would hike to the top of a
specific hill, where a white blaze and a sign pointing toward
Harpers Ferry waited on a tree. Each time I came across it, I'd stop
and silently tell that tree that someday I would be back for it when
I hiked the entire Appalachian Trail. And here I was. I had finally
fulfilled my promise, to the tree and myself. I hugged that tree
tight while I sobbed, so proud of myself for making my dream a
reality, and for having made it this far.

I hiked through the infamous rollercoaster in this section
of trail, named for its constant ups and downs. Some new friends
handed me a can of Miller Light beer just before I entered it, and
we shared some laughs until they took an offer by a passerby to
yellow blaze, or take a car, around this section. They waved from
the back of a pickup truck as I marched into the roller coaster
alone.

I was greeted by a sign that said, "Hiker warning: you are
about to enter the rollercoaster, built and maintained by the

Trailboss and his crew of volunteers. Have a great ride, and we will see you at the Blackburn Trail Center." Just a little way in, I hit the 1,000-mile mark. I was astounded. I couldn't believe that little old me had hiked 1,000 miles. I remembered how incredibly difficult the first 100 miles of the trail were, and how long it had taken to reach that milestone. And now here I was, at the 1,000-mile mark. Time seemed to be speeding up and flying by. And it continued from here, whirling by faster and faster until I reached Katahdin.

I hummingbirded my way through the rollercoaster, and as a result, I thought its difficulty was overhyped. About halfway through the day, I stopped for a shower and not one, not two, but three sodas at Bear's Den Hostel. Then, I found a trail magic cooler of Gatorades not too far down the trail. I downed one and snagged another for the road. Fueled by sugar, I practically bounced down the trail that afternoon, very much enjoying my sugar high and the solitude on the trail. By the time I got to camp that night, I had just nine flat miles to Harpers Ferry, where I would find my tramily waiting for me in the morning.

On the way into town the next morning, I stopped at the border of Virginia and West Virginia for a moment to thank Virginia for all she'd done for me. So much had happened since I'd crossed the border into Virginia from Tennessee, and I felt like I'd grown so much as a backpacker since then. Despite the rain and the stomach bugs, I had loved this state, with all of its wildflowers, lush green forests, swimming holes, and quaint little towns, and I wasn't sure that I was ready to leave just yet. But the tramily was waiting, and so after a quick farewell, I marched on into West Virginia.

CHAPTER 22

I smiled as I crossed the bridge over the Potomac River into Harpers Ferry. Not only was I about to be reunited with my friends, I had also made it to the unofficial halfway point of the trail. The Appalachian Trail Conservancy (ATC) is headquartered in downtown Harpers Ferry, and they invite thru-hikers to stop by when they get into town to get their halfway photos taken. They also hand out new hiker numbers to signify which number you are to have reached this point so far in the year. If you start at Amicalola Falls State Park in Georgia, you first get a number there, so you can compare how those numbers have changed. I moved up a few hundred numbers from Amicalola to Harpers Ferry, probably because a number of people had dropped out by that point. The ATC also had a fully stocked fridge full of cold lemonades and sodas that hikers could purchase for just $1 each, so I helped myself to two cans of lemonade while I was there, one plain and one pink.

I took a seat in the air-conditioned hiker room in the back as I waited for the tramily to come to collect me. Ibex strolled in first, running into my arms and giving me a chipper welcome. Chef came in just behind her and locked me into a huge bear hug. They didn't seem to mind that I was dripping with sweat. It was clear that they were as thrilled to see me as I was to see them. Wintergreen came a few minutes behind them and, unlike the

others, gave me a double fist bump. Not exactly the reunion that I
was hoping for. I was disappointed, to say the least.

They led me to Tumblina's place, a former thru-hiker who
now put hikers up in bunks in her basement. Tumblina was
incredibly sweet, a cute, blonde hippie who loved live music and
the festival scene. It was 90 degrees and humid outside, and the
basement was stuffy. But Tumblina was a welcoming host and
these were by far the cheapest accommodations in Harpers Ferry.
She also had a lawn where we could wash our gear. Mine
desperately needed it. Summer had arrived and my pack took on a
worse and worse odor as the daytime temperatures increased.
Tumblina and her boyfriend, Wahoo, a local rafting guide whom
she had met while hiking the AT, hosted a barbecue later that day
for family and friends. We were invited to attend.

After a shower and some time spent scrubbing my pack,
Ibex, Chef, Wintergreen, and I walked down to the main part of
town to grab some food. I was of course starving from the
weekend of keeping next to nothing down in my stomach followed
by the week of 20-plus-mile days. Just a teeny meal before the
barbecue couldn't hurt, I reasoned.

Over lunch, Chef animatedly told me about his 54-mile
day, how he had pushed himself through, and how he could barely
walk for the two days after. On day three, he was just now
recovering. But he had done it! I also learned that Chef had gone
on a Tinder date after I'd left the trail in Virginia. It was fun, he
explained, but now she was threatening to show up in Harpers
Ferry with her friends. He didn't know how to handle the situation
so he was avoiding his phone. They'd spent the night in his tent,
him unshowered, and she was into it. She liked his "man musk,"
she'd told him.

We returned after our meal to help set up for the picnic.
While we were hanging out there, Mark from Alabama, whom we
hadn't seen since Georgia, showed up with his friend Baby,

another 20-something software developer from Virginia. Mark told us he'd had to get off trail for a week back in Georgia because of a knee injury and had been trying to catch up to us ever since. We had no idea. Mark still didn't have a trail name, so Ibex fixed that. She'd thought of a trail name weeks prior that she'd been waiting to bestow upon someone without one. It didn't matter who, she just really wanted to be able to call someone Fancy Horse. And suddenly, here was Mark without a trail name. It ended up really suiting him.

Each summer while living in D.C., I'd come up to Harpers Ferry with my friends to go tubing on the Shenandoah River. Now that the tramily was back together, I insisted that we must go before leaving town. Wahoo kindly volunteered to drive us to the river, so Ibex, Wintergreen, Fancy Horse, and I got to it. It was hot and sticky—the perfect day to be out on the river. We floated for hours, relaxing in the sun and catching up. It was glorious. Wahoo returned to collect us when we were done, dropping us back at the ATC to collect our packs and Chef. And then, we were on our way as a fivesome.

We hiked through high humidity under a blazing sun for six miles to the next shelter. I was drenched in sweat by the time we got there. This was the weather that made me hate D.C. summers and I hoped we'd be able to hike north out of it before too long. Tumblina and Wahoo showed up at camp with beers for all of us. "You all made such an impression on us," Tumblina said. "We weren't ready to say goodbye just yet." I felt the same way. I wished we could take them with us.

The trail through West Virginia is only a few miles, so we crossed the border into Maryland just a few minutes after leaving Harpers Ferry. Maryland isn't much longer, only 40 miles and two days of hiking for us. The trail was well-kept and the hiking was easy, but it continued to be hot, humid, and crowded with day hikers. I knew from living in D.C. that the mid-Atlantic was busy and overcrowded, so I wasn't too surprised by the number of people using the trail. But I was ready to hike onward and escape it. I tried to appreciate the history of the area as I hiked through it. Several Civil War monuments adorned the parks that we walked through, and we passed by the original Washington Monument, a 40-foot stone tower that had been built in 1827. We camped at Annapolis Rocks, allegedly the most used campsite on the entire Appalachian Trail.

There, we met Dubs, a friendly 20-something guy from Denver with beautiful shoulder-length hair who would end up hiking around us for a few weeks. Somehow, I ended up sharing a campsite with just Wintergreen. I was hoping we could talk; we still hadn't since Devil's Backbone, but by the time I returned from the long climb downhill to collect water, the lights were all out in his tent and there was nothing but quiet.

The next morning, on June 20, the three-month anniversary of when Ibex and I started the trail, we had a scavenger hunt to participate in. Before I left D.C., my coworker, Kelly, brought a treasure map to my desk. Her friend had hiked the AT the year before and she'd buried a bottle of whiskey just off the trail for him in Maryland. He was never able to find it. So she bestowed the map upon me during my last week of work, and wished me luck in my journey. I carried that map with me all the way from Amicalola, and today was the day for glory.

Ibex, Fancy Horse, and I rushed out of camp; we wanted to find that whiskey. We were looking for a particular dead tree that Kelly had drawn out, at a particular mile mark, where the whiskey was buried. Wintergreen showed up to tell us not to take too long; his uncle was waiting for us ahead. After a few false starts, I began to dig beneath a felled tree and triumphantly pulled the bottle out of the ground, safe and sound inside of a Ziploc bag. I whooped in victory. Ibex, Fancy Horse, and Wintergreen gathered around to take a sip. "Happy three months!" I said happily, passing around the bottle.

Wintergreen's Uncle Ray was waiting for us with a full picnic spread at Pen Mark Park, just south of the Mason-Dixon line, where we'd cross into Pennsylvania. He'd driven up from Virginia to visit and put us up in a hotel for the night and took us out for a lovely Japanese dinner. He was a ton of fun. Wintergreen had a great family. We all swam in the hotel pool together that evening, and because the hotel hot tub was broken, Ibex and I put on our bathing suits and hopped into the bathtub together while Wintergreen sat on the sink, hanging out with us. While Ibex was taking a quick shower, I walked over to Wintergreen's bed and kissed him. He kissed me back. I hoped that might move things along between us.

While picnicking with Uncle Ray in Pen Mar Park, we got to meet another trail celebrity: Miss Janet. Miss Janet is the most famous AT trail angel of all. Each hiking season, she follows the hiker bubble north, offering whatever help she can to hikers along the way. Ibex and I insisted on getting a photo with her, and she bestowed upon us some sage advice. "You're going to get to New Hampshire feeling like you're 10 feet tall," she told us. "You will have accomplished so much of the trail by then. But the Whites are different, and they're going to be difficult. Be ready for that. Make sure you're eating enough, and not just ramen. If you start to smell like ammonia, you need more protein."

The next day, we officially crossed the Mason-Dixon Line into Pennsylvania and the North. It was the summer solstice, which also happens to be National Hike Naked Day. Ibex and I had been toying with the idea of participating, at least for a few minutes, but we weren't deep in the wilderness as we had been farther south on the trail. We were in the mid-Atlantic and too close for comfort to Waynesboro, Pennsylvania, so we decided against it. We ran into Dubs and his friend Foreman, who were participating, which made us feel a little left out. But we confirmed that we'd made the right decision when we ran into both a Boy Scout and Girl Scout troop. *That could have been bad*, I thought.

Pennsylvania felt noticeably different from the rest of the trail. It was grittier, seedier, rockier.… Hikers often refer to Pennsylvania not-so-fondly as "Rocksylvania" because the trail across the entire state is covered in jagged rocks. My feet felt constantly bruised during my time there, and I broke one of my trekking poles catching my fall on some especially spikey stones. There was also a ton of farmland that the trail would pass straight through, and many of the water sources were bright orange with mining pollution. We'd often hear mysterious booms in the night. I liked Pennsylvania, though, for the most part. There was a ton of wildlife—porcupines, deer, and beavers—and aside from the rocks, the terrain was far easier than any of the previous states.

Pennsylvania also has another claim to fame. It is home to the Half-Gallon Challenge. As hikers pass through Pine Grove Furnace State Park around mile 1,100, they are invited to stop by the Pine Grove General Store to purchase a half gallon of ice cream and eat it as quickly as they can in the name of glory. Each participant receives a small wooden spoon and the winner's name and time is posted on the wall until a faster eater comes by and destroys their record. My stomach can't handle heavy dairy, so I cleaned up in the nearby shower house while my tramily devoured their ice cream.

By the time I returned from my shower, Chef had made a name for himself by becoming the fastest ice cream eater so far that year. He finished his half gallon in just 12 minutes and 50 seconds. His name and time were posted on the wall of the store, and Jukebox 2 told us it was still there when he came through several days later. Chef was burping up ice cream for the rest of the day.

I replaced my hiking boots for the first time at a Boiling Springs outfitter. I'd been needing new shoes for hundreds of miles, but unlike many of the southern towns, the mid-Atlantic ones didn't seem to cater to hikers, and I hadn't passed by an outdoor store in a long while. It didn't help that I'd been rushing through northern Virginia to catch the tramily. My boots were waterproof and giving me heat rash now that summer was in full force. After trying on several pairs, I switched out my sturdy Asolo high tops for some breathable, non-waterproof low tops from Oboz. I tossed my old shoes in the trash and breathed a sigh of relief. I hoped this was the end of my heat rash. I even treated myself to a new pair of Darn Tough socks.

Boiling Springs was a cute, walkable little town, and our bodies were beginning to ache, signaling the need for a rest day. We considered staying for the night, but it was a Sunday and many of the shops and restaurants in town were closed. So we decided to push on to Duncannon. What we didn't know was that Duncannon was not the kind of place where we'd like to spend more time than we needed to. It was a necessary stop; the trail passed directly through town, and it was the home of the historic Doyle Hotel.

The hotel was built in 1905, and I'm pretty sure it hadn't been updated since. It was a dive, and infamous among hikers, one of those places you just had to stop by. We ducked in for lunch, but the kitchen was closed, so we had a quick drink and then moved across the street for calzones instead. I heard horror stories from friends who stayed there of dirty water leaking down into their showers while they were trying to bathe, so I was happy not to stay there. There was also a church in town with a hiker center in the basement with free showers and coffee, a place to charge your electronics, and Wi-Fi. I took advantage on my way out of town; my shower was clean, lovely, and free.

Dubs and Foreman had been hiking around us and camping with us often in this area. I liked them; they were fun,

funny, and easy to be around. But something was suddenly up with
Foreman. The 10-mile hike into Duncannon was easy and all
downhill, yet it took him several hours to complete. Dubs was
beyond frustrated. Foreman was a hammocker and on more than
one occasion had found ticks crawling up his legs in the mornings.
As he hobbled into the hiker center in town, I noticed that his face
was ashy white and he told me that all of his joints hurt. "You look
awful," I told him. We looked up the symptoms of Lyme Disease.
Check, check, and check. "You need to get some antibiotics," I
said.

According to the Centers for Disease Control and
Prevention (CDC), Lyme Disease is the most common vector-
borne illness in the United States. It is spread to humans through
deer tick bites, which tend to hang out in grassy, brushy, and
wooded areas, which are plentiful on the AT, and in the U.S., cases
are concentrated in the Northeast, mid-Atlantic, and Midwest.
Early treatment with antibiotics is imperative because if left
untreated, the illness can spread to the joints, nervous system, and
heart, wreaking all kinds of havoc and having some unpleasant
long-term effects.

Many hikers, including myself, treated their gear and
clothing with Permethrin, an insecticide, to keep the ticks away.
But even so, spending this much time outdoors felt risky on the
Lyme front. As soon as the temperatures on the trail rose above
freezing, Ibex and I became vigilant about giving each other tick
checks each evening, searching for signs of the pests along each
other's hairlines and behind the ears. We'd also check our waist
bands, belly buttons, and areas behind the knees, all places that
ticks commonly attach to humans.

I mapped out where the closest urgent care center was,
then used my AWOL guide to find Foreman a shuttle service. It
was 17 miles away, but this was an emergency. He protested, but
Dubs and I forced him to make the call to the shuttle. He texted me

a few days later. They hadn't been able to test for Lyme at the urgent care, he told me, but they concurred it was probably Lyme, and sent him on his way with a long course of antibiotics. He was already feeling like a new man after a few days of taking the pills. "It probably wasn't Lyme," he told me. "I might stop taking the antibiotics." I chastised him, realizing then that denial seems to be a symptom of Lyme, along with fever, headache, fatigue, joint pain, and if you're lucky, the signature bull's eye rash. This would not be the last time I would see the Lyme denial.

Despite originally wanting to stay in town for the night, Ibex and I did not dilly-dally once we'd completed our town chores in Duncannon. As we hiked out of town, the trail passed by a gentlemen's club. When I lived in D.C., I had driven through Pennsylvania to get home to Western New York dozens of times, always noticing the billboards for strip clubs and porn shops that adorned the highways in the state. It made Pennsylvania seem like the seedier cousin to the surrounding states. I wondered what was up with that as I hiked by.

There were a lot of snakes in Pennsylvania, especially rattlesnakes. Chef almost stepped on one while hiking and swiping on the Tinder dating app one day. He'd begun to feel like he either needed to fight or fuck someone and as he had no one to fight, Tinder it was. He would change the settings on the app to place him in the next town up the trail and swipe left and right on his prospects while he was hiking. I would not recommend this method if you're looking for love in a trail town. One day, as he was doing this, he nearly stepped on a gargantuan rattlesnake that was hiding under some thick plants hanging over the trail. He noticed the snake and shifted his footing just in the nick of time.

The trail through Pennsylvania was 230 miles long, but it went by quickly. We had hit our stride by this point, and we were moving fast, regularly pulling 20-mile days. I started to get a runner's high by the end of many of our hiking days as a result of this. Horse became a solid member of our group during this time, and the two of us hiked together fairly often. He was quirky and fun to have around. As soon as he joined the group though, Horse began to make some demands. He was on a leave of absence from work, so he had to finish the AT by a certain date. Every single day, he wanted to hike 15 miles. No more, no less. Yet, he was always stressed about not making enough miles. He was Wintergreen 2.0, except that Wintergreen *did* actually want to make big miles.

The rain that plagued us in Virginia continued through Pennsylvania. It was hot, and it was soggy. Yet somehow, we'd often have to hike a mile off trail to find a water source and were often forced to do long water carries despite the rainfall. One night at camp, Ibex and I volunteered to collect water for the entire tramily. We wanted to birdbath in the cold spring water anyway, so we hiked the mile down to the water solo with our empty packs, filled them with our own full water bags plus some for Chef, Wintergreen, and Horse, then hauled them back up the hill. Just one liter of water weighs 2.2 pounds, so taking on this chore was a generous offering. The next night, as I walked out of camp to go fill my bottles, Wintergreen stuck his empty water bag into the air. "Can you get some for me, too?" he asked.

"I got yours last night," I responded indignantly. "What have you done for me lately?" I continued down to the water without his bag.

One night, we arrived at a shelter to find a vagabond living inside. While he wasn't the first nor last person I saw living in a shelter, for some reason, he made the hairs on the back of my neck stand up. There was supposed to be a storm rolling in that night, so Ibex, Wintergreen, and Horse were planning to hunker down in the shelter. Though I hated sleeping in shelters because of the snoring, mice, and lack of privacy, I had planned to join them for just that night, which would have made it my third night on the entire trail in a shelter. But that man made me so uncomfortable that I ended up opting to camp with Chef instead. Chef hated shelters possibly even more than I did.

That night, I experienced the wildest, most intense thunderstorm of my life. Gentle rumblings of thunder in the distance morphed into explosions over my head. Lightning lit up the inside of my tent at two-minute intervals. The storm raged above us and stagnated there for five hours. I opened up the weather app on my phone and found a huge blob of red sitting directly over top of where we were posted up. Around midnight, I watched as a pond began to form at the base of my tent near my feet. The water crept closer and closer, getting deeper and deeper. I ignored it, not knowing what to do, until I no longer had the option to do so. I packed my sleeping bag and sleeping pad into dry bags and stuffed them into my pack, then pulled on my rain pants and jacket. I unzipped the door to my tent, then my vestibule, and crawled out, braving the storm.

I pulled my tent into a field of tall grass on higher ground and glanced around with my headlamp, finding that the entire campsite was waterlogged. I left my rain layers on as I repositioned my sleeping bag inside my tent and tried to go to sleep. An hour later, water started to infiltrate my tent again. But from where I was now parked, there was no higher ground to move to. I prayed that the storm would soon pass. Water licked the bottom of my sleeping pad, soaking it. I left my sleeping bag inside my pack, safe in its dry bag. Chef texted me. "Are you alright over there?" I told him I was, but that I'd been flooded out and it was starting to happen again. His Zpacks Duplex tent, with its bathtub floor, floated on top of the water. "I feel like I'm sleeping in a waterbed!" he bragged. He couldn't sleep either though, with the storm erupting so fiercely around us, so he spent the night watching movies and calling all of his girlfriends back in Hawaii.

When I crawled out of my tent in the morning, feeling like I'd been through battle, I found the entire campsite flooded. Wintergreen came by to check on us as we were eating breakfast. "I was worried about you guys last night," he told us. "I thought about coming out here but didn't figure there was anything I could do." He called a shuttle to pick us up at a road crossing four miles down the trail so that we could go into Hamburg and dry out our gear. Chef generously handed me a strong coffee. I practically ran the four miles down to the gap. Everyone started calling me "Bro-stick." In my tramily, we referred to hikers who pushed big miles and bragged about it constantly as "bros."

We didn't have to wait at the road crossing for long before a teenager pulled up in a beige SUV to pick us up. He was working on behalf of his father's shuttle service. But there was one problem: he had a flat tire. Chef jumped in to help fix it, crawling under the backside of the vehicle and getting to work, while Horse and Wintergreen stood closely by, providing moral support, and Ibex and I laughed and took photos. Once Chef had the tire switched out, we got on the road. As we made our way to Hamburg, we passed by raging streams, rivers creeping over their banks, and patches of road that were completely submerged in water. We were relieved to land safely in Hamburg. I was able to replace my broken trekking pole from Cabela's and snag a sub from Wawa, which I'd been dreaming about for several states. That night, I wandered outside of our hotel to catch a glimpse of the full moon. It was a rare treat to be able to see it; most months, the sky was covered in thick clouds.

The next day, once mine and Chef's gear had dried out, we returned to the trail. It was still flooded in some places, so our feet got soaked and our shoes got covered in mud. About six miles in, we found a rope swing hanging from a tree over a deep blue

swimming hole. Ibex and I jumped at the chance to test it out. I
quickly changed into my suit and went for it, holding on tight to
the rope as I launched myself over the water. I let go only as I
hung above the middle of the pool, free-falling into the turquoise
water. I came up gasping for breath. It was shockingly frigid!

Ibex and I wanted to camp there for the night, but the guys
wanted to push miles, and they always seemed to get their way. I
was getting more and more fed up with the pace. They never
seemed to want to stop for anything fun. It was late June and we
were halfway through the trail; we had plenty of time to spare. But
it didn't matter. They always wanted to forge ahead.

The next day though was particularly hot. Suddenly, the
guys wanted to stop the hiking day short and spend it in Port
Clinton, a tiny town with a diner that the AT passed through. Still
angry about missing out on camping at the swimming hole, I threw
a fit and forced them to hike a 22-mile day through the heat. If
Ibex and I didn't get to have our half-day at the swimming hole,
then they wouldn't get theirs in town. I hate-hiked all day long,
using my frustration to propel me forward. I was the first to camp
and the most energized when I got there. They had pissed me off,
but at least it had helped my hiking. There had been some boulder
hopping that day, so I'd needed all the help I could get.

That day, I leapfrogged with two young guys who looked
like they couldn't have even been out of high school. I saw them
smoking and giggling on the side of the trail as I passed by,
making me roll my eyes and laugh. Later, I learned that they were
18-year-old best friends from New Hampshire, and they'd finished
high school a few months early to hike the trail together. Their
names were Steak and Walker. We also ran into Horse's friend
Baby that we'd met in Harpers Ferry, who was hiking with
Monica, now named Moss, who we hadn't seen since the early
days of the trail. We figured that Moss would be way ahead by
now, because she and her original hiking partner had been pushing

miles already when we met them in Georgia. But Moss had gotten off the trail to work as a bus driver for a university program for two weeks, and she had just returned.

Because he was the strongest hiker, Chef always got first pick of the tent sites when we arrived at camp. On this particular day, he arrived last, which was usually my role. He angrily stomped around camp, declaring that there were no suitable sites left and that he was going to hike on alone. I rolled my eyes. I was going to enjoy having the best site for once.

The heat in Pennsylvania was oppressive, and it was so humid that I usually started sweating before I even started hiking for the day. As a result, alcohol no longer had the same appeal that it did earlier in the trail, at least for me. Ibex and I had secretly bought the guys some small bottles of whiskey in hopes of luring them into taking a "nearo," or short hiking day, with us somewhere near a nice swimming hole. But that hadn't happened, and we'd been carrying the drinks for a week, uninterested in doing so any longer. The four of us—Horse, Wintergreen, Ibex, and I—decided to polish them off in order to get rid of them after Chef left to find his own camping spot.

I tried to keep my drinking to a minimum, but the liquor went straight to my head after a long day of sweating buckets. A frustrating day turned into a merry evening, but we decided it was time to retreat to our tents after Horse almost knocked us all out with a dead tree branch that he'd inadvertently pulled down from above our heads. After brushing my teeth and changing into my pajamas, I decided I'd better finally go talk to Wintergreen while I had a little liquid courage running through my veins.

I tiptoed over to his tent, lest the others hear me. "Wintergreen?" I asked. "Yeah?" he responded. "Can we talk?"

I crawled into his tent and asked him what was going on between us and why he'd been so distant. I asked point-blank if he was no longer interested in me. He told me that he was though, and

he just hadn't found the right time to address what had happened.
"But you haven't done anything about it," I said.

"You can come to me too, you know," he responded. The
next thing I knew, we were making out ferociously. I dragged my
sleeping pad into his tent, and we shed our clothes, pressing our
bodies together. After a passionate night, I woke up with his arms
wrapped around me. We watched as a deer dined in the field
beyond our campsite in the early hours of the morning. Then, I
tiptoed back to my tent, hoping that we hadn't woken anyone up in
the night. I crawled into my tent and found a text from Ibex
waiting. "I'm glad y'all finally hooked up, but could you keep it
down over there?! I'm trying to sleep!" Well, the cat was out of the
bag. I giggled to myself in my tent.

Despite all of the drinking we'd been doing in trail towns,
we were rarely hungover. Hiking every day was like a superpower.
The booze burned right through us. We'd get a little buzz, and then
it would be gone as quick as it arrived. I can barely have a single
drink in normal life without a hangover, but on the trail, it wasn't
an issue. Well, it wasn't an issue most of the time. This day,
though, was different. None of us moved from camp until after
11:00 am. My head pounded unforgivingly and my stomach turned
as I finally emerged from my tent. What had I done?

I was afraid Chef was going to give me a taste of my own
medicine and make me hike a full day, as I had done to him the
day before. He'd missed the night of festivities and was feeling
just fine. But thankfully, he took pity on us and only made us hike
a few miles. Ibex and I looked around and realized we had been
here before. We'd made it to the spot where we'd met up for our
practice hike the previous fall. We were really making it up the
trail.

Anxious to escape Pennsylvania and its rocks and heat, we
continued to do some big-mile days after we recovered from our

collective hangovers. We were all splitting up for a few days between July 4 and mid-July for various things, so we tried to push some bigger miles before then. Chef was going off to spend a few days with his parents. Wintergreen was meeting up with his sister and her family. Ibex was going to the beach with her boyfriend. I was going to a wine festival in the Finger Lakes in New York, something I did every year with my brothers and a big group of friends. Horse was planning a trip to New York City to see a college friend. We planned to break up for those few days and then reconvene.

Wintergreen was the first to take off. He hiked ahead of the rest of us to pull some big miles before he met up with his sister for an Independence Day celebration. "Hurry back!" I texted him with a winky face. He didn't respond. He had T-Mobile and rarely had cell phone service except when we were in towns, so I tried to tell myself that must be why. But I had knots in my stomach over it for the next few days.

The night before Chef and Ibex were scheduled to get off the trail for their various activities, I fell ill again. I was sitting at camp eating a Knorr pasta side in the 90-degree heat when suddenly, I started to feel chilly. I snagged my puffy out of my tent, threw it on, and zipped it up, returning to my dinner. I sat back down and started to shiver. I decided to retreat to my tent for the evening so that I could snuggle into my sleeping bag. I put on every piece of clothing that I had with me, buried myself deep down into my sleeping bag and liner, and proceeded to shiver violently for the rest of the night. I sweat through everything, soaking my layers all the way down to my sleeping pad. I was dizzy, my joints hurt, and I could barely walk. I was covered in mosquito bites, so I wondered if there could be a link.

We were just a few miles south of Delaware Water Gap, and I told the gang to go on. I'd try to make the last few miles to town later that day, after some additional rest, but I couldn't hike in this state. After falling back asleep for a few hours, I attempted the trek into town. I made it a mile or two to a huge field overlooking the town when I collapsed onto my knees. I would be camping here for the night; I could go no further.

I set up my tent and dragged myself inside, napping the day away. As dusk fell, I began to hear a series of booms in the distance. It was the fourth of July. Soon after the fireworks started, I began to hear voices. I peeked out of my tent and found a huge group of teenagers rolling into the field. They started out tame enough, keeping to themselves across the way. But as they cracked open their beers, there was a significant shift in their noise levels and behavior. They got progressively louder and wilder as the night wore on, and a girl peed directly outside of my tent, drunkenly calling to her friends to let them know she'd fallen over. I pushed in my earplugs and tried to get some sleep, worried that one of them might fall into my tent. They didn't seem to have enough flashlights to go around and also couldn't seem to stay on their feet. The next morning, I got a text from Ibex, with a photo of a waffle piled high with maple syrup, berries, and whipped cream. "You're really missing out!" she told me. *Thanks a lot, Ibex*, I thought.

I packed up my things, wanting to escape before the teenagers woke up. I couldn't handle an awkward encounter, and I'd never felt so disgusting in my life. The sickly sweat from my bout of chills left me feeling grody and gritty, as if there was a scummy, salty film wrapping my skin. I needed a shower. I was still struggling, but my physical state was much improved from the day of rest. I could walk, I just needed to take it slow.

I descended into Delaware Water Gap, a picturesque little town that sits on the border between Pennsylvania and New Jersey on the Delaware River. I hightailed it to the local church, which runs a hiker hostel, to catch a shower. The pastor made small talk with me, asking me questions about the trail. Normally, I would have loved to tell him every single detail about my journey so far, but in this case, I had other priorities. I kept finishing each answer with, "So can I head back to the shower?" I was desperate. Finally, he led the way.

The shower was stocked with shampoo, conditioner, and body wash, and I was tremendously grateful. I stayed in there for a half hour, and when I finally emerged, I felt like a new woman. I spent the morning scrubbing my gear and laid it out on the church lawn to dry. Luckily, the day was sunny. After grabbing some food and a quick resupply, I returned to the hostel to chill out on a well-worn couch while I pondered what to do next. I wanted to stay and get some more rest, but I knew that I had to start making some miles to get ahead of the tramily before I got off the trail for the wine festival.

While there, I hung out with Starburst, a 30-something nurse from Virginia whom I'd met on the trail that morning, and Baba Ghanoush, a 30-something merchant mariner from New York. Baba had mailed himself a package and it was full of high-end treats—fancy chocolates, macadamia nuts, and dark roast coffee. He'd sent too much, so began to hand out his extra goodies, reminding me of a very young Santa Claus. He was charismatic and gregarious. I liked him immediately. Shortly thereafter, I visited the local ice cream parlor for some lemon sorbet and hit the trail. New Jersey wasn't going to hike itself.

CHAPTER 23

I can't say that I was terribly excited as I crossed the Delaware Water Gap Toll Bridge into New Jersey. Jersey doesn't exactly have the best reputation as far as states go. Despite its designation as the "Garden State," I had my suspicions about how much wilderness I'd really encounter there. But as I hiked over the river and into the recreation area across the border, several people stopped their cars to ask if I needed water, snacks, or a ride. I had a surprisingly warm welcome into New Jersey.

That first evening in the state, I hiked a few miles up the trail and set up my tent in an empty campsite, intending on a quiet evening to continue my recovery. Soon after, as I was cooking dinner outside my tent, a large group of preteen boys shuffled into camp, led by a couple of teenagers. They were backpacking as part of a summer camp. *Oh no*, I thought. *So much for my quiet evening.* Luckily, the campsite was huge, so there was plenty of space. But there was no water. One of the counselors had to backtrack two miles to go find some while the others set up.

Initially, I was a bit annoyed. I hadn't counted on sharing the space with a bunch of kids. But slowly, one by one, they crept over to me and won me over. They asked what I was doing, and why I was there all alone. I explained that I was hiking the entire Appalachian Trail and that I'd been doing this for a few months by now. Their eyes widened. For the rest of the evening, I was their hero. They had about a million questions, and more than anything, they wanted to know about my experiences with bears and other wildlife.

Their counselors tried in vain to keep them on their side of the camp, but the kids were just so excited to learn about my journey and had so many questions. I laughed as I answered every single one in detail. They told me that they'd lost two campers that day and that their counselor had almost stepped on a rattlesnake. I couldn't help but laugh. They were a hoot and a half. Surprisingly, I found that I was sad to wave goodbye to them the next morning.

It wasn't too far into the state that I decided New Jersey did deserve its designation as the garden state after all. I began to pass lakes each day, it was incredibly green, the views were lovely, and there was more wildlife than I'd seen in any other state so far. On top of that, the trail was easy and well-maintained, with well-constructed boardwalks protecting hikers from marshes and swamps. It was what I needed after falling so sick again in the couple days prior. Until arriving in New Jersey, I'd yet to see a trail bear; the only bears I'd seen were from vehicles in the Smokies and the Shenandoah. But in Jersey, I saw my first two trail bears on the same day.

I had decided that in order to put some miles between me and my tramily before I got off trail for the wine festival, I needed to hike a marathon day. Previously, my longest day of hiking had been 24 miles, but I wanted to make it 26.2 in one day. I had two things working against me: I hate getting up early, and I'm not the fastest hiker, especially up hills. But because the terrain in Jersey is fairly chill, this seemed like the place to do it. I set my alarm for 5:45 am and asked Ace, a section hiker who was camping with me for the evening, if he'd give me a shout if he was awake before me. He wasn't, and I did not rise until almost 7:00 am. That was not a great start.

But as I started marching up the trail that morning, I found myself in a spectacular mood, full of energy. Whatever the mystery illness had been that had taken me out so rapidly and intensely, it was long gone now. I was back, baby! The sun shone brightly and there wasn't a cloud in the sky.

Only a few miles into my hike, I rounded a corner, and there it was, an enormous black bear seated in the middle of the trail. It took one look at me and sprinted off in terror. *Wow!* My first trail bear! A few moments later, I ran into Stan the Man, a section hiker aspiring to eventually thru-hike. He'd brought a cooler of drinks out to the trail for the hikers, and I helped myself to an ice-cold Gatorade and a Coca-Cola. I downed the Gatorade as we chatted about life and the trail. He was enthusiastic to hear my story and his love for the AT was obvious. He told me he came out to do trail magic every year. As I said goodbye, I silently asked the trail gods to give this man the amazing experience that he deserved when he finally retired and could thru-hike himself.

I saved the Coke for a few miles later and drank it while I snacked under a fire tower. The carbonation and sugar were magic on my tongue. As I was finishing up, Horse texted to let me know there was big trail magic seven miles ahead. That lit a fire under me. I was trying to catch up with Horse anyway, so the lure of trail magic combined with the caffeine and sugar of the soda did the trick. I practically flew down the trail. I caught Horse at the trail magic, which was miraculously still set up, and helped myself to a heaping plate of picnic fare, much needed on this already double-digit-mile day.

In addition to Horse, I found Baba Ghanoush, Moss, Walker, and Steak there, chatting away and enjoying second and third portions. Baba told me that they planned to make it several more miles to a secret shelter on a farm that night and invited me to join them. They headed out shortly after I had arrived, having already been there for a couple of hours, but encouraged me to catch up later. If I made it, that would make 27.5 miles for the day.

I ate so much delicious food at the trail magic—veggie burgers, pasta salad, potato salad, fruit, and cake—that I practically had to roll myself out of there when I was finished. I packed myself out another Coca-Cola for later and got back to the trail. I drank the soda as evening began to fall and an incredible pink and orange sunset lit up the farmland around me. I saw my second trail bear, running through an open field toward a farmhouse. I was glad it was heading in the opposite direction as the trail and I was suddenly happy to do some extra miles from here, not wanting to camp near the bear.

I pulled out my phone and pressed play on Dua Lipa's self-titled album, both to help me pass the time and to warn any animals that might be out and about that I was near. Night fell, and I pushed on, grooving to the poppy music until I was stopped dead in my tracks. About a mile away from the secret shelter, as I was completely alone in the dark of the night, a pair of bright green, glowing eyes suddenly appeared up the trail. I couldn't tell what they belonged to, but I knew it was *big*. I clapped, I stomped, I yelled, and I shined my light up toward it, but it didn't budge. I stood, terrified, for several moments. I wasn't sure what to do.

Eventually, upon realizing that whatever it was wasn't going to move along on its own, I bravely charged forward. As I crept closer, I discovered that the owner of those huge, ominous eyes belonged to nothing more than a very large deer. It snorted at me and went on its way. I breathed a massive sigh of relief, chuckling as I continued up the trail. I had places to be.

I hiked through a big open field, decorated with the blinking lights of hundreds of fireflies. Fireworks lit up the night sky overhead. I felt like I must be sleepwalking; this was a dream. I soon completed my marathon day at the secret shelter on the farm where my friends still lay awake, waiting for me. They cheered as I walked up, arms raised in victory.

For the rest of the state, Horse, Baba, Steak, Walker, Moss, and I stayed together. This eclectic crew of two teens, two 20-somethings, and two 30-somethings was a blast. I hadn't laughed so hard since we'd lost Jukebox 2 in Virginia, and my worries about Wintergreen melted away. When I'd met Walker and Steak in Pennsylvania, I kind of dismissed them. What could I possibly have in common with two teenage boys? But in New Jersey, they quickly became dear friends. They were hilarious, lighthearted, and playful, and I adored them. And they worshiped Baba. While he tried to act as if they were pests following him up the trail, it was clear that he enjoyed having them around. They started calling him "Dad." I laughed hysterically the first time I heard it. Then, Baba changed Walker's name to Tortilla. He'd run out of toilet paper and had an emergency situation in the woods after eating some questionable meat from the grocery store. Not having the proper supplies, he used tortillas. And Tortilla was born.

A couple of nights into forming the New Jersey tramily, Baba got a wild idea. He'd heard that there was a drive-in movie theater in nearby Warwick, New York, and there was a rumor floating around that they let thru-hikers camp on site. The theater was just a few miles away by car. He thought we should go check it out. The others quickly agreed, but I was unsure. What if we got out there, and were stranded? Also, I was supposed to be making miles…. But the next thing I knew, Steak and Tortilla started taunting me with a new nickname, "Blowstick." "Blowstick is no fun," they teased me. That did it, I was in.

There was a farm store with treats for sale at the road crossing that led to Warwick. We stopped in for a popsicle and a cold beverage, and Baba began to chat up a couple of the young women who worked there, asking if they had any intel about the drive-in. They offered to drive us there in a couple of hours when they got off work.

As we strolled up to the drive-in entrance, packs strapped to our backs, a middle-aged man in a branded shirt walked up to us. He directed us to a line of cars where we could pay. About two seconds later, he called us back over, laughing. "I'm just kidding, you guys," he said. "For you, it's free. And you can camp on the top of that hill." He pointed and handed us a radio. From where I stood, it looked like the best seat in the house. He told us that we were welcome to set up and then take a trip over to the grocery store just a couple of blocks away. "We don't normally encourage that sort of thing," he told us. "But we know you guys are hungry." We had a blast, enjoying the warm summer evening as we huddled around the radio watching movies until deep in the night.

Hitchhiking is illegal in New York State, and we were warned that they were particularly strict about it in Warwick. So after a quick stop at a bagel shop in the morning, we made the executive decision to call a taxi to shepherd us back to the trail in New Jersey. After the day's hike, we officially crossed the border on the trail into New York, and I left this lively band of misfits behind.

We had a last supper of ice cream and frozen yogurt at a creamery just off the trail, and afterward, my friends hiked on as I stayed and waited for my friend Kristin to come to collect me. It was a sad goodbye, but Kristin was my best friend from college and still one of my most cherished friends, and because she lived several states away and was also a new mother, I didn't get to see her nearly as often as I would have liked. It was fitting that I'd get to see her while hiking the trail because Kristin was actually the very first person in my life to encourage me to follow my dream and hike the AT.

A few years before my trek, when I first started talking seriously about it, most people that I told brushed the idea off. But

Kristin found a book about the AT from the 1980s in a vintage bookstore. She bought it for me and stuck several notes inside of places that I should visit and of tasks that I should complete along the way, like getting my photo taken at McAfee Knob in Virginia. She mailed it to me in D.C., and I was over the moon. I showed it proudly to my then-boyfriend of two years. He decided to break up with me pretty much on the spot. He realized I might actually be serious about this undertaking, which meant that we were highly incompatible.

I promised to come for a visit as I hiked through New York, and in return, Kristin promised to whip me up a heaping plate full of strawberry shortcake. She lived on an apple orchard with her husband, Tim, and their young son, Lukas, about an hour's drive from the ice cream shop. I wanted to stop for my visit with her before the wine festival, so this was the time for it. I watched a bit forlornly as my friends marched off one by one. I was really going to miss them.

"You don't smell nearly as bad as I thought you would!" Kristin told me on the drive to her house. She even let me hug her. As someone who tried her best to have decent hygiene on the trail, this was a high compliment. I did insist on showering before all else once we arrived at her place, however. This was not an easy decision, because I knew that treats were waiting.

Kristin is an amazing cook, so she was the perfect person to visit along my journey. Every dish that she put in front of me was incredible. Each time she piled something new and delicious in front of me, such as her tortellini and fresh mozzarella salad, she laughed off my praise and proclaimed that these were the simplest of dishes. But I was in heaven. I ate to my heart's content and then I ate some more. It was glorious.

In between meals though, I had to get a few chores done. My gear had started to smell pretty rancid by this point, so Kristin hooked me up with a hose, a sponge, and a bucket of soapy water. I changed into my bikini, put my clothes in the washer, then headed for the backyard. I scrubbed and scrubbed the stench and stains out of my gear while enjoying a killer view of the Shawangunk Mountains. Kristin sat in the sun a safe distance away. "I've never seen you so happy," she told me.

After my chores were finished, I got some much-needed downtime as I filled Kristin in on everything that had happened on trail so far. My zero day on the farm flew by way too fast, and before I knew it, she was driving me back to the trail. I had just three days of hiking to go before my brother and sister-in-law would scoop me up for the Finger Lakes Wine Festival.

CHAPTER 24

I'm a native New Yorker so I feel guilty admitting this, but New York was my least favorite state on the entire Appalachian Trail. It was oppressively hot and muggy, had countless busy road crossings and pointless ups and downs, and the creek beds were nothing but dry, cracked mud flats. There was no water to be had except for the caches of gallon jugs that trail angels left behind. Those trail angels made hiking through the state possible when conditions otherwise wouldn't have allowed it. This was not the wilderness that I had cherished so much earlier on the trail. This was civilization.

I'd been having too much fun with the New Jersey crew, so when Kristin dropped me back on trail, I had to pull a couple of big-mile days to make it on time to the pickup locale for the wine festival. I hiked up and over the "stairway to heaven" and around the "lemon squeezer," a narrow passageway through huge rocks left behind long ago by glaciers. Most people hike through the squeezer, but with my oversized pack, I didn't think I'd fit, so I took a side trail around it. I also hiked through the zoo at Bear Mountain State Park, hitting the lowest point on the AT at 124 feet above sea level, and then across the Hudson River via the Bear Mountain Bridge.

The night before I was scheduled to get off trail for the festival, I camped on the grounds of the Graymoor Spiritual Life Center, the headquarters of the Franciscan Friars and Sisters of the

Atonement, a religious congregation of the Catholic Church. There, I ran into Foreman. I had not seen him since I sent him to the urgent care center in Pennsylvania to get treated for Lyme Disease, and I couldn't believe how different he looked. His face was full of color; tan replaced white. And he had so much more energy than I remembered. The antibiotics had done him good!

That Friday, as I popped out of the woods at AT mile 1,415, I found my brother, Andy, sister-in-law, Helena, niece, Corinne, and old buddy, JP, standing outside of their car, waiting for me. I'd wanted to bring Horse to the festival with me, but unfortunately, there was no room in the car for him and his pack, so he headed to New York City for the weekend instead. After hugs all around, I hopped into the back seat of the car and was handed a blue freezie pop. Corinne, just a year and a half old, sat next to me and insisted that I share my freezie pop with her. I obliged.

After a few hours on the road, we arrived in beautiful Watkins Glen for the festival. We set up our tents on the festival grounds, then headed to the local state park, where my parents had a huge, delicious barbecue dinner waiting. My mom, like Kristin, is also an amazing cook, and she loves to feed people, so she was another perfect person to visit while my hiker hunger was raging. My parents were there to watch Corinne and Shamrock, my younger brother Bryan's sweet beagle, while the rest of us enjoyed the festival for the weekend.

When we made it back to the festival grounds, several more of my friends were there waiting. I felt like the honored guest of the weekend. Everyone wanted to see me and hear firsthand how my trek was going. I felt like a celebrity. For the first time in months, I got to put on normal, non-hiking clothes. "You bitch!" said Jenn, one of my roommates from college. "You look so damn good." And I felt good. I finally had the body that I had always wanted. It had only taken 1,400 miles of hiking and three bouts of illness to get there. I put on some tight denim shorts, a crop top, and a sparkly tiara that I had thrown into the duffle that I packed for the festival before leaving D.C. for the trail. I was going to enjoy my trail body while it lasted.

The weekend went by in a flash. I had a blast reuniting with family and old friends, but alas, after we'd all had a little too much fun, it was time to head out. My dad generously drove me the four hours back to the trail. When we arrived back at mile marker 1,415, I asked if he'd like to come say hi to the trail with me. I wanted to share this big meaningful thing with him. He declined, laughing, and waved goodbye as he told me to be safe. *The ones who get it, get it,* I thought. *And the ones who don't, don't.*

I was soaked in sweat within five minutes of arriving back on trail. It was oppressively hot and muggy. But I heard from a couple of hikers hanging around a spigot not too far from where I got dropped off that Chef and Ibex were near, so that perked me up. Just a few trail miles ahead, I found them stealth camping in a stand of maple trees. They cheered as I hiked into camp, embracing me one after the other and lifting me off my feet into the air. I hadn't seen them in almost two weeks; we had so much to catch up on! Wintergreen, on the other hand, was nowhere to be seen. I hadn't heard from him since Delaware Water Gap. *He's avoiding me,* I thought. But a happy reunion ensued with Chef and Ibex as we swapped stories. That night, a medium-sized animal ran into the side of my tent. I peeked out to try to see what it was, but it was too quick for me. Whatever it was, it was clumsy.

There were two good things about New York. Number one, there were lakes everywhere. This was a huge help because it was so gosh darn hot there. Just when I thought I might puke from heat exhaustion, I'd stumble upon a lake that I could take a dip in to cool off. Number two, there were delis everywhere, often very near to the trail. Some of them even let hikers camp on their grounds, so you could wake up in the morning and snag a real coffee and a breakfast sandwich. I spent so much money in New York at those delis, but every penny was worth it.

In the morning, we planned to meet Wintergreen for a swim at Canopus Lake. It was another terribly hot and humid day, as all of the days on trail in New York were, and by the time I got to the lake, I was completely drenched in sweat again. I was relieved that this lake, with a swimming beach and outdoor showers, would be our first stop of the day. Wintergreen gave me a short, awkward hello when I found him at the snack bar, then wandered off. As had been the case in Harpers Ferry, this was not the reunion that I had been hoping for. I asked Chef if he thought I should try to talk to him. Chef had been thrilled when he found out that Wintergreen and I had gotten together; the man loves love. "You just got back," he told me. "I'd give him some time to come around. I can tell that he likes you. I think it will all work out."

So instead, I changed into my bikini and dipped into the cool waters of Canopus Lake with Ibex. As I waded back toward the shore, Chef called me over to where he was lying out on a towel. He asked me to work a knot out of his back by digging into it with a trekking pole. He groaned as I pushed down hard on the trekking pole, moving the handle around in a circular motion at his instruction.

Eddie, who we hadn't seen since Virginia, showed up with Tickle Me Elmo, her hiking partner who had, at the beginning of the trail, been a member of Warrior Expeditions, a nonprofit outdoor therapy program that takes veterans on long-distance outdoor expeditions. Elmo was traveling with his service dog, Kara, another of the few well-taken care of dogs that I met on the AT. They took a dip and then hung out with us on the beach for a while.

We tore ourselves away from the beach only after Ibex stood up in a panic, frantically brushing some invisible nuisance from her legs. "Ticks!" she cried. "A bunch of them!" She suspected that she'd stumbled into a nest. Just when I had begun to think New York might not be so bad.

This was high Lyme Disease country, and we weren't taking any chances. We quickly gathered our things and then headed to the changing rooms to get hiking ready. We hit the trail, intending to camp at a deli that night.

En route, we passed by a shelter, where we had no intention of stopping, but we were lured inside by a group of retirees who ran a volunteer trail crew. They were holding a picnic for hikers, with all the fixings. Chef, Ibex, and I sat with Eddie and Elmo and stuffed our faces. Wintergreen hiked onward, having no idea that the trail magic was there. We ate to our heart's content then began the arduous five-mile climb to the deli, which was about a half-mile off trail.

It was pitch dark by the time I got to the road crossing near the deli, so I was a bit nervous about making it there by myself. But I found Starburst just before the road crossing, so she joined me en route to the deli, and we camped next to each other for the night. The campsite behind the deli was loud, hot, buggy, and full of hikers. But it had a hose where we could rinse off, and of course, a deli breakfast waiting for us in the morning.

The next day, we hiked 15 miles to a road crossing, where Chef's dad waited to pick us up. Chef had talked his parents into letting us stay at their place for a couple of days while we slackpacked the trail. They were incredibly welcoming and accommodating, driving us to the trail each morning and picking us up each afternoon that we stayed with them. They lived in a massive, historic farmhouse on hundreds of acres of forest, had two adorable dogs, Diesel and Blackjack, and the best part was that they had an Olympic-sized in-ground pool on the premises. Diesel, their sweet, goofy German Shepherd, would run circles around the pool as we took turns jumping off the diving board.

We finished the New York section of the trail while we stayed with them and hiked through the majority of Connecticut's 50 miles as well. Horse rejoined us during this time. He'd gotten a bit farther ahead on the trail with Baba and crew because Baba had begun to push some 20-plus mile days. This pace made Horse anxious, so he decided to slow down and wait for us. Slowing down and waiting also made him anxious. Wintergreen continued to keep his distance from me, which left me feeling disheartened.

Connecticut was gentle on us, especially since we didn't have to carry our full packs. The terrain was fairly flat, the air temperatures were a tad cooler than in New York, we often hiked next to a river or a stream, and there were wildflowers, like daisies and bee balm, every which way that we looked. In our days after slackpacking, we'd come home to Chef's parents' house and there would be snacks waiting for us, like chips and homemade French onion dip. We were living the high life.

I weighed myself while at Chef's parents' house. I was down to 119 pounds. I was just 15 pounds lighter than when I started the trail, but my body had completely changed. My legs were pure muscle and my ribs were poking out. At that moment, I thought I looked fantastic. But looking back on photos, I can see how unhealthily thin I was getting. The big miles and illnesses were beginning to take a toll on my physical health.

Despite the wonderful time that I had at Chef's parents' house, whenever I was away from the trail, even to stay at a gorgeous mansion in the countryside, I missed it. Chef's parents were incredible to us, and I deeply loved their swimming pool. But I missed being able to set my tent up anywhere that I wanted and the freedom to set my own hiking pace. I couldn't dilly-dally in the woods while we were slackpacking, or I'd make everyone wait, including Chef's dad. So when Chef's parents decided that it was time to take us back to the trail for good, I was relieved.

CHAPTER 25

I could feel a difference in the terrain and the ecosystem immediately as I crossed into Massachusetts. We'd been spoiled by fairly flat terrain since West Virginia, but in Massachusetts, the marshes, bogs, and farms that we'd grown accustomed to were slowly replaced with higher mountains, deep ravines, and pine forests. My legs had to learn to climb again; they'd gotten spoiled and weak by the flatter terrain throughout the mid-Atlantic and the slackpacking in New York and Connecticut.

Zack, Ibex's boyfriend, showed up for a visit as we crossed into Massachusetts. We'd been waiting for his arrival for one special reason: so that we could throw a forest rave! We'd decided that our tramily needed some bonding time, and what better way to bond than dancing the night away? On our first night in Massachusetts, we found the perfect secluded pine grove in which to do it.

Ibex and I had been trying to throw our rave for a few states now, but the timing had just never worked out with all of us in one place at one time and in the right mindset to do it. But in Massachusetts, we were finally all back together, Zack was able to join us, and now, we just needed to find the perfect spot for the party. A couple of states back, I had ordered a big package of glow sticks, a portable speaker, and some brightly colored, flashing jelly rings from Amazon. I had them delivered to one of the trail towns that we passed through and Ibex helped me to convince the other tramily members to carry some of the supplies in their packs. Many hands make light work, after all.

We passed around the party favors, then stood in a circle, waiting for the rollercoaster to come. Zack acted as the DJ for the night, pumping out electronic dance music. I attempted to crack some glow sticks, which Chef had been carrying, to find that every single one of them had already been cracked, and they emitted no light. I wondered if he had broken them out of spite since he was such a weight weenie.

One time in Virginia, I had snuck a tiny tube of liquid soap into his pack because his processed meat and cheese sweats were getting to me. I could usually smell Chef before I saw him. Some people on the trail smelled very little, despite not showering, and some smelled quite a bit. Chef was one of those people who smelled quite a bit. I thought the soap could help. But he could immediately tell there was something extra in his pack and disposed of it. He was like the Princess and the Pea. So I suspected he wasn't too keen on carrying those glow sticks for us.

Not to be kept down, I started handing out flashing jelly rings to everyone and attaching the extras to trekking poles, which Ibex and I assembled into a circle. Not long after, a wave of warm, fuzzy energy washed over me. I hugged each and every one of my tramily members and told them that I loved them, so very much. "I knew you were going to be like this," said Ibex. But she squeezed me tight, smiling.

Chef was shocked to find himself getting in touch with his feelings. Except he didn't call them feelings, he called them "ideas." He kept calling me and Ibex over to wrap us in big bear hugs and to tell us that he had many "ideas" about us. "You two are the sisters I never had," he told us. Our hearts melted. We loved him too.

Horse, though, was possibly the most high-spirited of the bunch. He was able to truly let loose, riding a flashing trekking pole around as if *it* were the horse. And he inserted himself into the middle of the group hugs that Chef initiated. It was incredibly touching to watch him and Chef bond. It made me love them so much more to see that they also loved each other. The group of us danced for hours, enjoying the cool summer breeze on our skin and reaching our hands up toward the starry sky.

Wintergreen was the most muted of the crew. He didn't seem to be as affected by the festivities of the night as the rest of us. Or maybe he just didn't have strong feelings for us, I don't know.

At the end of the night though, Wintergreen came to my tent. "Do you wanna snuggle?" he asked. I was surprised. I had thought whatever had been between us was long over. He was barely speaking to me these days and I couldn't remember the last time he'd looked into my eyes. I thought I'd caught him checking Ibex out in her bikini at Chef's parents' house. But I decided to give it one last shot. He came with me into my tent, immediately kissing me. My skin was on fire with his touch. It was the most intense night of my life. For the entire time that we were together, I felt like my body was going to explode into stardust and I was going to become part of the night sky. I had never felt that way physically, before or since. It was incredible.

I could have stayed locked in his embrace forever. But eventually, he got overheated and pushed me away. I probably should have asked the hard questions at that moment, but I was in no state to do so. This is also a pattern that I struggle to break in relationships; I often can't bring myself to initiate difficult conversations until they reach a boiling point. I chugged some water and fell into a fitful sleep, under the light of a flashing jelly ring that was still attached to the top of my tent, which a huge moth was flitting around.

Wintergreen tried to force us to hike 17 miles the next day. Even after a rave, when we stayed up most of the night and didn't

leave camp until 10:30 am, he couldn't relax and let us take it easy.
But none of us were really in the right form to be pushing miles;
we'd barely gotten any sleep and we were dehydrated. Ibex and
Zack ducked into Great Barrington to visit with her mom and pick
up some pastries. Meanwhile, Wintergreen rushed ahead as Horse
tried to keep up. Chef and I took the caboose and took our time. I
watched as a young bear sprinted across a golden field and was
briefly stuck waiting for several minutes as a gargantuan eastern
diamondback rattlesnake stretched itself out in the middle of the
trail.

Wintergreen and Horse camped together that night at Tom
Leonard Shelter. Chef and I stealth camped together a couple of
miles south of that. And Ibex camped alone back near Great
Barrington. I ate not one, not two, but three packs of Indomie that
night for dinner. My hiker hunger was starting to get out of
control.

The next day, Wintergreen demanded via text that we
make it to the Upper Goose Pond Cabin, 21 miles ahead for him,
and 23 miles ahead for me and Chef. Thru-hikers can sleep inside
the cabin, which sits on Upper Goose Pond, and are served a
pancake breakfast in the morning by the caretaker. I was extremely
frustrated. Chef and I were two miles behind, and Ibex was even
further behind than us, and Wintergreen wanted us to do a 20-plus-
mile day. And for what? Because he wanted to get to the next town
so he could park himself in front of a television and drink beer and
eat a cheeseburger.

Chef and I hiked on our own for most of the morning, and
he found me sitting on a rock face, 13 miles into the day,
despondent. "I'm so tired," I told him. "I don't know how I'm
going to hike 10 more miles, and I don't know why I should! And
who knows when Ibex is going to be able to catch up! I'm so sick
of going at his pace."

Chef listened, as he did so well, and made me a strong coffee, adding some mochaccino-flavored protein powder. He was always worried that I wasn't getting enough protein. "Let's hike together for a while," he suggested. A couple of miles later, he asked how I was feeling. "Better," I said.

And then he asked me, "Hey, didn't you tell me that you wanted to do a 30-mile day at some point on the trail?" I told him that I had, but now that we were back in the higher mountains, hiking tougher terrain, I figured I had missed my chance.

The next thing I knew, Chef and I were plotting to hike 30 miles that very day, in secret. We'd stop to cook dinner on the side of the trail around 7:00 pm, and he'd make me another coffee. We'd pass Upper Goose Pond Cabin right on by, and we'd simply tell Wintergreen that we were camping on the side of the trail and that we'd catch him tomorrow. He would assume that we were behind him, but in reality, we would be several miles ahead of him. Bright and early in the morning, we'd hike the remaining 14 miles into Dalton.

Wintergreen *loved* being the first to reach town. It was his favorite thing. But if we could pull this off, we'd get there hours ahead of him. It would drive him crazy. We wouldn't tell him where we were until we were already in town so that he couldn't rush and catch us. We already had a hotel room booked, and this way, we would actually get some time to spend in it and relax instead of arriving around nightfall and being rushed out the next morning by Wintergreen. It was diabolical, and I was in. Nothing energized me like a strong "bro coffee" and an evil plan.

Chef stayed with me for the rest of the day and night, helping to push me forward. We took turns playing songs, tried to identify glowing animal eyes in the night, talked about anything and everything under the sun, and giggled and giggled about our trickery.

Around 10:00 pm, about two hours before we'd finish our 30-mile day in a soft pine grove, as our energy levels were waning, the trail gods outdid themselves. We hiked up on a huge metal trash can sitting in between two coolers on the side of the trail, with a sign letting us know this was trail magic from someone named Commander. First, we peeked into the coolers. Nothing was inside but some jugs of water. "Bummer," I said. But we figured since we were there, we might as well fill up our water bottles and throw out our trash.

I unhooked the chain from the top of the trash can and pulled it open. My eyes widened in shock. It wasn't trash inside. It was every kind of treat that you could imagine. Chips, cupcakes, Twinkies, maple sugar candy, Pop-Tarts, pastries, you name it. We must have stood there for half an hour, gobbling down as many treats as we could stomach. With 26 miles down and four more to go, this sugar rush was more than I ever could have hoped for. I couldn't believe our luck. The trail was really looking out for us that night.

It was a beautiful night, and thanks to Commander and Little Debbie, the next four miles came much easier than the last few. We set up our tents in the dark and lay down to rest in a perfect pine grove next to a babbling brook. I slept the night through until Chef woke me up at 6:00 am to crank out the last 14 miles to Dalton. I was exhausted and stiff, but I knew that we had to get a move on if we wanted to ensure that Wintergreen didn't catch us before Dalton.

Our first stop in town was the local sub shop, where we got a foot-long sub each to celebrate. We snapped a selfie, and Chef texted it to the group. We couldn't stop laughing. We knew that Wintergreen was going to be pissed. We, on the other hand, were thrilled with ourselves.

After we finished our hard-earned meal, we scooted over to our hotel room, which was booked under Wintergreen's name.

We checked in, took showers, and kicked back with a shared six-pack of beer. When Wintergreen showed up hours later, he grilled us on how we were able to check into *his* hotel room. Rather than complain directly about our devious behavior and rush to town ahead of him, he focused instead on the hotel room, sighing loudly and threatening to complain to management about it. Ibex caught up before we checked out the next morning.

A couple of days later, we ascended Mount Greylock, the highest point in the state at 3,491 feet. I was reunited with Tortilla on the climb up, and we posed for a rainy, foggy photo in front of the Mount Greylock Veterans War Memorial Tower at the top together. He joined my tramily as we got a hot lunch at the lodge inside. The day was surprisingly cold, so we were especially grateful for the warm meal. Ten miles and a few hours later, I found myself standing at the Vermont border, where a big wooden sign welcomed passersby to the Long Trail. This was no longer just the AT; we'd be sharing the trail with Long Trail hikers for the next 105 miles. From there, the trails would split. The AT would continue on another 500 miles to Maine, and the Long Trail would continue another 165 miles to the Canadian border of Vermont.

CHAPTER 26

I was excited to hike into Vermont for a couple of reasons. First and foremost, it was a state that I'd never been to before, and I'd always heard that it was stunning. Second, we were finally going to get to meet the Twelve Tribes and stay at their hiker hostel. I was incredibly curious about them, especially after they ignored us at Trail Days.

Vermont was immediately much muddier than Massachusetts. Just as Pennsylvania becomes Rocksylvania to hikers, Vermont becomes Vermud. It absolutely covered the trail. Sometimes, the mud would be thigh deep. I felt like I was always covered in it and would wade into a stream each night that I could to wash the stuff off my legs before crawling into my tent. The climbs also suddenly became much higher and more difficult, and the mix of trees that we'd seen in the woods of Massachusetts turned into pine-dominant forests in Vermont. There were ponds and lakes everywhere. We were finally back in the wilderness, as we had been in the South, and wildlife started to become more prevalent. Beavers dammed up creeks, we started to hear the forlorn calls of loons in the evenings when we camped near water, and we began to see moose prints and droppings on the trail. I was dying to see a moose. We watched as several naked hikers passed by us on the trail. Apparently, hiking naked is a popular pastime in Vermont.

We started to see the first southbound thru-hikers of the season in Vermont, and people who were keen to get a move on with finishing the trail started to rush by us. Easy, the Manhattanite who'd lost his bear bag in the Grayson Highlands in southwest Virginia, camped with me and Ibex for a night after a 25-mile day. He was planning to hike another 25 miles the next day.

Again, I was getting increasingly fed up with the pace that we were hiking. This had been an ongoing issue since North Carolina, but it was coming to a head. Each day was another push, another rush to the next town. I was constantly exhausted, and I was frustrated and felt like I didn't have a voice in the tramily when it came to how many miles we'd hike each day. I had no time to stop and smell the roses and swim in any of the gorgeous swimming holes that we were passing. I'd voice my frustrations, and nothing would change. When Ibex and I tried to protest the mileage planned for one day, Horse said to us, "Well we got you this far."

"No, we got ourselves this far," I said indignantly. I wasn't going to let him take credit for my accomplishments. It wasn't him hiking 20-plus-mile days into the night after two bouts of the stomach flu in Virginia. Or him hiking a marathon to the secret shelter in New Jersey, haunted by glowing eyes in the night. Or him dragging himself into Delaware Water Gap after sweating through all of his clothes and his sleeping bag and while feeling like dying. Or him hiking a 30-mile day fueled by Chef's bro coffee. He could go fly a kite.

Each time we'd get back into the woods from town, Wintergreen would have a new excuse as to why we'd have to rush to the next town. A new piece of gear would be waiting, he needed to make an important phone call, he needed to handle something for his condo that he was renting out while he was on trail... there was always another reason that we all had to run ahead to civilization.

Wintergreen's tent started to leak, so he slept in my tent for a couple of nights before he was able to pick up some seam sealer in town. He didn't touch me. He barely even spoke to me even while lying two inches from me. I heard through the grapevine that he was flirting with Jukebox over text and trying to get her to come catch up and hike with him. He was still trying to finish the trail by Labor Day. One day, he changed the group plan of where we were going to camp out for the night. He told everyone but me.

I wandered around the shelter where we had been planning to stay for a half hour before I gave up and continued up the trail. The whole tramily was at the next campsite. I had no idea that they were going to be there, and no one had bothered to tell me. There was also no space for me. "I thought you knew that the plan had changed," Ibex told me. But I didn't, and it wasn't the first time in recent days that something like this had happened. I was hurt. I continued up the trail for another few tenths of a mile, throwing my stuff down in a pine grove near the Glastenbury Mountain Lookout tower. I needed some space. I sulked in my tent as some friendly, sweet guys camping nearby who I had not met before— Sherpa, Bernie, and Bad Bunny—kindly tried to coax me out.

I climbed up to the top of the tower, looking out at the pine-covered mountains in the distance and enjoying the sunset as the summer breeze blew through my hair. Ibex, Horse, and Wintergreen came up a little while later to check out the tower. They joined me at the top, and we took the last ever photo of the four of us. I'm smiling in the photo, but I wasn't smiling on the inside.

A couple of days later, after a fantastic day of hiking, I showed up at camp, and the same thing happened again. They weren't there. I had been hiking in the back of the group, but again, I found myself abandoned. I was at a loss. A Long Trail hiker told me they'd overheard them saying that they were going to hike into Manchester Center that night. I was enraged; we weren't supposed to hike there until tomorrow, and no one had told me. I felt like a fool.

I hadn't wanted to stay at that particular campsite anyway because the tent sites were on wooden platforms, and those did not work well for my semi-freestanding tent. I had to stake the back of the tent out, and I couldn't do that on planks of wood. So I shouldered my pack and decided that I was going to hike as close to Manchester Center as possible and have a night to myself. I'd go into town bright and early in the morning to do my laundry and get some food. I wasn't interested in staying in a crowded hotel room in town; I wanted to be in the woods. I'd do what I needed to do and get back out on trail. The tramily could do what they wanted.

I found a gorgeous, secluded campsite between two streams, and set up for the night. It was a little way off the trail so I wasn't worried that someone would walk up on me, so I did something that I had yet to do on the entire AT. I stripped down and rushed into the cool stream completely naked, submerging my body completely under the water. It was incredibly freeing, and the cold water helped to wash away some of the frustration that I was feeling. I scrubbed my face and brushed my hair, and lay out on my camp towel to dry, still sans clothes.

In the morning, I walked the short distance to the closest road crossing to town, put my knife and my wallet in my pocket, and did another first. I stuck out my thumb, hitchhiking solo. I was picked up by the first car that passed. I asked my driver, a friendly college-aged man, to drop me off at the laundromat. I put my clothes in the washer and wandered over to the bakery next door for some breakfast. I hung out there until my laundry was done, then I packed up my things and walked uptown to the grocery store to resupply. I ran into Horse and Baby, who we hadn't seen since Pennsylvania, and joined them at a Thai restaurant for lunch.

I tried to talk with Horse about how I was feeling and why I was upset, but he didn't seem to get it or want to listen. He told me that they had not actually come to Manchester the night before. They'd all taken a break together, sitting on some boulders and chatting with some Long Trailers a couple of miles before the campsite. That was why I hadn't seen them. I had overreacted in this instance, but I was still really upset. I felt like I was getting left behind more and more often, and in truth, I thought that Wintergreen was purposefully trying to push me out of the tramily. He wanted everything to be his way or the highway, and I challenged that. Plus, it was pretty clear that he'd lost interest in me. And I was angry at Ibex too because I felt like she was letting him call all of the shots, and she stood by while he tried to get rid of me.

As I was walking through downtown Manchester Center, I heard someone call my name. But it wasn't Glowstick that I heard, it was Audrey. I turned, confused. "Are you the Audrey that worked at Camp JK?" asked a large blond man, towering over me. "Yeah…," I responded. "I'm Carl. I was a counselor-in-training when you worked there. You look exactly the same!" It couldn't be. The Carl that I remembered looked nothing like this Carl. That Carl had definitely been less tall and had decidedly less hair, and a baby face. But this Carl was huge and hairy and full-grown! Of course, he'd been just 15 when I first met him at camp. That was a decade ago. I supposed that he must be in his mid-20s now. My, how things change. "I go by the Professor now," he told me. We chatted for a bit, and I told him that I hoped to run into him out on the trail to catch up more.

Horse told me and Baby that Chef was going on a Tinder date in town. We caught a glimpse of him standing with a brunette in street clothes next to a beat-up red car. Baby and I decided to spy on them a bit and followed them into a breakfast restaurant. We sipped coffee and munched on pastries while occasionally glancing over to see how things were going. I thought she was cute and that he seemed engaged. Maybe Chef would find love on the trail after all. Once we finished our coffees, we rushed out of there, giggling. We'd had our fun.

Ibex and Wintergreen showed up as we were hanging out in the town square, but I was still too angry about the events of the previous week to speak to them. I decided that I was going to head back to the trail, so I started walking back to the other side of town to catch a ride. Baby asked if he could hike out with me and, of course, I agreed. Horse caught up before we'd managed to snag a ride, so he came along as well. We got back to the trail and hiked over a mountain located at the Bromley Mountain ski resort together, and onward a few miles down to a shelter next to a creek. We got a text from Chef saying that he was planning to stay in town for the night with his date. We didn't hear a peep from Ibex and Wintergreen and wondered if they would show up at the shelter.

Horse got off the trail the next day to visit a friend. He'd catch us by Rutland, the next town, he told me. Baby and I hiked together all week. We talked about life, jobs, and relationships, and he let me vent about what was going on with the tramily and offered up some perspective and sage advice. He was much younger than me, only in his mid-20s, but he was wise beyond his years and a huge comfort. And he was a ton of fun. We swam in every lake and pond that we could that week, split a small box of red wine as we leaned against some trees at camp one night, chatting into the dark, and tried to gather intel from the southbounders as they passed by. One particularly helpful southbounder shared a key piece of information with us: the Yellow Deli Restaurant would close at 3:00 pm on Friday and would not reopen until noon on Sunday. We were loosely scheduled to arrive there on a Saturday, so we knew that we had to find a way to get there sooner.

Chef caught up with us a couple of days later. I laid out the
incidents that had upset me so much lately, and Chef listened
intently, nodding. He understood. He apologized and proposed that
he talk with the tramily about our recent lack of communication,
how it needed to be improved, and how everyone needed to have a
say in our daily plans. Because I was still so upset, he volunteered
to lead the conversation. I felt much better. I had Chef back. He
also regaled Baby and I with tales of his date and went into detail
about their romantic encounter under a bridge. I will leave it at
that.

We checked out our trail guides and realized that we could
get to Rutland a little sooner without pushing any huge miles if we
exited the trail at Killington Mountain, rather than the road
crossing that we had been planning to hitch in from. We could
walk .2 miles uphill from a shelter, then catch the gondola at the
top of the mountain, which the resort lets thru-hikers ride for free.
It would take us to the bottom of the resort, where there was a
public bus that we could take into Rutland.

We set up our tents at Cooper Lodge Shelter on Thursday
night, then carried out this plan in the morning. Chef was
especially excited to ride the gondola because he'd been skiing at
Killington as a kid. I was just excited to get to the Yellow Deli
before it closed.

We arrived at the Twelve Tribes hostel to be greeted by a
short, middle-aged, charismatic man named Aish. He was one of
the warmest people that I had ever met. He told us that the hostel
was by donation, guests weren't required to pay, and that we were
encouraged to help around the hostel for free snacks and treats. He
handed us each a glass of the most delicious iced tea that I'd ever
tasted. It was fresh and fruity, and I thought I detected notes of
lemongrass. He gave us a tour of the hostel and showed us to our
quarters. There was a men's bunkroom and a women's bunkroom,
so I was on my own. We promised to meet in the restaurant below

in a few minutes. The women's bunkroom was nearly empty, so I had my pick of the beds. The only other person inside was a sweet, pretty 20-something named Blackbird. She was hiking the trail with her fiancé, and he was across the hall in the men's room.

Chef, Baby, and I met downstairs in the Yellow Deli restaurant and ordered just about everything on the menu. We were served by a young woman named Derusha. We learned that she had originally been hiking the AT southbound the year before, but when she arrived at the Yellow Deli, she stayed. She seemed happy; she was friendly and always had a smile on her face, but I thought I caught a glimpse of her dropping the mask a couple of times.

I've read that when they join the community, Twelve Tribes members have to give up all of their money and worldly possessions to the group. They also get a new name, and they're supposed to cut contact with outsiders. Allegedly, they don't treat their women or children very well. There were also dark rumors about them swirling on the trail. For example, I was told by another hiker that if you stay at the hostel for more than two nights, they assign you a secret "special friend" that would show up in places they thought you'd be. You were meant to think these surprise meetings were serendipitous when in reality, they were completely calculated and used as tools to suck you in. I'm not sure if this is true, but this and other things that I've heard about them would certainly give me pause if I was considering joining the group or one like it.

However, the food was incredible, and the members were certainly kind to us hikers. I'm still dreaming about their sweet potato pound cake. Aish even invited us to their Friday night Sabbath celebration, a festive dinner, singalong, and dancing event at their community house. Baby, Chef, and I took them up on it, piling into their bus with several other hikers who were staying at the hostel that evening.

From the moment we arrived, they started pouring us tea, and they didn't stop pouring us tea until we left. We were all asked to stand in a circle with the community members, and people were invited to talk about what they were thankful for that week. Next, the community members sang joyful group songs in unison. They served us a delicious meal made with fresh ingredients from their farm, and each table of hikers had at least one community member seated with them. They invited us to ask any questions that we'd like about life in the community. We sat with Love, the chapter's baker. He gave us a bit of his back story and explained that the community can send a member to any chapter that might need them. This chapter needed a baker, which is how he ended up in Rutland. After dinner, we were invited to take part in group dances. We swung each other around and around and around. I found myself howling with laughter. It was so much fun.

After the celebration, as the bus dropped us back off at the hostel, Chef grabbed me and Baby and told us that we were going to get a drink with Ibex, Wintergreen, Horse, and Zack, who was back for a visit, at a nearby bar. I sat at the opposite end of the table from Ibex and Wintergreen. I was still angry with them, especially after they had disappeared for the week without so much as a text and I didn't want to pretend that everything was okay. I learned that while Chef had told them to hop off the trail at Killington so that we could all go back out to hike together, they'd ignored his instructions and hiked six more miles up the trail to a different road crossing. Then, Wintergreen had set up a day of slackpacking for just the four of them. I was fuming. Even Chef was cross. Baby was just trying not to get caught in the crossfire.

I had a chat with some of the women in my bunkhouse later, telling them about all that had transpired. "Oh girl, you need to get away from him," they said. I knew they were right. It didn't seem like it was going to be that hard to do so, either, since Wintergreen was making alternate plans without me and Chef.

The next morning, after I picked up an overstuffed care package of delicious snacks from my aunt Kay at the post office, Chef, Baby, and I caught a ride back to the trail and resumed hiking northbound. Chef would handle everything regarding the tramily, he told me. And he said that he could tell that Ibex was upset too, and that I was going to have to talk to her. I knew that he was right.

Before we left, Chef received a handwritten letter from his date in Manchester Center. His hiking shorts were coming apart at the seams and she had included a piece of fabric to sew them up with. Apparently, she had rubbed it against her "naughty bits" for good luck. Chef drove women crazy. They were always giving him snacks, offering him rides, or complimenting him. But you couldn't even fault them, because Chef is such a genuinely kind, genuinely sweet person. I think he just exudes that energy out into the universe and people pick up on it. He was touched by her letter, but when she started texting him about moving to Maui, he knew he needed to be direct and cut her loose.

Because Ibex, Zack, Wintergreen, and Horse were slackpacking, they were moving southbound. So inevitably, we ran into them on the trail that day. Wintergreen was first. I was hiking with Chef at the time, so I hid halfway behind him. Chef made small talk, but he was mad that Wintergreen had gone behind his back to plan the slackpack without us. Wintergreen barely glanced in my direction. A while later, I ran into Ibex and Zack and I stopped to talk with them. I didn't want to be fighting with Ibex. This was our first and only real fight of the entire trail, and it sucked. We began to hash things out. Zack has a calming presence, so his being there helped. Ibex asked if Wintergreen had talked to me. I told her that no, he had not. She seemed flustered. "He was supposed to talk to you!" she said.

"Well, he didn't," I told her. Hesitantly, she told me what she'd learned over the past week while hiking with him. They'd secretly stayed the night in Manchester Center while Baby and I hiked out because Wintergreen wanted to watch a soccer game on TV. He grilled her about why I was so grumpy all of a sudden. "Are you kidding me?" she asked. "This is your fault!"

She called him out on his behavior, and he denied that he was to blame. "I don't have any feelings for her," he said coldly. "I was never looking for any romantic involvement on the trail."

When Ibex relayed this to me, my heart shattered into a million pieces. This was nothing that I hadn't gathered on my own after the way he'd been behaving. But to hear it out loud from someone else was devastating. I cried for a week. He'd been so different in the South when he would set his tent up next to mine each night, wait for me at shady water crossings, and gaze deep into my eyes. I'd hiked with him for almost five months by this point, and I felt like I didn't know him at all. What I had initially liked so much about Wintergreen was how kind, genuine, and open he seemed. Before anything had happened between us, we had been friends. And while Chef trolled Tinder for ladies, Wintergreen had signaled a distaste for that behavior. On top of that, his parents were amazing to us. I suddenly felt like it had all been a façade.

"I'm done with him," I said. "I'm not doing this anymore." I told Ibex and Zack that I would not continue to hike with Wintergreen, though I would not pressure Ibex to leave the group if that's not what she wanted. Personally, though, I was no longer going to be pushed into doing huge miles so that Wintergreen could make it from town to town as quickly as possible. I wasn't going to stand around while he texted other women, inviting them to come hike with him. And I wasn't going to pretend that nothing was wrong.

Ibex didn't even have to think about it, bless her soul. "I started the trail with you," she told me. "And I'm going to finish it with you. I'll tell him and Horse tonight."

I had to have the same difficult conversation with Chef at camp that night. I knew that Chef was closer with me and Ibex than with Wintergreen and Horse, but I also knew that he wasn't ready to give up on the tramily. "I'll talk to him," he told me. "If we can't work this out, I don't know, maybe I'll go off on my own. I don't want to upset anyone or take sides." I was devastated. I couldn't lose Chef too.

Ibex relayed the information to Horse and Wintergreen over beers at the Long Trail Inn. They were completely shocked. Horse chose to stay with Wintergreen as I knew that he would. They were both on a schedule and wanted to finish the trail sooner rather than later.

A couple of days later, once Ibex had rejoined us and Horse and Wintergreen had gone ahead of us on the trail, I received an angry, accusatory text from Wintergreen. It sent me into another fit of tears. I showed it to Chef, and he got angry.

"What the hell!" he shouted. "I told him what he needed to do to fix this. I told him that he needed to talk to you and apologize for hurting you. This is not what we talked about!" I hoped this would change his mind about leaving and going off on his own.

I sat by a water source, refilling my bottles later that day, when Chef and Ibex hiked down into the ravine from above. Ibex had caught me crying in my tent that morning, and I could hear her telling Chef about it. "I'm right here," I called. This was not a conversation that I wanted to eavesdrop on. I felt bad enough about the situation as it was. I told them I'd let them talk as I headed up the trail, bound in just a few miles for the New Hampshire border.

But first, we had a stop to make. Ibex and I had missed out on jumping off the James River Footbridge in Virginia, but we had another chance to get our thrills. The AT crosses the White River about 10 miles south of the New Hampshire border. There is tape on the bridge over the river signifying where it is allegedly safe to jump from and we'd heard of hikers ahead of us doing it, including

Wintergreen and Horse. So when we arrived at the bridge, we changed into our swimsuits and walked back up to the bridge. I was ready to feel anything but heartbreak, and there was no way I was going to wimp out when Wintergreen had done it. Plus, I figured the adrenaline would certainly take my mind off things.

I was scared out of my mind. Ibex and I made Baby go first, seeing as how he was the youngest and therefore would recover best if something went wrong. He didn't hesitate. He hopped over the bridge and plunged into the water below, cheering as he resurfaced. I was next. I climbed over the handrails of the bridge, shaking. I put my feet on the tape as I held on tight to the rails with my hands. It took me three tries to get myself to let go of the bridge, but I finally leaped off the bridge into the water. Before I knew it, I was popping back up to the surface. It was such a rush. I felt like I could do anything. I swam to shore and Ibex followed me into the deep channel. Baby and I whooped as she jumped.

Later that day, we marched over the Connecticut River bridge, crossing from Vermont into Hanover, New Hampshire. Vermont, though spectacularly beautiful, had been rough on me. But I had made it through, and I was still incredibly grateful to be living this life of adventure on trail. Heartbreak or not, the AT was still where I was supposed to be.

CHAPTER *27*

A couple of days into New Hampshire, Ibex and I lay
under a waterfall, letting the cold water wash over us. It felt like
the clean start that I needed.

   I tried to reach out to Horse in the days that followed the
tramily breakup, but he wouldn't talk to me. He was angry at me
for breaking up the tramily, and not considering his feelings in the
process. At least, that's what I heard from Chef and Ibex. I knew
that I had put him in an unfair position, and since he wouldn't
answer his phone, I tried to express over text how sorry I was. It
was evident from his silent treatment how much I had hurt him.
This was unfortunately the end of my friendship with Horse; we
never spoke again. I deeply regretted that, and it was something
that haunted me as I worked to get over the Wintergreen situation
and move on with my life. I knew this was all partially my fault,
and I hated that by breaking up the tramily, I had inadvertently
broken the hearts of these people that I had come to love so much.
Ibex was sad, Chef was sad, Horse was sad, and I was sad. I never
wanted that.

   I was so deeply grateful to Ibex and Chef for sticking with
me through such a tough situation. They didn't have to, and I knew
that. I was also grateful that we had picked up Baby just as we lost
Horse and Wintergreen. We needed some fresh blood, and it felt
like the trail was throwing us a bone in bringing Baby to us at
exactly the right time.

While Vermont had been challenging, New Hampshire was next level. As we entered the White Mountains, the climbs got steeper, the trail got rockier, and the air temperatures got colder. This section through the Whites of New Hampshire and Southern Maine is widely recognized as the most difficult of the entire Appalachian Trail. For many hikers, it's also their favorite section of the trail. We were about to find out what we were made of.

Our first climb into the Whites was Mount Moosilauke. That ascent requires hikers to climb 3,500 feet over about 4.5 miles. I had hiked up to the top of this mountain years ago with my brother, Andy, and sister-in-law, Helena, when I was in decidedly worse shape, so I knew that I would be fine. Helena, not much of a hiker, had even made it to the top back then. I thought she might break up with Andy by the time we got back to the car though.

I was right to be confident; I cruised easily up this climb. Several hikers that I'd met at the Yellow Deli, including Blackbird, were standing at the Moosilauke sign. They cheered me on as I finished my ascent. This would turn out to be one of the easiest climbs of this entire section though. The climbs to follow were the ones that I needed to be worried about.

Baba Ghanoush was ahead of me by about a week by this point, and he was sending intel backward. "The Kinsmans are the toughest climbs out here," he told me. "Be ready for that." South Kinsman was especially brutal, he said.

He wasn't kidding. You wouldn't know it from looking at their elevation profiles, but getting to the top of the Kinsmans doesn't require hiking. It requires scrambling up and down slick boulders. My short stature gave me a huge disadvantage in this section. While Chef was often able to step right up from one boulder to the next, I was climbing hands over feet. I thought back to Miss Janet, and how she told me that the Whites humble even the strongest of hikers. I'd only just arrived, and I could already tell that she was right.

As I made it, huffing and puffing, to the top of South Kinsman, I looked out into the distance. All I could see in any direction was white. The mountain was completely socked in. The same thing happened a couple of days later, when I climbed up to the top of Franconia Ridge, allegedly one of the most incredible views of the entire AT. Aside from a few peekaboo glimpses at the mountains as the wind blew the mist briefly out of place, I couldn't see a darn thing at the top of the ridge. That was after climbing up stone step after stone step for hours to get there.

When the weather cooperated, New Hampshire was incredible. The day that I hiked through the Presidential Range and up Mount Washington, which allegedly has "the worst weather in the world," was one of the best days I had on the entire trail. The mountain is rumored to have just five perfect weather days per year, and I got one of them. My tramily got a gorgeous, shirtless, blue-sky photo at the Mount Washington sign at the top. We were freezing cold during the photo shoot, but still. Chef, Ibex, and I, determined to get a clear view of the Perseids meteor shower at its peak, camped above tree line that night. I didn't see any shooting stars, and we froze that night, but our spectacularly clear view of the Milky Way made it worth it.

In addition, there were wild alpine cranberries and huckleberries everywhere that you looked. I stopped to pick them whenever I could, often shoving a handful of them mixed together into my mouth, enjoying the combination of tangy and sweet. They were divine.

When the weather didn't cooperate though, New Hampshire was brutal. Because the trail was mostly rock, even the tiniest bit of rain made the trail slick and dangerous. And it was mentally draining to complete incredibly tough climb after incredibly tough climb just to catch a view of some nice fog at the top. We passed the time by starting a tramily book club. We each downloaded the same audiobook, "Pirate Hunters: Treasure, Obsession, and the Search for a Legendary Pirate Ship" by Robert Kurson, chosen by Chef, which we'd listen to each day and discuss each night at camp. The book was adventurous and hilarious, and it gave us much to discuss and was a surprising source of joy during the tough slogs up and down peaks each day.

Because the terrain was so tough in this section, my hiker hunger ramped up like crazy. And it had already been insane by this point to begin with. The Appalachian Mountain Club huts were a saving grace. These huts offer costly bunks to guests, who reserve them far in advance. Sometimes, they'll take in hikers for the night to help out with chores in exchange for a bunk. I wasn't one of those lucky hikers, but several times, as I hiked by the huts in the mornings, the staff would call me over and offer me leftover breakfast foods and coffee. Usually, this meant pancakes and eggs, which I would always gratefully wolf down along with my own breakfast foods. They also sometimes sold cheap baked goods to the hikers. I truly believe that all the hut food that I consumed played a part in getting me through New Hampshire.

We were lucky in New Hampshire to be hiking around a fantastic group of people for the majority of the state. Sherpa, Big Bunny, and Bernie, the three friendly dudes that I'd met at the fire tower in Vermont, regularly hiked and camped near us. We reconnected with Moss and Tortilla, and I bought Tortilla ice cream for losing a bet several states back. And our friendships deepened with Baby.

My body was beaten down by the end of the state though. While I had hiked 20-plus-mile days in other states, I struggled to hike 12 miles per day in the Whites. As we descended out of the Presidential range down to Pinkham Notch, I thought things were about to get a little easier again. I was so wrong. Immediately, we climbed up into the Wildcats, which were steeper, longer, and more jagged than anything I'd experienced before. If you were to ask me what I think the toughest area of the AT is, I would 100 percent say the Wildcats. Around this time, my sweat took on a sickly sweet smell which infested my clothes and much of my gear. It stuck around and lasted even past the finish line of the trail.

I ran into Fisher and his dog Forrest on my way into the Wildcats, whom I had not seen since Tennessee. They had flipped up to Katahdin and were now going southbound because Fisher was worried they'd been moving too slowly and wouldn't beat the weather window to the end of the trail.

Next, I ran into Tortilla, who was camping on the side of the trail alone. He'd gotten into an argument with Steak, and he was devastated, thinking that Steak didn't want to hike with him anymore. I told him that he was welcome to hike with me but he had already set up camp for the night so opted to stay put. Later, I found out that while I was there with Tortilla, Moss was in Gorham with Steak. Steak was also upset and thought that Tortilla didn't want to hike with *him* anymore. Thankfully, they later reconnected and finished the trail as a duo.

Because I had stopped to chat with these old friends for too long, I fell behind my tramily. Chef, Ibex, and Baby had charged up into the steep mountains while I dilly-dallied at the base. Night fell before I could make it to our planned campsite, and I wasn't willing to hike these craggy, rugged mountains in the dark. So I found a flat spot next to the trail and set up by myself, settling in for the night. I left my socks and sock liners inside of my shoes in my vestibule while I slept, and woke up in the morning to find that a rodent had chewed on my sock liners and had pulled one of them halfway down a hole in the ground. I stole it back and continued to wear it until the end of the trail.

The next day, I had to pull 16 miles to catch up with the tramily and meet them at camp. I didn't know how I was going to do it. I was exhausted three miles in and these mountains were insanely steep. I dug out the emergency reserves of energy chews with caffeine that were buried at the bottom of my pack and threw some in my mouth. Whenever I'd start to feel my energy wane, I'd eat more. And when I stopped for lunch, I made myself a strong coffee. Three middle-aged women who were out for a day hike together stopped me. "Are you a thru-hiker?" they asked. "I sure am," I replied. "Oh no you can't be, you seem way too clean and energized!" I laughed.

The sun had come out and it was a beautiful day, and the extra caffeine had done me wonders. I was having a great time, honestly. I had the trail to myself for the majority of the day and I was able to move at my own pace without worrying where the others were in relation to me. I also watched as a pine marten, an adorable weasel-like creature, popped out of the woods. It was the second one that I'd seen since entering the White Mountains.

When I finally caught my tramily around 8:00 pm, they were all fast asleep at camp. I was still hyped up and wanted to chat about all I had experienced that day, but I was out of luck. Instead, I sat by the river near camp, reflecting on my day as the sun went down. I crawled into my tent and dozed off into a deep sleep. We had just a couple of easy miles to the jump-off for Gorham the next day. I was ready for a break after all of this. I hoped against hope that we'd be able to find a hotel with an outdoor pool. I needed it.

On the way down to the road crossing in the morning, Chef stopped us. "Look," he said, pointing to some wrinkly black mushrooms on the ground. "Black trumpets. Let's pick a bunch and cook them in town." Chef and Ibex both knew a fair bit about wild mushrooms, and we'd been feasting on black trumpets and chanterelles for several states by then. We quickly fell to our hands and knees, gathering the ugly but tasty mushrooms.

Hitching into Gorham from US 2 was our hardest hitch of the entire trail. While we usually got picked up within a few minutes, this time it took hours. My usual trick if we weren't getting a hitch right away was to whip off my tank top. This was both to say, "Look, I'm a harmless woman!" and "No weapons in here!" But even that didn't seem to speed things along. At long last though, a car pulled over and scooped us up. We finally made it into Gorham, and there was an outdoor pool with lounge chairs waiting for us. The trail provides.

We spent the next two days relaxing, swimming, playing mini golf, and cooking. We made crispy, buttery garlic bread topped with black trumpets. I picked up a brand-new pair of Oboz from the hostel in town, which allowed hikers to send a package there for a small fee. We vowed to get good and rested before the next hiking day, when we'd climb up into the great state of Maine.

CHAPTER 28

Maine was everything that I wanted the rest of the AT to be, and more. The wilderness was remote and stunning, there were endless places to swim, the sun was always shining, we picked up some new, fun members in our crew, and the state's people were deeply kind. On more than one occasion, as we'd cross a road on the trail, a pickup truck would pull to the side of the road, and the driver would poke their head out, calling to us, "You guys need anything?" It rained a total of two out of the 25 days that we spent hiking in the state, one of those being the very first day that we crossed the state line. Though the trail through Maine is under 300 miles, we slowed our pace way down once we got there and stayed for almost a month. In addition to the terrain being tough, we just plain weren't ready to finish the AT yet.

As high as my spirits were though, my body was falling apart. I felt like I could never shove enough food into my mouth. My energy levels were at an all-time low, despite being in incredible shape, and my hair started to fall out in big clumps. Every time I showered and ran a brush through my hair, I came out with a giant fistful of it to toss in the trash. I was burned out. Ibex and I both became obsessed with peanut butter. We'd barely eaten it for the entire trail, and suddenly, it was all our bodies wanted. I'd run through a jar of it in three days, spreading the stuff on absolutely everything, and when I'd run out, I'd be desperate for more. I was like an addict.

Maine boasts the "hardest mile on the entire AT" in the form of the Mahoosuc Notch. Hikers have to climb up and over huge boulders and leap across chasms between rocks for a full mile. Ibex, Chef, and I hiked through together, and honestly had a blast.

We also ran into Eddie and Elmo about halfway through, so we hiked the rest of it with them, making it an even more social occasion. The trail through the boulders was fairly flat, so I didn't think it compared to the difficulty of the Wildcats and Kinsmans in New Hampshire. Chef lent me a hand a couple of times as I climbed up through the rocks, which helped. I lost one of my water bottles to a deep fissure in the rock as it fell out of my pack, so I was a one-bottle woman until the next town. And someone had taken the liberty of taking a number two right there in the middle of the trail, so we had to find our way up and over some huge boulders to get around the mess. I would not crown this mile as the toughest on the AT, but I would say it was one of the most fun. Aside from the number two.

Baby hiked ahead of us through the notch, and we were planning to camp on the far side of it, so when we popped out, we dropped our packs and went searching for him. We found him camping with Candyman, one of the most handsome men I'd ever seen in real life. And I had met a lot of actors while I was working in movie publicity in D.C. He was an Adonis. He was tall, dark, handsome, and had the most gorgeous dimples and a five o'clock shadow. While most of the male northbounders were starting to look a little emaciated by this point, he was toned and muscled. He was incredibly friendly, and he also played the guitar. But, he was also married. Hearts were broken everywhere when they found out, I am sure.

Candyman was a philosophy professor who was section hiking; he came out to the trail for two weeks each year, eventually hoping to complete it. He hiked and camped around us for a couple of days, until finally, he'd start asking each morning what "our" plan was for the day. He was an easy addition to our tramily and brought a lot of laughs and joy for the couple of weeks that he was on trail. He also humored me by agreeing to a sassy photo together in a lake in our bathing suits, just in case any past tramily members who shall remain unnamed were paying attention to my social media accounts. Yes, I was that petty. We originally planned to pose "Dirty Dancing" style, with him lifting me over his head in the water, but he somehow managed to fracture his hand that week on trail and couldn't do the lifting. So I settled for one where I was in my bikini, and his arm was wrapped around me.

The next day, we planned to hike 17 miles. But there was so much elevation gain, and it was so steep, that after stopping for a long lunch with Moss and her current hiking crew, which included hikers named Naps, Dori, and Venus, I knew I wasn't going to make it before dark. I settled in at a shelter with the four of them, plus Candyman. Shortly after, a group of dozens of college freshmen showed up, setting up a city right there in the forest. We'd seen numerous groups of college kids in the preceding days because they were hiking as part of freshmen orientation at various schools. They tended to completely take over any space that they stopped at, simply by nature of there being so many of them. Luckily, we'd already claimed the shelter area at this spot, so they found a big open space 30 or so feet away to set up their parachute-sized tents.

As we sat around the fire ring in front of the shelter, having dinner, Candyman offered each of us a hard candy infused with marijuana. I don't know how, but Candyman somehow convinced me to try it one more time, despite my distaste for it. "This is the good stuff," he told me. "You'll like it." Everyone else had already popped a candy into their mouths so I accepted a piece from Candyman and did the same, sucking on it. It was grape-flavored and tasty. My body was happy to have any extra sugar. But the next thing I knew, Candyman was laughing hysterically next to me, and I realized that I couldn't stand up. I was *high*.

I looked around the circle. Everyone else seemed fine but I was reeling with anxiety. Thankfully, by this time, darkness had fallen. I was unable to walk, so I crawled on my hands and knees to the safety of my tent, needing to lie down in private. I carried my half-empty pot with me to my tent, leaving the remainder of my Knorr side in my vestibule. I crawled, gratefully, into my sleeping bag and pulled it tight around me. I didn't feel well. Suddenly, I heard Moss say, "Is this supposed to make me feel any kind of way? I don't feel a thing." Meanwhile, the college kids began to chant loudly together under their giant tents. It echoed through the campsite, and I did my best not to panic. Confirmed: I do not like pot.

The next morning, Candyman asked what had happened to me. I told him how I'd had to crawl, paranoid, to my tent, and how I'd lain in my sleeping bag, practically paralyzed. "I should have told you to just eat half of the candy," he said apologetically. *Now he tells me.*

I had to hurry up the trail that day to try to catch up to Ibex, Baby, and Chef. They were planning to hitch into Andover for an all-you-can-eat Italian buffet, and I didn't want to be left behind. It was hard to move quickly though because the terrain was crazy steep and difficult. The last climb of the day was called Moody Mountain, but I renamed it Lucifer's Mountain in my mind. At one point, the soil caved in under my feet, causing my ankle to roll. For a second, I worried that I'd sprained it, but luckily, I was able to walk it off.

Just as I was about to reach the road crossing to get into Andover, where I hoped the gang was waiting, I was waylaid. Here was the best trail magic that I had seen on the entire AT. Trail magic had been few and far between since New Jersey. New

Englanders, for whatever reason, just didn't seem to know about and be as connected to the AT as the folks farther south were. The hitching was much harder in the north, and people seemed more surprised to learn what we were out there doing. But this trail magic made all the waiting across the past several states worth it.

The trail magic was run by a 2008 thru-hiker named Buzzard, a 2015 thru-hiker named Wallet, and a non-hiker named Mac, a father of four and the sweetest, most paternal man that I had ever met. Buzzard had been running trail magic weekends for years, and one year, Mac happened to be camping nearby. He was curious and came over to investigate. He loved the idea of being a part of something like that and asked Buzzard if he could join in. From then on, Mac showed up every single year for trail magic, growing special foods in his garden to bring to the hikers, and cooking up homemade dish after homemade dish over a big camp stove. He mixed up a fresh summer vegetable pasta right in front of us and served us heaping portions of homemade blueberry pie with whipped cream. I scarfed down three pieces. His youngest was heading off to college, he told us, choking up, so he was finding other ways to take care of people beyond raising children.

There were camp chairs available for all of the hikers that showed up, and I sat with Naps, Venus, Dori, and Moss, most of whom I had known from earlier on the trail. We began to leapfrog with them in Maine, and I hiked or camped with them some days when my tramily got too far ahead of me on the steep climbs. Chef volunteered to pick up some food for me in Andover, so I was free to enjoy the trail magic for the rest of the afternoon. We camped there for the night and enjoyed a pancake breakfast with homemade jam the next morning, courtesy of Mac. I semi-regretted having Chef pick out my food though, as he brought me back heavy cans of fruit to carry up and over the mountains.

We hiked out that morning, bellies full of pancakes. It was a fairly easy day of hiking as far as that part of the trail went, but I was somehow still exhausted after just 12 miles. Baby was getting frustrated. He was around the halfway point of his hike because he was a flip-flopper who had started in Virginia, so he was hitting his stride and wanted to speed up. My body, though, was screaming at me. I had hit a wall and didn't know how to push through it. I wished that I could just sleep for a few days. But that would have to wait until after Katahdin. Chef, despite being such a strong hiker, was also suddenly fine with a slower pace. It felt nice to chill out a little bit and take it easy, he told us.

We slept in a beautiful pine grove next to a stream that night, joined by Moss, Dori, and Candyman. The next morning, we hitched into Rangeley, a tiny little town that sits on Rangeley Lake, for a quick shower, laundry, and resupply. The hitch took a half hour. We were finally picked up by a self-proclaimed trail angel who seemed drunk, high, or both. But we made it safely to town. A local gym had showers for a fee, so we didn't need to stay in a hotel or hostel in town to get clean. Rangeley was also known for having the last "real" grocery store on the AT, so we all overstuffed our packs with food. Baby had an anxiety attack in town and somehow managed to lose his shorts. We got in for our chores and a quick meal then got back to the trail.

CHAPTER 29

Saddleback Mountain, at 4,121 feet, is one of the steepest mountains in the state of Maine. A week into the state, we went up and over it, along with the Horn and Saddleback Junior. I felt surprisingly strong, energized by the incredible views surrounding me. We stopped as a group for lunch, and I made a hot lunch of tortillas with mashed potatoes and cheese. At the bottom of Saddleback Junior, we had to rock hop across a wide stream. In rainier seasons, hikers must ford this creek. But for us, it was smooth sailing.

I noticed a nice swimming hole as I passed by, vowing to return for a dip after I'd set up camp. My peanut butter addiction was doing me good. I'd begun to feel much more energized since I'd started polishing off a jar every three days, and the sickly sweet sweat smell that had been plaguing me had begun to subside, though it didn't disappear entirely.

We set up camp on a logging road next to a waterfall, and before I could make it back to the swimming hole, a thunderstorm rolled in. I ate cheese and crackers in my tent while playing a Decemberists album through my phone speaker as Ibex and I sang along. Once the rain passed, Ibex, Baby and I returned to the swimming hole. I stretched my body out as far as it could go into a back float. Baby tried to perfect the hair flip. Dori and Moss joined our tramily for good here, as Venus and Naps sped up to finish the trail. While I had initially thought Moss was a "bro" when I met her way back in Georgia, I was wrong. She was chill, fun, and a good listener. Dori was easygoing, always down for a party, and great comic relief.

Eddie stopped to say her final goodbyes the next morning. She and Elmo were on a schedule to finish and had some big days of hiking ahead.

Two days later, we hit the 2,000-mile mark. Ibex, Baby, and I danced gleefully around to The Proclaimers' "I'm Gonna Be (500 Miles)." While Baby hadn't actually hiked 2,000 miles yet since he was a flip-flopper, this was his halfway point, so he wanted to celebrate too. He did so by completing his own half-gallon challenge in Stratton later that day. He finished his half gallon of ice cream in under seven minutes, blowing Chef's record out of the water.

Candyman played "Wagon Wheel" by Old Crow Medicine Show on a guitar that he'd borrowed from another hiker as we watched Baby inhale his ice cream. And there, seated on a patch of grass in the middle of town, Ibex and I were reunited with our old friends Katie and Francis, whom we had met on our very first day down in Georgia. Like Fisher and Forest, they had flipped up, worried about the weather window. We couldn't believe that we had run into them. We stuck to Katie's side, catching up, until it was time to hike out of town.

Chef and I had gotten into a small spat the day before in Rangeley. I had left my external battery, which I used to charge my phone while in the wilderness, plugged into an electrical outlet at the laundromat while I went to shower. He promised to keep an eye on it, but had instead inadvertently knocked it out of the wall when he plugged his own devices in. I was mad, because every precious minute of charging it was crucial, and I gave him a hard time about it. He gave me an attitude right back.

That evening, next to the waterfall, Chef crawled into his tent and stayed there, antisocial. And the next morning, he stayed in bed until after the rest of us had broken down camp, had breakfast, and hit the trail. It was like this all week. We barely saw him. He'd arrive at camp, set up his tent, and he'd be in for the night. When we left in the morning, he'd still be sound asleep. Or at least hiding from us. I suspected that he was still fuming at me about the charger incident, but we all speculated that he also didn't like Candyman. Chef was the big strong manly man of the group, and I think he liked that role. But with Candyman around… we now had two big strong men. And one of them was a novelty who we only got to keep for two weeks.

The following Saturday, we hiked through the Bigelows, Maine's last big mountain range before Katahdin. They were incredible—some of the wildest, most incredible stretches of mountains that I'd seen on trail. And the perfect Maine weather continued to bless us. Ibex, Baby, Moss, and I stuck together for most of the day, and Candyman joined us for lunch at the top of a mountain. Chef and Dori met us at camp.

We'd hardly caught a glimpse of Chef all week. Finally, Ibex, Baby, Dori, Moss, Candyman, and I sat around camp, talking and joking together, celebrating Candyman's last night on the trail. His wife would pick him up around noon the next day, whisking him back to civilization for the start of his teaching semester. Suddenly, Chef emerged from his tent. I was shocked by his appearance. He seemed to have lost a significant amount of weight since the last time I'd really looked at him. His face was the color of ash, and his cheeks were sunken in, giving him a hollowed-out appearance.

"I have an announcement," he told us dramatically. "This is going to be my last night with the tramily." We were stunned. Everyone was silent for a full 30 seconds. I began to apologize for yelling at him in Rangeley for knocking my charger off the wall.

Baby, Dori, Moss, and Candyman gaped at him for a moment, then headed to their tents. They didn't want to be involved. Ibex looked at him, stone-faced. He told us that he was going to plan a trip to Germany right after the trail, and that he needed to get back to civilization and Wi-Fi to plan it.

The real reason though, was that Chef realized he probably had Lyme Disease. We'd suspected for the past few weeks that he might. He'd been complaining about mild joint pain, and his energy levels had been lower than normal; he'd let us take the trail at a slower pace without argument. During the past week though, the illness seemed to progress. His joints were on fire, and he was completely devoid of energy. When his elbows started to ache, that's when he realized it was probably serious. All he wanted to do was sleep. That's why he'd been hiding out in his tent so much. "I'm allergic to the antibiotics used to treat it," he told us. He'd had Lyme before and ended up with a mouth full of blisters because of the Doxycycline. "That can't happen while I'm on trail," he said. "I'm going to rush to the end of the trail, by myself. I've mapped it out, and I think I can finish by September 11."

I was sobbing, my face now buried in Chef's coat. Over the past few months, he had become one of my best friends. We had been together almost every single day and he was a huge part of my AT world, which at that time, was my *entire* world. And now he was leaving, with no warning. Emotions were already heightened as we marched closer and closer to Katahdin, and Ibex was not about to let him leave without a fight. She was irate. "I can't believe you didn't talk to us about this first, before making your decision," she said. "I don't want you to go," I cried.

Chef's resolve crumbled and we compromised. The next day, we were scheduled to be picked up by Ibex's best friends from New York, Megan and Ryan. They wanted to come visit her before she finished the trail, and it was Labor Day weekend. They rented us a house back in Rangeley for two nights and would deliver us there from the trail, picking us up on Sunday and returning us on Tuesday. Ibex had a course of Doxycycline that she'd been carrying since Georgia, just in case. Chef could start to take it in Rangeley, while he was safely in town, to make sure he didn't have an extreme reaction. Then, he could make his decision. The only thing between us and our ride to civilization was Little Bigelow Mountain, which we made quick work of.

As we stopped at a road crossing to get picked up by Megan and Ryan the next day, we said a fond farewell to Candyman. We told Dori and Moss not to hike too fast up the trail, and that we'd see them soon. We crowded into the backseat of Megan's car and pulled up to our rental house in Rangeley an hour and a half later. Chef, after stepping out of the shower, threw his shirt at me and told me to smell it. I obliged, almost gagging as I did so. It smelled like straight ammonia. Miss Janet had warned us back in Pennsylvania that this is a sign that your body is breaking down muscle tissue to use as energy. So much for Chef holding onto his bodybuilder physique.

After just two days of antibiotics, there was already a significant change in Chef's attitude and energy levels. He was still a little sleepier than usual, but quickly returning to the Chef that we knew and loved. When he began to chatter on about all of his girlfriends, I knew that he would be fine.

I also got a much-needed respite in Rangeley. Our first morning, we cooked a huge pancake breakfast, fueling up for a day of kayaking on Rangeley River. Baby stayed behind to do laundry, and Chef to rest and do some research for his trip to Germany, but Megan, Ryan, Ibex, and I headed out to the local outfitter to pick up our rentals. We were the only people on the river; we didn't see a single other soul out there. It felt untouched by people. I didn't notice a single piece of trash or a drop of pollution. I saw two blue herons standing in mud flats and a few ducks floating on the top of the water. We jumped out of our kayaks a few times to swim. Our relaxing run was only interrupted when, as we neared our exit point, it began to thunder. We paddled hard to beat the rain back to our car.

We cooked up a huge spaghetti dinner together that night and watched "Close Encounters of the Third Kind." Chef whipped us up some amazing French toast in the morning, and after we'd cleaned up the kitchen, we retreated to our rooms to pack up our things. And then, we were on the road to head back to the trail. I enjoyed the rest, but as always, I was anxious to get back to the woods.

The day that we returned to the trail, we swam in three separate ponds, taking a nap on the beach of the second one and camping at the third one with Big Bunny, Sherpa, and Bernie. I fell asleep to the mournful calls of loons.

The next morning, we hiked an easy four miles down to the "ferry" that would shuttle us across the mighty Kennebec River. Hikers are encouraged to take the ferry, which is really just one person manning a canoe, because dam releases upstream can cause swift changes in the water depth and current, making it dangerous to cross on foot. On the other side of the river, we were greeted by a sweet golden retriever puppy that was anxious to say hello to everyone that passed by. Then, we took a short, half-mile detour to the Caratunk House, a small resupply store, bed-and-breakfast, and grill in a historic house, for important business: to buy Baby a birthday milkshake. He turned 24 years old that day. I of course indulged there as well, inhaling a veggie burger, two cokes, and a generous slice of chocolate cake with peanut butter frosting and walnuts while Ibex and Baby chowed down on pulled pork sandwiches.

I arrived at Moxie Pond a few hours later to find Ibex splashing around in the water. I dropped my pack and threw off my clothes, leaving them on the beach as I jogged into the pond naked.

The day had been hot, and I wanted to wash the sweat away. I dunked in the black tannin water, then returned to shore, pulling my clothes back on about one minute before Baby arrived. I followed him up the trail to camp and set up. As we sat around, eating dinner, someone told me that Horse and Wintergreen had summited Mount Katahdin that day. I was relieved to learn that Wintergreen would no longer be on the trail.

CHAPTER 30

We headed straight for the local barbecue joint as we arrived in Monson, Maine, our last trail town. I sat at a table after ordering, waiting for my number to be called signifying that my food was ready. Ibex plugged her phone into an empty outlet. Suddenly, the bartender who had taken our orders stormed over, yanking her cord out of the outlet. "Y'all haven't had bats!" she screamed.

"Bats?" I asked. *Like the animals?* I was so confused. "Yeah, you stink! Everyone in here can smell you. You need to go to the hostel and get bats!" We grabbed our food and hustled out, vowing to leave a nasty review. I regretted the tip that I'd already left her when I placed and paid for my order.

We did as she asked though and cut across town to Shaw's Hiker Hostel, one of the most well-known hostels on trail. It is run by two former thru-hikers, Poet and Hippie Chick, who are raising a family there. Their hostel had everything that we could need, including washers and dryers, a scale, town clothes to wear while we did laundry, multiple bathrooms, a bunkhouse, and a resupply room where we could purchase hiker food. The best part though was the Maine blueberry pancake breakfast that they served every morning. The pancakes were all-you-can-eat, and they were stacked high in the shape of cairns. We opted to sleep in our tents on the hostel grounds for just $12.

Upon stepping on the scale at Shaw's, I learned that I was back up to 126 pounds. All of the climbing that I had done since entering the Whites and all of the peanut butter that I had consumed in Maine had changed my body again. While I had been getting skinny in the mid-Atlantic and southern New England, I built some muscle in New Hampshire and Maine.

From the very beginning of Maine, Ibex and I insisted that we couldn't finish the AT at Mount Katahdin on a Saturday. It was the busiest hiking day of the week, and we didn't want to share our precious last moments on trail with vacationers. We had nothing against day hikers of course; we just wanted to be among our own for one last special day. Chef, however, began to insist that we finish the following Saturday. His parents would be coming to pick him up as he finished the trail, and Saturday was easiest for them. Ibex and I debated about what to do for days. He wouldn't budge. Yet, that was our only request about our final day, that it not be on a Saturday. To the very end, even after we had ditched Wintergreen for good, our tramily was still arguing about pace.

As I headed upstairs to take a shower, Ibex hurriedly told Chef that she and I would in fact not be finishing the trail on a Saturday, and that if he needed to finish that day, he could hike on his own. He got upset and stormed off, and she was left in tears. As I came down from the shower, the rest of the Maine tramily, Baby, Moss, and Dori, eyed us angrily as if we were villains. Ibex deflated like a puppy who'd been kicked.

I strolled over to the grocery store with Dori to pick up a six-pack of beers to split with everyone. I thought we could all use one. After the cashier rang up my beers and we came back outside, I found Chef sitting alone on a curb, looking forlorn as he wolfed down a sandwich. I handed Dori the beers and told him I'd meet him back at Shaw's. "Save me at least one of those!" I said, pointing at the beers.

I walked over and sat next to Chef. "Hey," I said. "Hey," he responded, looking down at his sandwich. "Can we talk?" I asked. He shrugged his shoulders. "I don't want you to be upset and I don't want to break up the tramily," I said. "I just don't want to finish the trail on a Saturday."

"I feel like you guys dropped a bomb on me," he said. "We're supposed to be working on communicating better!" We came to a compromise. We'd finish on Katahdin on Sunday, September 16, but we'd get up at 4:00 am and hike through sunrise to do it. That way, his parents could still get home in time to do whatever it was they needed to do to get ready for their Monday and the week ahead. It was a deal. He went to call his parents to let them know the plan and told me he'd meet me back at Shaw's. I walked back to let everyone know the new plan. They were relieved, though perhaps still a little irritated at me and Ibex for causing the drama. Crisis averted.

In the morning, after our blueberry pancake breakfast, Poet gave us a lift back to the trail, where we'd continue north into the 100-Mile Wilderness. Before we ventured into the forest, he snapped a photo of us and offered some sage advice—to enjoy the journey that we'd come so far on and to carry it forward with us after we'd finished. He also recited a poem for us that he'd written before waving goodbye and sending us on our way.

As we entered the 100-Mile Wilderness, we were greeted by a wooden sign, which had been installed by the Maine Appalachian Trail Club. It read, "There are no places to obtain supplies or get help until Abol Bridge 100 miles north. Do not attempt this section unless you have a minimum of 10 days of supplies and are fully equipped. This is the longest wilderness section of the entire AT and its difficulty should not be underestimated. Good hiking!"

The 100-Mile Wilderness was a challenge. Ibex, Moss, and I had opted to carry our food for the entire 100 miles on our backs, whereas Chef, Baby, and Dori opted to pay for an expensive food drop about halfway through, so I was really feeling the weight on my back. There was also a significant amount of elevation gain and loss, especially during the first 50 miles, with lots of tough climbs. And it felt like summer was replaced by autumn overnight. The nights were once again chilly, forcing me to burrow deep down into my sleeping bag each night, and there was a day or two when I didn't even want to swim.

In many ways though, the 100-Mile Wilderness was a dream come true. It was remote, untamed, and lush. It was the wilderness experience that I had been hoping for the entire trail. It turned out to be my favorite section of the AT and the perfect end to a beautiful journey.

On our second day in, upon coming across the sign to leave the AT and join the Gulf Hagas trail, Ibex and I took it. It wasn't often, especially by then, that we were willing to hike off-trail miles. But in this case, we'd heard that Gulf Hagas hosted a series of gorgeous waterfalls, so we took the detour. The trail followed a river that cut a gorge deep into the Earth, featuring a series of huge waterfalls. What we'd heard was true, and it was absolutely magical. To top it off, Ibex found a lion's mane mushroom growing from a tree, which she harvested for us to enjoy over dinner. It was delectable—rich, buttery, and fresh. Back on the AT, from the top of White Cap Mountain, I caught my first glimpse of Mount Katahdin. It gave me goosebumps.

The next morning, I awoke to rain pitter-pattering on the ceiling of my tent. I groaned. The campsite had flooded overnight, and all of my gear was soaked. Maine had spoiled me; this was only the second rainy hiking day in the state. After just a few miles, Chef, Moss, Baby, and Dori posted up inside a shelter, keen to wait out the rain as long as it took. Ibex and I, on the other hand, didn't want to waste time in a shelter that could later be used for swimming. So she and I carried on through the storm, hiking a 20-

mile day, and settling in at Antlers campsite, a favorite among
thru-hikers. We had the entire campsite to ourselves. We set up in
a pine grove, the lake surrounding us on two sides. Around 10:00
pm, I heard splashing in the water. Hoping that it might be a moose
looking for a midnight snack, I dragged Ibex out of her tent to help
me investigate. Forget my bear pact with Wintergreen, Ibex and I
now had a moose pact. But alas, it was only the wind. We were
rewarded for our efforts though. The night was pitch black, aside
from the sky full of twinkling stars above our heads. We removed
the rain flies from our tents, sleeping under their bright lights. And
in the morning, I ate candy for breakfast and we dove into the
water like mermaids.

The next night, after an easy 13 miles of hiking through
the soft pine forest, we found an even better campsite on the shore
of Nahmakanta Lake. A lone kayak sat just a few feet away from
where we set up our tents. Because we were the only people in
sight, we figured it couldn't hurt to take it out for a little spin. We
carried it to the water's edge, and I slipped inside. Ibex sat up on
the bow, readying herself to jump into the waves as soon as we got
into deep enough waters. We rode around in the kayak, observing
the loons as they dove under the water then resurfaced, chattering
to their friends, until the sun began to set.

After we pulled the kayak back to shore and took a seat
next to our tents, we watched the sunset and enjoyed our dinners.
Soon, Dori stumbled into camp. He'd nearly run out of food and
was going to book it to the Abol Bridge Campground and Store 23
miles away. I offered him the little extra food that I had, but he
wouldn't take it. "I can make it," he said. He loved night hiking,
and this was one of his last chances to do it. He took off in a flash.

A father and son duo named Mouse House and Skyward
showed up when we were on the water, setting up camp next to our
tents. The father of the group told us that he'd hiked from Virginia

to Monson 31 years prior, back in 1987. He'd been waiting for his
chance to hike the entire trail ever since. He choked up as he told
us how much it had been worth the wait. "It makes me emotional,"
he told us. Tears sprang to my eyes. I had only had to wait a few
years, and it made me emotional, too.

On our final full day in the 100-Mile Wilderness, Ibex and
I hiked just 10 easy miles from Nahmakanta Lake to Rainbow
Lake Dam. Katahdin was looming ever closer, and we had a view
of the mountain from camp. We swam in the lake, fell asleep to the
sounds of beavers gnawing at trees and loons calling into the night,
and watched as stars shot across the night sky. Of all the campsites
on the AT, these last three in the 100-Mile Wilderness were my
favorites—Antlers, Nahmakanta Lake, and Rainbow Lake Dam.

I awoke at sunrise to a tangerine sky, beavers still hard at
work. I curled up inside my sleeping bag on a rock overhanging
the water, watching as the sun shot up over Katahdin. After we had
our coffee and breakfast, just as Ibex and I were about to strip
naked for a photo shoot in front of the lake, Moss and Baby hiked
into camp. The two of us began to howl with laughter. "What's so
funny?" they asked. We let them know that they'd been about 30
seconds away from seeing us completely in the buff. They started
chuckling as well, but then looked at each other, and then looked
back at us. They asked to join us. So the four of us took turns
stripping down and posing, showing off the rock-hard trail bodies
that we worked so hard for over the last several months.

We hiked on for a few miles, stopping on the other side of
the lake for another swim. Chef caught up, and he and Baby rushed
ahead. They'd both run out of food and were keen to grab some
lunch at Abol Bridge. Eventually, after I'd had my fill of
swimming, I meandered back to the trail. As I hiked over the
Rainbow Ledges, I noticed signs of fall around me. The leaves of
the trees were starting to transform from the forest green that I'd
grown so accustomed to over these many months to brilliant reds,

oranges, and yellows. The tips of the blueberry bushes were shifting to a deep maroon, and the world was turning golden. Autumn was coming, and my journey was almost complete. I strolled down the trail and out of the 100-Mile Wilderness.

That night, we stealth camped on the banks of the Penobscot River. Dori was there in his hammock waiting for us when we popped out of the wilderness. It was a short walk across Abol Bridge to enjoy the luxuries of the camp store and restaurant, and we dined on burgers, fries, and beers for dinner. Baby was suddenly a ball of anxiety. He wasn't finishing the AT yet, but he was about to lose the only tramily that he'd had as we summited Katahdin. I was freaking out inside. I was about to lose my whole world. I loved this trail, this life, these friends.... I wasn't ready to leave just yet. But the time was drawing near.

CHAPTER 31

On our second-to-last morning on the trail, I awoke to the sounds of the Penobscot River. I pulled on my clothes and then dashed across the Abol Bridge, bound for the campground restaurant, which had an all-you-can-eat breakfast buffet. Inside, I wolfed down five pieces of French toast, a bagel, a huge bowl of mixed fruit, a glass of orange juice, and a mug of coffee. When I was finished, I tossed a load of laundry into the washer and paid the $6 fee for the shower house, which was in the back. I watched huge clumps of my hair fall to the shower floor as I shampooed it. While I wasn't emotionally ready to leave the trail, I pondered that perhaps my body was telling me it was time to go. As I walked back across the bridge to pack up my tent, I looked across the water and found Mount Katahdin staring back at me. I sighed.

Once we were all packed up, we walked, as a group, across the bridge and into Baxter State Park, where Katahdin was waiting. We had just 10 miles to hike to Katahdin Stream Campground, where we would pick up our permits at a ranger station to hike up Mount Katahdin the following day. En route, we slid down a natural water slide, jumped into a deep pool, and tanned on the shores of the river. We snapped photos of Big and Little Niagara Falls, and dove into Daicey Pond.

As we arrived at Katahdin Stream Campground, Zack pulled up in his car. Ibex ran to him, squealing, "My buddy is here! My buddy is here!" and wrapping him in a full-body hug. Then, he

unloaded the Trader Joe's snacks that he'd brought for us—
Scandinavian swimmers, dried pineapple, dried mango, and pizzas
for us to enjoy for dinner.

We piled into the tiny ranger station, and one by one, the
ranger handed out red cards with our names and finish numbers,
permitting us to hike up Katahdin the next morning. We filled our
water bottles in the creek below, and sat at a nearby picnic table,
tucking into the pizzas. Chef had some "ideas" to share—he told
us that he would definitely be up for having a tramily again on
another long trail and that he deeply appreciated experiencing the
AT with us.

There wasn't enough room for all of us to stay at the
Birches, a pay-to-stay shelter specifically for thru-hikers just down
the way from Katahdin Stream. Katahdin Stream Campground was
also full. Baxter State Park has a strict no-stealth-camping policy,
so Zack booked a campsite for the night a few miles away, taking
me and Ibex with him. Chef, Moss, and Dori stayed behind at the
Birches.

My alarm buzzed at 3:30 the next morning. Ibex, Zack,
and I swiftly packed up our things and hopped into Zack's car,
heading back to Katahdin Stream. There, we found Moss, Dori,
and Chef waiting for us, headlamps on. From here, we had 5.2
miles and about 4,000 feet of elevation gain between us and the top
of Mount Katahdin, the official ending point of the Appalachian
Trail.

The first hour, we hiked through complete darkness, our
headlamps lighting our way. Soon, the songbirds began to chirp,
and dawn's early light crept into the woods. We climbed through
thick forest and up and over boulders, putting hands over feet once
more, as the trail rose above the tree line. As the world slept, we
marched, closer and closer to the finish line of our great
Appalachian adventure. We stayed together as a group of seven for
most of those five miles, but as we neared the top of the climb,

Chef pushed ahead, and Baby and Moss fell behind. Ibex and I had left most of our gear behind; we were slackpacking this last climb. Baby and Moss had elected to bring their full, heavy packs. I didn't understand it; Katahdin was one of the hardest, if not the hardest, climbs of the entire trail, even sans gear. But that was their prerogative.

As we ascended above the tree line, orange, pink, and yellow light began to fill the sky and fluffy white clouds framed the imposing mountains surrounding us. Dori DJed for us, loudly playing the soundtrack to "Dungeons and Dragons." During the last mile of the climb, a heavy pea soup of fog rolled in. We were finishing the trail in the same way that we had experienced so much of it—completely socked in.

I finished the climb as if I was in a trance. As I got to the top, I marched over to the wooden Mount Katahdin sign that signifies the end of the AT, placing both of my hands on it. I bowed my head, and tears sprang to my eyes. I couldn't believe that I was here. I turned to my right as cheers erupted. Bernie, Sherpa, and Big Bunny were there to greet us. I dug the celebratory root beer that I had brought for me and Ibex to split out of my pack. I cracked it open, raising it first toward the mountains, then toward my friends, and finally to my lips. We had done it. Together.

EPILOGUE

After Chef watched each of us tag the Mount Katahdin sign and we snapped a few group photos, he gave us each a big hug and turned back toward the trail, disappearing down the mountain. His family was waiting. I stood, watching as he climbed down the mountain out of sight and out of our lives. Big Bunny gave me a sympathetic glance. "Wow, I felt that," he said.

"He's been with us since Georgia," I replied, tears streaming down my face. He was leaving us behind, for real this time.

The rest of us stayed up at the top of Mount Katahdin, cheering on the hikers who came behind us for the next two hours. At 5,200 feet above sea level, it was frigid up there. When I began to shake from the cold, Big Bunny wrapped his sleeping bag around my shoulders. Eventually, we all headed back down the mountain. We made our way out of the park, and onward to Portland, where Ibex, Zack, Baby, Dori, Moss, and I spent a couple of days brunching to our heart's content and not doing any hiking at all. Afterward, Zack drove us on to Boston, where we scattered like the wind.

Zack and Ibex went home to New York, Baby and Dori caught the Amtrak together down to Virginia and Georgia, respectively, Moss went west to Amherst, and I caught the commuter rail up to Salem to visit my brother, sister-in-law, and niece before flying home to Western New York.

Less than one in four people who set out to hike the entire Appalachian Trail succeed. But somehow, of the people that Ibex and I had bonded with way back in the South, most of them made it the entire way. Wintergreen and Horse summited a week and a half before us, missing Wintergreen's Labor Day concert even without us slowing him down. Jukebox summited just the day after we did. Girl Scout, Double Stack, and Workhorse finished a few days behind us. Of our original crew, Butterstuff was the only person who quit early, and from what I heard, that was because he was sick with Lyme Disease. Our other crooner, Jukebox 2, hopped off the trail in Rutland, Vermont, but he'd never been gunning for Katahdin anyhow.

There was just one thing though—I had some unfinished business. Eleven miles of unfinished business, to be more precise. So after a two-week break from the trail, I hopped in my red Ford Focus hatchback and drove south from New York to Virginia. I found Baby waiting for me at a pull-off on US 60. He'd flipped down to Virginia and was continuing his journey southbound. And I was filling in the miles that I had missed during my first bout of the stomach flu all those months before.

Although I summited Mount Katahdin on September 16, I officially completed the trail at Punchbowl Mountain Overlook on the Blue Ridge Parkway on September 30, with Baby by my side.

As I turned around to hike the 11 miles back to my car, Baby pressed on, continuing south toward Georgia. As I passed cheerful southbounder after cheerful southbounder, I felt deep in my bones that it was time to go home. This was their trail now; my hike was over.

A NOTE FROM THE AUTHOR:

If you enjoyed this book, **please** leave a positive review on Amazon or Kindle. It will help it to become more visible, and it will be very much appreciated. Thank you so much!

If you'd like to follow my adventures, find me on YouTube at Audrey Adventures and on Instagram at instagram.com/audipayne. Visit my website at audrey-adventures.com.

ACKNOWLEDGEMENTS

Thank you thank you thank you to my early readers, makeshift editors, and dear friends Cassidy Glover, Tia Pedretti, Corey Danvir, Sharon Lane, and Natalie "Ibex" Parker. You're all brilliant and I am eternally grateful for the generosity that you showed by reading my book and offering feedback and encouragement when I was terrified to let anyone see it. Extra thanks to Sharon for formatting the inside of this book and making it look so much more beautiful than if I had done it alone!

Thank you to my wildly talented artist friend Monica "Moss" Aguilar for designing the gorgeous cover of this book and the fantastic map of the Appalachian Trail that sits inside. Check out more of her work at ChasingTrailsArt.com and Instagram.com/chasingtrailsart.

Thank you to the orthopedic surgeon, Dr. Joseph O'Brien, who fixed my spine. I owe my life to you.

Thank you to the many people who helped me in ways big and small on the trail, including the trail angels who shared food and gave me rides to town, the friends and family who sent encouragement and treats along the way, those who contributed to my "gear replacement fund," and every single person who made the adventure just a little bit more sparkly.

Thank you to Kelsey Peters for leaving work to drive four hours roundtrip to pick me up in the Shenandoah because I wanted to go to a music festival and for bringing me the most delicious homemade brown butter cookies that I have ever tasted, to Jessica Monroe for rescuing me from Storm Xanto and hosting Ibex and I for two days while we vacationed in Asheville, to Kristin Dressel for always encouraging my dreams and for serving me a heaping plate full of homemade strawberry shortcake in the midst of my hiker hunger, to Allison Branca for sending me a monthly "allowance" and offering to make the long journey up to Mount Katahdin to meet me if I needed her to, to Andrea Drusch for driving across the state of Virginia in the pouring rain to visit me at Trail Days and for returning me to the trail after Bonnaroo, to Alysha and Seth Love Anderson for helping me to get my feet ready for the trail by climbing regularly with me during the lead up, to Dave Millican for hosting my entire tramily before Trail Days, to Jolie Parker for driving Natalie and I to the start of the trail, to Zack Kerr for collecting the tramily in Baxter State Park and driving us back to civilization (even if we weren't ready to go), to Andy and Helena Payne for picking me up and driving me to wine fest, to Kellie and Tim Krzos for letting me store my stuff in your basement while I was on the trail, and to everyone else who helped in some way—there are far too many of you to mention!

Thank you to my brothers, Andy and Bryan Payne, for being excellent partners in crime, for providing a fantastic support system, and for never telling me quite how crazy they think my ideas are. Thank you to my dad, Jim Payne, for educating me about the plants and the trees, for making life in the country a grand adventure, for teaching me how to swim so I could become the mermaid that I am, for making me laugh more than anyone in the world, and for making me feel like I always have someone in my corner. Thank you to my mom, Penny Payne, for showing me how to be fearless when coming face to face with a bear, for constantly telling me to go play outside when I was a kid (and going out plenty with me), for planning all of our family camping trips, for being my biggest cheerleader, and for encouraging me for the last two decades to write a book. I love you all!

Thank you, deeply, to my trail family for making hiking up and down mountains all day every day so damn fun, especially Erik "Head Chef" Grumet, Sarah "Girl Scout" Kurtz, Joshua Stephen "Baby" Epstein, Alex "Dori" Schenck, Monica "Moss" Aguilar, and Anthony "Jukebox" Shaheen (I know, I know, you never officially joined the tramily). Thank you to all of the other amazing friends that I met along the way as well.

And most of all, thank you to Ibex, for sharing my dream, for helping to make it a reality, and for sticking with me from Georgia to Maine. I will be forever grateful.

Audrey Payne

Where the Rhododendrons Bloom

Audrey Payne was born and raised in rural Western New York and now lives in beautiful Boulder, Colorado. She caught the travel bug early in life when she was selected for a scholarship for an exchange program in New Zealand as a teenager. While she has lived in various places around the United States and the world, the Appalachian Trail has been her favorite adventure so far. This is her first book.

Made in the USA
Monee, IL
15 September 2024

65826541R10166